LIVING
WORTH

Critical Global Health:
Evidence, Efficacy, and Ethnography

Vincanne Adams and João Biehl, editors

LIVING
WORTH

Value and Values in
Global Pharmaceutical Markets

Stefan Ecks

Duke University Press
Durham and London
2022

Library of Congress Cataloging-in-Publication Data
Names: Ecks, Stefan, author.
Title: Living worth: value and values in global pharmaceutical markets / Stefan Ecks.
Other titles: Critical global health.
Description: Durham: Duke University Press, 2022. | Series: Critical global health: evidence, efficacy, ethnography | Includes bibliographical references and index.
Identifiers: LCCN 2021025276 (print)
LCCN 2021025277 (ebook)
ISBN 9781478015048 (hardcover)
ISBN 9781478017677 (paperback)
ISBN 9781478022282 (ebook)
Subjects: LCSH: Depressed persons—India. | Antidepressants—India. | Antidepressants—Economic aspects—India. | Mental health—Economic aspects—India. | Depression, Mental—Treatment—India. | Pharmaceutical industry—Economic aspects—India. | Pharmaceutical industry—Moral and ethical aspects—India. |
BISAC: SOCIAL SCIENCE / Anthropology / Cultural & Social | HISTORY / Asia / India & South Asia
Classification: LCC RC537.E257 2022 (print) | LCC RC537 (ebook) |
DDC 338.4/761510954—dc23
LC record available at https://lccn.loc.gov/2021025276
LC ebook record available at https://lccn.loc.gov/2021025277

Cover art: Design and composition by Lara Minja / Lime Design. Pill illustration by gomolach / Shutterstock.

for Christine, Carlotta, and Noah

Contents

Acknowledgments

SINCE THIS RESEARCH BEGAN, I have interviewed and spent time with different kinds of biomedical prescribers (psychiatrists, general practitioners, rural medical practitioners); with people at Indian pharmaceutical companies (especially those working in marketing); and with pharmacists, distributors, and health policy experts. The fieldwork and writing were supported by the Economic and Social Science Research Council; the Medical Research Council; the Brocher Foundation; the Studienstiftung des Deutschen Volkes; and the School of Social and Political Science, University of Edinburgh. I was fortunate to present ideas and earlier versions of book chapters in Aberdeen, Amsterdam, Berkeley, Berlin, Bielefeld, Brighton, Cambridge, Chiang Mai, Chicago, Copenhagen, Denver, Dehradun, Durham, Frankfurt, Glasgow, Greifswald, Heidelberg, Hermance, Honolulu, Istanbul, Kathmandu, Kolkata, Konstanz, Lancaster, Leiden, Liverpool, London, Oxford, Malta, Maynooth, Mérida, Minneapolis, Montreal, New Delhi, New Haven, Paris, Prague, Rotterdam, San Francisco, Santa Fe, Sheffield, Vancouver, Washington, DC, Waterville, York, and Zurich. My thanks to all of the wonderful hosts and organizers. Some material that this book draws on has previously been published in journals (Ecks 2005, 2008, 2015) and edited volumes (Ecks 2010, 2011, 2017, 2021).

This book on value could not have been written without the invaluable support of friends and colleagues. First, I thank all of my fieldwork respondents in India for sharing with me what matters in their lives. Among so many friends in India I want to give special thanks to Anirban Das and Rumela Roy for their incredible help and inspiration. Dodo Lahiri and the late Shanu Lahiri gave me a home away from home. Tea with Suhasini Kejriwal was always a highlight. Soumita Basu has been an outstanding research assistant and collaborator over many years. For all their feedback, ideas, and puzzled questions I thank Vincanne Adams, Marcos Andrade Neves, Kalman Applbaum, Daan Beekers, Dominique Béhague, Dorte Bemme, Katrin Beushausen, Sanjoy Bhattacharya, João

Biehl, Cristobal Bonelli, Tom Boylston, Bridget Bradley, Petra Brhlikova, Carlo Caduff, Claire Carlisle, Janet Carsten, Arijit Chakraborty, Partha Chatterjee, Haidan Chen, Nancy Chen, Lawrence Cohen, Nathan Coombs, Rachel Cooper, Jacob Copeman, Magnus Course, Ivan Crozier, Thomas Csordas, Kit Davis, Carl Denig, Klaus Ebmeier, Alex Edmonds, Susan Erikson, Wendy Espeland, Kirk Fiereck, Tine Gammeltoft, Danya Glabau, David Graeber, Tapati Guha-Thakurta, Murphy Halliburton, Anita Hardon, Rachel Harkness, Ian Harper, John Harris, Cori Hayden, David Healy, Julia Hornberger, Ema Hrešanová, Elisabeth Hsu, Juli Huang, Tim Ingold, Sushrut Jadhav, Sumeet Jain, Deborah James, Janis Jenkins, Kriti Kapila, Lilian Kennedy, Karina Kielmann, Laurence Kirmayer, Junko Kitanaka, Madlen Kobi, James Laidlaw, Claudia Lang, Zohar Lederman, Annette Leibing, Julie Livingston, Angus MacBeth, Donald MacKenzie, Roslyn Malcolm, Rebecca Marsland, Emily Martin, Kaaren Mathias, Sandra Matz, Linsey McGoey, Jonathan Metzl, Axel Michaels, China Mills, Jim Mills, James Mittra, Annemarie Mol, Projit Mukharji, Mark Nichter, Michael Oldani, Aihwa Ong, David Orr, Martyn Pickersgill, Stacey Pigg, Laurent Pordié, Johannes Quack, Mohan Rao, Ophra Rebiere, Peter Redfield, Tobias Rees, Gael Robertson, Nikolas Rose, Emilia Sanabria, Jamie Saris, Bo Sax, Ulrich Schwabach, Lesley Sharp, Margaret Sleeboom-Faulkner, Matthew Smith, Wolfgang Sofksy, Alice Street, Steve Sturdy, Samuel Taylor Alexander, Maya Unnithan, Ross Upshur, Ayo Wahlberg, and Thomas Widlok. I thank the late Hubert Dreyfus for discussing Heidegger's *Mitsein* with me. Trenholme Junghans's workshop in Cambridge changed my perspective on commensuration and value—thank you. I am greatful to all the great staff at Duke University Press, especially Ken Wissoker and Elizabeth Ault. Preparing the Valuing Health conference in 2018 pushed me to think through value more than ever before; many thanks to all the participants. I also thank my students, especially those in my medical and economic anthropology classes at Edinburgh University. Trigger warning: this book will mention biocommensuration.

Introduction

IN THIS BOOK I think through depression and the use of antidepressants in India to develop a new theory of value. Depressive disorder is a problem of value because it questions how the self is valued, how the world is valued, and how life itself is valued as worth living. In turn, the value of antidepressant medications depends on how much they are able to enhance life. Physicians value antidepressants for reducing suffering. Pharmaceutical companies value antidepressants as commodities in a multibillion-dollar global market. Depression and antidepressants are both products of a multitude of valuations. I argue that value practices can be best understood when they are brought back to embodiment. To create value means to enhance embodied life. Value is created when lives are made better, but not all actions that claim to make lives better actually do so. I conceptualize embodied value practices as *biocommensurations*: social practices that allow value to be measured, exchanged, substituted, or redistributed. Through different case studies on depression and the global circulation of psychopharmaceuticals I show how the value of lives and the value of things are entangled.

Previous value theories assume that humans are the only creatures that value. Both philosophical and economic value theories take for granted that valuing belongs exclusively to humans. But if *life is value*, then valuing is what all living beings do. If embodied value goes beyond humans, it does not have to be based solely on ethnography. The theory I outline comes from conceptualizing life both with and without language, abstraction, and reflexive consciousness. Embodied value theory is applicable to the whole range of anthropological inquiries into what humans think they do, what they say they do, and what they actually do. This value theory is about embodiment and about practice, but the bodies do not have to be human bodies, and the practices do not have to be human practices. Embodiment allows for a more-than-anthropological value theory.

Other theories hold that value is subjective and expressed in money or that value can be measured in labor. I propose an embodied value theory that traces value to bodily being-in-the-world, comparison, and relevance. To live means to value, and to value means to compare. Comparisons become meaningful as *relevant to life*. Every comparison values because it must have a pragmatic goal. Comparisons are the basis of specific actions, including direct exchanges, substitutions, distributions, or correlations. Whenever a specific pragmatic goal guides a comparison, we can speak of a commensuration. In biocommensurations, at least one entity of the comparison is a living being or some aspect of a living being. In biocommensuration, embodied value comes full circle.

My argument starts from the thesis that life values living. I explain why valuing is intrinsic to all forms of life. From there I outline a theory of comparison. Everything can be compared to everything else in infinite ways; hence, there is neither incomparability nor incommensurability. The problem is not whether one thing can be compared with another, but whether the comparison is useful. Relevance for life makes comparisons possible. Comparisons with a specific pragmatic goal are commensurations. Two entities can be compared and evaluated for purposes of exchange, but there are several other possible goals of comparison, such as correlation, redistribution, substitution, or compensation. That is why I argue for expanding value theory beyond exchange. I analyze economic value theories and bring out how neither the Marxian labor theory nor the mainstream "subjective" theory of value as price is sufficient.

Most of this book presents fieldwork in philosophy—or, as the anthropologist Paul Rabinow (2003: 83) calls it, *Wissensarbeitsforschung* (a science of "knowledge work"). Field philosophy bases conceptual work within empirical work. It is a pragmatic, situated practice that takes questions from fieldwork and thinks through fieldwork findings with concepts developed for a context. It is a "mediated experience" that "operates in proximity to concrete situations" (3).

The concepts I work through spring from long-term fieldwork on pharmaceutical practices in India. I started to work on antidepressants in India because I was fascinated by the contrast with the United States. In the United States, direct-to-consumer marketing for antidepressants ("Zoloft is not habit-forming. Talk to *your* doctor about Zoloft") are everywhere. The United States has long been a country where psychiatry and psychotropics are part of everyday life (Herzberg 2009; Metzl 2003; Tone 2009). The launch of Prozac in the late 1980s pushed this public awareness to a new level (Elliott and Chambers 2004). The cover of the March 26, 1990, issue of *Newsweek* magazine featured a green-and-white capsule and the headline, "Prozac: A Breakthrough Drug for Depression." In 1993, Woody Allen told Diane Keaton in *Manhattan Murder Mystery*, "You don't need to see a shrink. There is nothing wrong with you that can't be cured with a little Prozac and a polo mallet." Psychiatric books for nonacademic audiences, such as Peter Kramer's *Listening to Prozac* (1993), were on the top of best-seller lists. Elizabeth Wurtzel's autobiography *Prozac Nation* (1994) was made into a movie, and Tony Soprano could be seen taking Prozac in 1999. Antidepressants, along with antipsychotics, stimulants, and tranquilizers, were becoming ever more widely used in the United States. By 2010, these drugs accounted for 11.4 percent of total US spending on pharmaceuticals (King and Essick 2013).

In India, meanwhile, I had hardly ever heard anyone talk about antidepressants. Indian newspapers carry large sections on health and often feature content from the *New York Times* and other leading US news media, but I had not read anything about antidepressants. If mental health problems were discussed in the news, they were always dubbed "hidden" or "secret." Some of the biomedical doctors I was working with would mention that patients with long-term digestive problems could be helped by psychotropics. A gastroenterologist said that he prescribed a lot of tranquilizers to his patients: "Initially I never believed in these, but I found that the stress level is so high, even in people who don't come across that way . . . , you have to treat the brain if you want to get the stomach OK." But there was no public debate about these medications. India did not look like it was on Prozac at the beginning of the twenty-first century.

Shortly after I arrived in Kolkata in 2005, I met two friends, Leela and Amit (all names in this volume are pseudonyms), a married couple in their early thirties. We were having dinner when they asked about what I wanted to study during my trip. I told them I was interested in how mental health problems such as "depression" are treated in India. Amit, an economics lecturer at a provincial college two hundred kilometers north of Kolkata, asked what kinds of treatments I was thinking of. I said that there are various kinds of "antidepressants" and that one of the most widely used was called fluoxetine (Prozac). Amit looked at me with a frown and said that I must have gotten the name of the medicine wrong: fluoxetine was not an "antidepressant." From next to the table he grabbed a little basket that contained an assortment of pills and his cigarettes and pulled out a packet of Pronil, an Indian-produced brand of fluoxetine.

Amit said he had been taking Pronil capsules regularly until recently but that he was no longer using it often. A year earlier he had gone to see a heart specialist in Kolkata because he was feeling "stressed" and had been gaining weight. Leela and Amit's first child was born around that time. Amit had a grueling commute to his college job: five hours for the return journey, five times a week. On the long train rides, he ate a lot of sweets and fatty snacks because he was bored. He and his doctor spoke at some length about his life stresses and eating patterns. The doctor diagnosed "greedy eating" as the main problem and prescribed a medicine to keep Amit's appetite in check. The doctor's prescription for Pronil covered only the first month, but he also told Amit to take the drug for as long as he felt he needed it. The medication could take a couple of weeks to kick in, the doctor said, so Amit should not stop taking it before one month was over.

Amit was happy with the medicine, feeling that it curbed his hunger on the train rides. A year later he stopped taking Pronil regularly because he did not feel the same desire for sweet and fatty food. The price of the medicine was never a reason for stopping: a daily dose cost less than one rupee (one cent). Amit went on to say that if I wanted to study antidepressants, then I should look at other drugs, because Pronil was obviously a medication for the belly and not a medication for the mind. I said that I still believed that fluoxetine is usually considered a drug for depression, but maybe the doctor found a new way to prescribe it.

This chance conversation about a drug that is classified as an antidepressant but was not called one by the doctor seemed at first like an outlier, but over years of research I found that this is typical for how these drugs are spreading in India. Amit's story about how he was first prescribed fluoxetine and how he continued to take the drug exemplifies how these substances are used in daily practice in India. Amit obtained the prescription from a private, not a public-sector, prescriber. He did not visit a psychiatrist but a nonspecialist who also prescribes psychopharmaceuticals (in his case, a cardiologist). The consultation focused not on "mental" health but on physical symptoms, eating habits, and daily routines. During the consultation, the doctor never mentioned depression, and he never said that the drug was an antidepressant. The prescribed medication is an easily affordable and widely available generic drug produced by a domestic pharmaceutical company. It was easy for Amit to continue taking it for as long as he wanted because he never had to return to the doctor to get a fresh supply. All he needed to do was to go to a private medicine shop and either present the original prescription or say the brand name. By law, psychopharmaceuticals are to be taken exclusively by prescription from a licensed doctor, but in practice no pharmacist is bothered by this (only tranquilizers and opioids are restricted). Also typical is that Amit got a prescription and never returned to the doctor to reassess the treatment. He just stopped taking the pill when he thought the problem did not need drug treatment any longer. There was no issue of stigma because the drug was for a bad habit ("greedy eating") rather than a feared chronic mental disease. The packet of medicine was not hidden away but stored openly. Anyone in the house could reach the drugs, and it is possible that others helped themselves to a few of the capsules when they heard that it worked for "controlling appetite" and helping one to lose weight. In Kolkata homes, little baskets containing medicine are a regular item, and it is a common practice to pass them around at mealtimes.

Each chapter unfolds different forms of value practices that relate to depression and pharmaceutical markets. The first three chapters are largely conceptual: the first outlines valuing as a social practice in pragmatic context; the second looks at cultural value theories and the problem of incommensurability; and the third analyzes different economic value theories and asks about the relation between depression and capitalism.

Chapter 1 introduces the concept of biocommensuration through three case studies on how pharmaceuticals and biopolitical interventions are valued. Biocommensurations are transactions between humans (as individuals or groups), and between humans and nonhumans, that aim to make life better. I unfold why valuing can be seen as a series of answers to questions about similarity and relevance. Valuing is modulated by power differences; proximity of transactants; boundaries between the subjects of valuing; time; and possibilities of transcendence. I go on to show that the ground of all valuing is embodied being-in-the-world and that a general theory of value reaches beyond humans.

In chapter 2, I analyze how anthropologists have theorized value so far. Through a reading of works by Clyde Kluckhohn, Louis Dumont, and David Graeber I argue that comparative value theories forgot to ask what it even means "to compare" different values. My analysis of comparison starts with different forms and different degrees of "similarity."

Different kinds of similarity may be numerically quantified, but in most cases similarities are established only as a relative "more or less" of a shared feature. Comparisons are always possible, and they can always be valued by one side being better or having more than the other, even if not all comparisons are, or ought to be, numerically quantified. This leads into a discussion of philosophical works on comparability, commensurability, and scalability. Comparisons are always possible because any two things share an infinite number of similarities (see chapter 2). What matters is the pragmatic relevance of the similarity. Alongside Nelson Goodman's (1992: 14) analysis of similarity as "relative, variable, culture-dependent," I argue that absolute incommensurability does not exist, but that communities can turn some values into quasi-incommensurables through cultural consensus.

The false juxtaposition between cultural values and economic value is the theme of chapter 3. I start by analyzing the core idea of mainstream economics, the subjective theory of value (STV). This theory proposes that price in a market is the only expression of value and that price is relative to subjective demand. Economists expose an extreme value relativism by arguing that values are ever-changing and that only free-market exchanges can optimize the fulfillment of demands. Free-market economists think about value in a way such that "economic value" does not even exist. Such a market-based value theory has serious problems, however. One of them is that it cannot recognize or measure any form of value creation outside of markets. Price-based valuations of life and health reveal a flaw of STV: it cannot recognize health-enhancing and life-sustaining work if it happens outside of markets. Another problem is that STV appears to force all goods of exchange into the form of alienable commodities. The clearest articulation of this problem comes from Karl Marx. His labor theory of value (LTV) proposes an alternative to STV: all true value is created through labor. As I argue, however, Marxian LTV also has fatal blind spots. Although the labor theory allows some critical insights into alienation and exploitation, it suffers from an absurd reduction of all value creation to human labor. While labor is clearly a source of value, it cannot be the only source. The Marxian reduction of value to human labor renders it incapable of understanding value creation in the bioeconomy. I go on to discuss whether capitalism produces a global epidemic of depression by its excessive pressure to make value decisions. I discuss psychiatric descriptions of depression as indecisiveness and argue that problems making decisions could emerge as a serious pathology only under conditions of advanced capitalism. I explain why anthropology and economics have different views on inherent self-worth and how capitalist economies create a context in which no one can "live enough."

In chapter 4, I explore corporate campaigns to spread awareness of disease in India. Raising awareness is part of growing the market for antidepressants, as I show using the specific example of a corporate training workshop in India. Spreading awareness of disease is constructed as a form of corporate social responsibility and global corporate "citizenship." I broaden the discussion to how "value" has become a catch-all concept for the pharmaceutical industry since the 2010s. I argue that the corporate version of value is a form of *polyspherical heterarchy*: value that is created both in *and* beyond the market is claimed as belonging to the corporation. Instead of reducing value to a single metric, heterarchical corporations thrive on difference. Instead of laying claim only to value creation within the organization, pharmaceutical corporations now lay claim to value creation in spheres outside their boundaries.

While chapter 4 analyzes the pharmaceutical corporation–as–citizen, chapter 5 looks at the notion that consuming drugs constitutes a form of pharmaceutical citizenship. In policy discourse, ill health is defined as marginalization, and medicating is defined as a form of demarginalization. Bringing in suffering people from the margins to the center and giving them full citizenship is made possible by pharmaceuticals. I analyze how drug marketing in India taps into the narrative of demarginalization through consuming drugs. Taking pharmaceuticals becomes a comprehensive path out of both bodily marginality and socioeconomic marginality. Drugs, dubbed "a dose of life" by the industry, are portrayed as the "gift" of life itself. This is followed by a close reading of bioethical engagements with "authentic" happiness. A core argument is that depression and other mental illnesses marginalize sufferers from society. The only *authentic* way back into society appears to lie in stronger social ties. Drugs may help demarginalize people, but they can never be an authentic *substitute* for social ties. I argue that this crossing out of pharmaceuticals as inauthentic commodities is a form of socio-logocentrism. I then compare this sociocentric notion of authentic happiness with Indian philosophies of transcendence to show that Hinduism devalues social ties as obstacles to true liberation. Social ties are valued as "true" and "authentic" only within dualist cosmologies that take the difference between I and Thou as irreducible. Monist cosmologies, by contrast, see social Others as unnecessary for salvation.

Chapter 6 argues that drugs cocreate social spaces. These poly-spherical spaces appear in different places and have different shapes. First, I explore how antidepressants cocreate intimate spaces within the household, sometimes with extremely pathological effects. Then I move to the cocreation of global spaces through drugs. Psychiatric deinstitutionalization, as liberating people from the confined space of asylums, was facilitated by psychotropics. This spatial liberalization into the community ran parallel to market liberalization. Psychiatry underwent several phases of globalization: the metaphysical globalization of believing that all brains are the same in all places; the terrestrial globalization of spreading psychotropics around the world; and the communicative globalization of how the global South started to talk back to the North that tried to "cover" it with psychotropics in the first place. I end by showing that spatial proximity or distance between the lifeworlds of doctors and patients can make all the difference to treatments.

In chapter 7, I return to the question of why depression rates are rising around the world and present fieldwork data on how different types of Indian doctors answer this question. General practitioners (GPs) argue for a fundamental transformation of the lifeworlds of Indian people over the past two decades, triggered by global market liberalization. Habits are embodied structures that afford instant and nearly effortless valuing. The Indian doctors argue that market liberalization disrupts established habits and thus increases people's risk to get depressed. I explore what habits are and propose a new way of studying people called *habitography*. Building on new scholarship on habit, I show how some perennial conceptual problems of anthropology could be solved if anthropology made habit its central subject. Engaging with the recent proposal for a thinking through other minds (TTOM) framework, I argue that acting through other people's habits (ATOH) has even greater explanatory power. I conclude the chapter with a habitography of Indian GPs to show that a change in prescribing habits, afforded by the availability of "safe" antidepressants since the 1990s, is a more convincing explanation for the rise of depression risks than changes in patients' lifeworlds.

Chapter 8 continues thinking about habit, context, and valuation with questions about the place of "culture" in psychopathology. The analysis begins with the fierce criticisms of the fifth edition of the American Psychiatric Association's *Diagnostic and Statistical Manual of Mental Disorders* (DSM-5). I identify two major stands of critique, both of which are "culturalist." One attacks the DSM-5 for basing diagnostics on outward symptoms rather than on measurable biomarkers. The DSM-5's categories, including "depression," lack validity because they do not lead to solid biological causes for mental disorders. The DSM-5 is merely based on social "consensus" opinions. The second strand of critique accuses the DSM-5 of excessively medicalizing "normal" ways of grieving, worrying, and being indecisive. It undermines established cultural responses. I then analyze how the DSM-5 itself conceptualizes culture and psychopathology. The fifth edition presents an exceptionally complex notion of culture. However, the DSM's culture concept fails because it neglects how *nonhumans* matter in culture. The thing most sorely missing from this culture concept is the psychotropic medication.

Chapter 9 asks what "generic" medications are. Generics are things that depend even more than other things on the contexts that they are in. What a generic is depends on what it is contrasted to: a patent-protected drug, one of hundreds of other generic "brands," or an "authentic" drug. Similarities are copious, and only within contexts can it be said what is a generic and what is not. It is also only in contexts that the many similarities between good and bad copies can be decided. I work through various findings on how generics are regulated in India and beyond; on how drug marketing tries to make products that are similar look sufficiently different within markets; on how a glut of generic similarity gives too much choice and chokes Indian retailers; on generic substitutions in both prescribing and in retailing; and on how generics are internationally policed under the suspicion of being fakes and counterfeits. I end the chapter with an analysis of the latest attempts in global health policy to pin down "generics" without reference to any context. But contexts can never be excluded because no meaningful valuation can be done outside of them.

In chapter 10, I extend my analysis of mental health policies with a genealogy of global mental health (GMH). This field of policy and practice is the latest phase in the globalization of psychiatry and psychotropic medications. Global mental health continues, on a public health level, the global spreading of drugs that pharmaceutical corporations initiated decades ago. The guiding idea of GMH is that neither mental disorders nor their treatments have local specificity. The same ills can be found in all societies, and the same pills can be given to anyone in any culture. If social context has any significance, it does so only as a "barrier" to access or as source of "stigmatization." I focus on three of the pillars of GMH: epidemiology (how many people suffer), economics (how more wealth should mean better mental health), and service provision (how to mobilize more prescribers). Each of these pillars has its own history of emergence and its own evidence base. With each pillar, however, there is a serious mismatch between GMH policy claims and the empirical evidence on which these claims rest. The epidemiology turns out to be questionable; the assumed correlations between wealth and mental health are littered with paradoxes; and the argument on the lack of providers ignores where psychopharmaceuticals are actually prescribed.

In the last chapter, I explore why psychiatry has fallen into such a deep crisis in recent years. I start from the double crisis of symptoms-based diagnostics and psychopharmaceutical innovation. The DSM has been radically devalued by research psychiatrists for its lack of validity and its inability to commensurate biomarkers with symptoms. At the same time, psychopharmacological innovation has ground to a halt because investments in research and development could not be commensurated with financial value. I show why these two crises are deeply connected to each other, then link them to a range of other crises. Drawing on Ian Hacking's (2007) "ten engines of discovery," I list eight more crises in which psychiatry finds itself. All of these crises are failures of bio-commensuration in one way or another. There were two attempts at a paradigm shift in the last few years. First, there was a shift toward a research framework called the Research Domain Criteria Project (RDoC), built on the assumption that genetics, brain circuitry, and symptoms can all, somehow, be integrated with one another. The second shift was toward big data and hopes that algorithms could crunch billions of behavioral data points to come up with new syndrome clusters and possible new therapies. The fate of both of these projects is as yet undecided.

ONE

Embodied Value Theory

Biocommensuration as a Social Process

I am not feeling well. My doctor says he can prescribe a drug that will make me feel better. But I will have to take the medicine for a long time, for months or years. The medicine costs money. There are harmful side effects. Some of them are immediately visible; some are visible only after a while. Is it *worth* taking the drug? The answer to this question is a biocommensuration: a contextual decision about whether something makes life better or not. To create value means to enhance life. To enhance life, possibilities must be weighed against one another. To value means to compare two or more possibilities and to choose the one that enhances life more: "Two roads diverged in a wood and I— / I took the one less traveled by / And that has made all the difference" (Robert Frost, *The Road Not Taken*, 1916).

The process of weighing different possibilities against one another is a commensuration. To compare two possibilities for their relative worth, a criterion for comparison must be selected. This criterion is called *tertium comparationis,* the "third part" of the comparison. A commensuration compares two entities to determine which is better. A *bio*commensuration compares two entities to determine which is better at enhancing life. In biocommensurations, lively matters are valued toward pragmatic goals. Biocommensurations are processes that draw vitality, health, disease, and healing into transactions with living and nonliving entities. All commensurations are about life in one way or another because all value is created from life and directed toward enhancing life. All commensurations are also *bio*commensurations because they always refer to embodied life, either directly or indirectly. *Valuing* and *biocommensurating* are two different words for the same process. Analyzing biocommensurations means unpacking any valuing process.

Biocommensurations involve different transactions, either with other humans (as individuals or groups) or with nonhuman entities. Exchange is the most common form that biocommensurations take, but there are other possibilities, such as substitution, compensation, or reallocation. Exchanges include commodities, gifts, and countless other entities that can be transacted. A *dose* literally means a *gift* (Greek, *dosis*). In exchanges, at least two transactants (A, B) transact entities (y, z) that "can be human or animal, material or immaterial, words or things" (Carrier 2010: 271). To biocommensurate means putting two or more entities into a value comparison toward a pragmatic goal. In each case, biocommensurations arrive at valuations of people and things involved by answering six questions: What makes these entities similar? What is the degree of similarity between them? How are these similarities relevant? Why are these entities similar? To whom are these similarities relevant? What is the pragmatic operation that the comparison makes possible?

As social processes negotiated between different actants, biocommensurations rest on conventions of "good practice." What is valuable and what is not depends on the criteria for value, and these criteria are based on context (Espeland and Stevens 1998). What counts as good practice depends on different degrees of *recognition* from A and B. What A sees as good practice may differ or agree with what B recognizes as good practice. Recognition can be nuanced by direct *mutual* recognition between A and B and wider *social* recognition of the relation between A and B and of the entities transacted. *Trust* is a form of recognition that the other will behave in a manner consistent with past behavior. Further, there are different degrees of *transparency* about what is being valued and who is doing the valuing. Each dimension differs by how *routinized* commensurations are. This includes different degrees of *institutionalization*. Each differs by levels of *expertise* required to perform a convincing valuation. Levels of expertise, routinization, and institutionalization are tied to different forms of *technological elaboration*. When health is biocommensurated, the work of experts in institutions,

Biocommensuration

To biocommensurate means putting two or more entities (x, y) into a value comparison toward a pragmatic goal. At least one of these entities is a living being or some aspect of a living being.

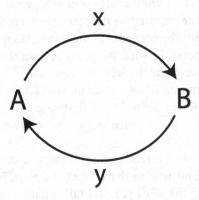

Transactants (A, B) arrive at valuations by answering six questions about transacted entities:

1. What makes transacted entities similar?
2. What is the degree of similarity between them?
3. How are these similarities relevant?
4. Why are these entities similar?
5. To whom are these similarities relevant?
6. What is the pragmatic operation that the comparison makes possible?

Foundations of good practice:

recognition
transparency
routinization
institutionalization
expertise
technological elaboration

Contextual dimensions:

status/power differences
   between A and B
proximity between A and B
in/dividuality of A and B
time of the transaction
inner/outerworldly orientations
   of transactants

and of the accounting technologies used, varies considerably. Questioning the *power* of institutional experts doing health metrics is a difficult task that requires substantial counter-expertise (Adams 2016; Murphy 2017). Critique does not need to attack metrification itself, but it needs to ask who is doing the metrification, with what methods, and to what ends.

Each chapter in this book analyzes how depression and antidepressants are biocommensurated in different contexts and with different pragmatic goals. But the concept of biocommensuration can be applied to any valuing process. In what follows, I present three case studies on how biocommensurations work in practice. These case studies involve two drugs, Sarafem and Glivec, and one population-level intervention, the Great Lockdown of 2020. In the first case study, I expand the dimensions that make a difference to whether biocommensurations are successful or not.

The first case study is on the value of Sarafem, a drug licensed to treat premenstrual dysphoric disorder (PMDD). In 2001, Eli Lilly won a US patent for the drug; the same year, Eli Lilly's patent for the drug Prozac expired. Sarafem contains fluoxetine hydrochloride 20 mg as its active ingredient. Prozac's active ingredient is also fluoxetine hydrochloride 20 mg. That means that Sarafem is *identical* to Prozac, except in packaging and color scheme. What is the value of introducing a drug that already exists?

When a pharmaceutical company wants to gain a product patent, it either needs to show that the new drug is significantly more effective than existing drugs or that the new drug is able to treat a condition no other drug can treat. Pharmaceutical regulation is all about comparing entities for whether one enhances life more than another. Regulation also has to consider novelty in the *market*, which introduces another set of potential differences. The task of pharmaceutical marketing is to make a product sufficiently distinctive from similar products. Any perceived parity between the "same" products must be turned into sufficient difference (Hayden 2013).

Eli Lilly gave different answers from the company's critics to the six valuing questions:

1. If Sarafem and Prozac are not identical, they are at least extremely similar for containing the same active medicinal ingredient in the same dosage. They are both produced by Eli Lilly. They differ in many other aspects: the look of the capsules, the packaging, the

only safe + effective if not more effective Index?

clinical indication, the price. According to the company, the two drugs are different because they have different "identities." An Eli Lilly representative said that PMDD is a disorder with its own identity, so the drug to treat it needed its own identity: "We asked women and physicians, and they told us that they wanted a treatment with its own identity. . . . Women do not look at their symptoms as a depression, and PMDD is not depression but a separate clinical entity" (Vedantam 2001).

2. The *degree* of similarity between Prozac and Sarafem is extremely high, if "active ingredient" is taken as the key criterion for comparison. If "brand identity" is taken as the criterion for comparison, the degree of similarity is lower.

3. The similarities are *relevant* in several ways. One of them is that women might be upset when they realize that the prescription they receive for PMDD is the *same* as the standard prescription for someone with depression. Patients might also feel it is unfair that patent-protected Sarafem is more expensive than generic fluoxetine.

4. Prozac and Sarafem are *similar* because of the primary oneness of the active ingredient.

5. These similarities are relevant to many *different parties*, including patients and the manufacturers, in different ways.

6. The pragmatic *purpose* of the comparison varies with who is making the comparison. For the company, the purposeful comparison is not between Prozac and Sarafem, but between Sarafem and available treatments for PMDD. Since there were no other drugs in the market, the patent application was successful.

Winning the Sarafem patent was a way for Eli Lilly to compensate for massive financial losses from the end of the Prozac patent. For corporations, profitability is about enhancing the life of the organization.

In the case of Sarafem, valuations of "better life" for patients can be found on every level. If a critic argues that Eli Lilly is trying to evergreen an expired patent by finding a spurious new disease category called PMDD, the company can reply that PMDD is a real disorder that causes real suffering, and Sarafem offers patients real relief. Eli Lilly would say that using Sarafem is the better choice because it is the life-enhancing choice. For Eli Lilly, Sarafem is *better* at treating PMDD than Prozac or generic fluoxetine. A former vice-president at Pfizer argues that politicians should not haggle with pharmaceutical companies about the value of drugs relative to corporate profits, all that mattered was how drugs enhance lives (LaMattina 2013).

There are five further contextual dimensions to how value is established. Each of them can shift how easy or difficult a biocommensuration is in practice:

1. *Status/power differences between A and B:* Biocommensurations differ by the relative social status of the actants. This is usually called "power," which is itself a congealing of many valuations. Power applies on all levels. It can be analyzed through embodied image schemata (see chap. 1). Image schemata for power are "verticality" and "distance": if A is more powerful than B, then A is "above" B. Being *up* means having *more* power. Michel Foucault's (1975) notion of "capillary" power changed the image schema to a diffused horizontal distribution. This capillary power drives both disciplinary and biopolitical modes of power (Foucault 2008). Centrality, where a powerful actant is at the center and weaker actants are on the margins, is another image for status differences (Raheja 1988). A type of biocommensuration with maximal power difference is slavery, which reduces the human body to a commodity that can be bought and sold. The enslaved person appears not as a seller ("A") in this transaction, but only as the object ("x") of the transaction, paid for with money ("y").

2. *Proximity between A and B:* Biocommensurations differ by how close actants are to each other. Proximity can take social, spatial, or temporal forms. The value of an entity can be seen as higher or lower if received from someone close. The basic image schemas of proximity are horizontal orientation and nearness. Earlier generations of economists defined a "market" by the *proximity* of actants. For example, the nineteenth-century English economist William S. Jevons ([1871] 2004: 427) defines *market* as "a body of persons who are in intimate business relations and carry on extensive transactions in any commodity." Later, the opposite became a truism: that commodity exchanges are maximally abstract, distant, and impersonal. By allowing "abstraction," the market allows "extraction" from the real value represented by "life energy" (Gudeman 2016: 24). In any commodity exchange, social proximity between seller and buyer is said to be "entirely irrelevant" because "we are simply comparing the value of two objects" (Graeber 2011: 103). But this is not always true. Imagine that a

"close" relative needs money for expensive surgery. The money is lent at a 0 percent interest rate. The same would not be done with someone "distant" or outside the family (Zelizer 2011). Or imagine transacting a lifesaving kidney to a relative: the proximity between donor and recipient makes all the difference (Kierans 2020).

3. *In/dividuals in transactions:* With low status differences and close proximity between A and B, the possibility opens up that the "identities" of A and B become coconstituted through their transactions. A and B do not have to be individuals; they can be *dividuals* (partible persons) modified by transactions (Haraway 2016; Marriott 1976; Strathern 1990). The image schema is that the inside and outside boundaries between A and B overlap or even merge. In/dividuality also makes a difference to whether items of transaction are seen as alienable or inalienable: if A gives x to B, this item x is not "alienated" if A and B are "of the same kind." For example, passing an heirloom to one's children does not alienate it because it is still in the family (Weiner 1992). The elementary form of dividuals in biocommensurations is kinship. Through kinship, different people are linked by a primary oneness of bodily material and bodily form that becomes a "mutuality of being" (Carsten 2013; Sahlins 2013).

4. *Time:* Biocommensurations are modulated by time. For example, it makes a difference to value if entities are compared for an immediate exchange or for a delayed exchange. Humans cannot imagine time *as* time; they can only imagine bodies moving through space, usually along a path (Johnson 2017). Economic time reckoning is usually about the "future" as a spatial "return" on investment. The time *of practice* modulates comparing and classifying because every time a similarity is decided, it conditions *future* decisions: "Every act of use of a kind term changes the associated similarity relation, which relation is implicated in the application not just of the term itself but of all associated kind terms. It follows that any act of use of a term is liable to condition all subsequent acts of use of all those associated terms" (Barnes et al. 1996: 59).

5. *Innerworldly and outerworldly orientations can come into play:* Value can be transcendent. For example, people who donate their blood do so more willingly if the merit accrued from the transaction is not only self-transcendent ("give blood, give life") but also

outerworldly and for good karma (Copeman 2008). The meaning of suffering, both bodily and mental, is a core theme of all religions (Weber [1904–1905] 2010). Disease, pain, and hardship are better suffered when they can be turned into "positively valenced forms of moral experience" (Throop 2010: 2).

Deciding the relative value of Sarafem was influenced by a significant power differential between the pharmaceutical industry, on the one hand, and regulators, on the other. It needed years of lobbying to get the new disease label "PMDD" recognized as a valid diagnosis. Eli Lilly could not have won a new patent for fluoxetine if there had not been changes to the *Diagnostic and Statistical Manual of Mental Disorders* (DSM) that established premenstrual dysphoric disorder. The label first appeared in an appendix to the DSM-III (Greenslit 2005). For some psychiatrists, the PMDD label "facilitated" the search for "useful" medications (Epperson et al. 2012). From a corporate point of view, opening new markets and keeping them exclusive to one's own products qualifies as "innovation." But from the point of view of clinical practice, being forced to prescribe a particular brand is not innovative. The closeness between the pharmaceutical industry and psychiatrists on DSM panels made all the difference. Conflicts of interest are an epidemic in psychiatry: a solid 100 percent of psychiatric experts writing clinical treatment guidelines have conflicts of interest due to receiving industry funding (Cosgrove et al. 2013; Lexchin 2018). Winning drug patents is all about getting the timing right. Sarafem was prepared for many years ahead of the expiration of the Prozac patent, and the patent application rested on Sarafem's being the "first" drug on the market for PMDD. Intellectual property is always conditioned by various time lines.

Eli Lilly spent $17 million to market Sarafem in 2001 (Vedantam 2001). The direct-to-consumer campaign achieved notoriety for its aggressiveness, and the company had to withdraw some TV spots because they trivialized premenstrual syndrome ("Think it's PMS? Think again. It could be PMDD"). Another reason for the low recognition was the perceived breach of trust and lack of transparency in rebranding an antidepressant drug to treat perimenstrual problems. Diagnoses of PMDD became more institutionalized over the years, and Sarafem prescriptions became more routinized (but not enough to make up for all the losses). In its 2003 annual report, Eli Lilly portrayed Prozac and Sarafem as a single segment, "fluoxetine products," and complained about declining sales "due to continuing generic competition" (Eli Lilly 2003: 11).

Despite a considerable power differential between the company and consumers, the introduction of Sarafem met with much derision and resistance. The recognition of both PMDD and Sarafem as a valid treatment was relatively weak. Sarafem was clearly an attempt to give a new lifeline to fluoxetine after the expiration of the Prozac patent.

Let me illustrate how biocommensurations work with two further examples beyond psychopharmaceuticals: first Glivec, then the COVID-19 lockdowns. Glivec is a flagship product of the Swiss pharmaceutical giant Novartis. The Glivec patent is worth billions of dollars every year. The patent application was filed in Switzerland in 1992 and soon *India* after in many other countries. In 1997, Novartis filed new patent applications for an improved "beta crystalline" version of Glivec in many countries across the world. In 2006, it filed for an Indian patent for the beta crystalline version. The Indian Patent Office rejected the application, arguing that the beta version of Glivec did not show significantly

Figure 1.2 | Advertisement for generic imatinib

better efficacy compared with the original version, which was already produced in generic form by several Indian companies (Ecks 2008; see fig. 1.2). Novartis's application was denied in reference to section 3(d) of the patent law, which says that any two medications will be treated as the same substance unless they have significantly enhanced efficacy. "The mere discovery of a new form of a known substance which does not result in the enhancement of the known efficacy of that substance," the law says, "or the mere discovery of any new property or new use for a known substance" is insufficient grounds for being granted a new patent. The case went through different courts, but Novartis eventually lost the battle. In its verdict issued in 2013, the Indian Supreme Court found that the beta version of Glivec was not "new" enough when compared with the generically available versions.

For Glivec alpha and beta, the Indian Supreme Court answered the six questions on value comparisons this way:

1. The two versions are identical in most respects but differ in a few details. For example, Novartis argued that the beta version of Glivec showed better bioavailability, meaning that the active ingredient was better metabolized in the beta version.

2. The *degree* of similarity and difference mattered for the outcome. Novartis said that the two versions are significantly different and that the new version deserves a new patent. The court ruled that the degree of similarity is too high to merit a new patent.

3. The different criteria that were compared mattered in different ways. For the court, the deal-breaking criterion was therapeutic efficacy. All other criteria were deemed *not relevant enough*.

4. Glivec alpha and beta are similar because they are nearly the same molecule manufactured by the same company.

5. The similarities between the two versions of Glivec mattered greatly to different parties involved. For Novartis, establishing enough difference would have meant billions of dollars in profits. For the critics, the company's financial profits mattered less than the lives of millions of people dependent on affordable medications.

6. The pragmatic goal of comparing Glivec alpha and beta were similar for both pro-Novartis and anti-Novartis stakeholders. Both asked whether the beta version was "new enough" to deserve a new patent. Was the beta version of Glivec so much more *valuable* to the lives of patients that it deserved the protection of intellectual

property rights? Novartis's goal was to convince the court that the new Glivec is substantially more valuable. The opposing side won the case by convincing the court that the difference between the alpha and the beta versions is *not valuable enough*.

Power relations were prominent in the Glivec case. Novartis tried to muscle its way outside the court to winning the argument inside the court. The company put pressure on Indian authorities by announcing that it would withdraw investments in India if the court ruled against it. In court, Novartis argued that it was close to patients. It referred to its extensive corporate social responsibility efforts, including the Glivec International Patient Assistance Program, which gave free access to the drug, and its work with a patient organization called the Max Foundation. In turn, there were many reasons to distrust Novartis's true intentions. Novartis fought for a Glivec patent, but what the company actually aimed for was the dismantling of legal safeguards against the evergreening of patents while simultaneously protecting its lucrative markets in Europe and North America (Ecks 2008).

The third case study of biocommensurations are the lockdown interventions that emerged in January 2020 to stem the spread of severe acute respiratory syndrome coronavirus 2 (SARS-CoV-2), more widely known as coronavirus disease 2019 (COVID-19). Until the first vaccines arrived in late 2020, no pharmaceutical therapy was available. The spread of COVID-19 reduced the scope of biomedicine to acute intensive care: trying to keep people alive if the infection took a bad turn. Intensive care medicine also hit limits: initially, only half of patients admitted to intensive care survived. The only interventions available were about population control. Some of these techniques included contact tracing and testing for acute infections. Others, such as border checks, travel bans (both internal and cross-border), quarantine (at home or in public facilities), physical distancing, closing of workplaces and educational institutions, canceling public events, closing public transport, and wearing face masks (Hale et al. 2020), controlled individual movement and behavior. Any of these measures could be advisory or mandatory. A "lockdown" is a maximal combination of these measures, with a focus on prohibiting citizens' physical movement outside their homes.

The alarming SARS-CoV-2 disease cluster was first detected in the city of Wuhan, in China's Hubei Province, in December 2019. For several weeks, the Chinese authorities suppressed news reporting about it. Li Wenliang, a doctor in Wuhan who used social media to alert medical colleagues about the disease, was forced by the police to retract what he had said; he contracted COVID-19 and died on February 7 (Buckley and Myers 2020). China officially notified the World Health Organization (WHO) of the outbreak on December 31, 2019. In early January, the WHO issued its first guidance on how to deal with the virus "based on experience with SARS and MERS and known modes of transmission of respiratory viruses" (WHO 2020). The first case outside China was confirmed in Thailand on January 13, 2020. The first WHO committee meeting on whether COVID-19 should be classified as a public health emergency of international concern (PHEIC) took place on January 22–23. A consensus was not found at the time, but one week later, the WHO decided that the outbreak was a PHEIC. On January 23, China's central government imposed a *fēng chéng* (blockade line), first on Wuhan, and soon on other Chinese cities. On March 11, the WHO reclassified the outbreak as a "pandemic." On March 13, the Chinese government partially lifted its lockdown and ended it officially on April 8, 2020.

Most other governments were initially skeptical of lockdown measures. Governments had asked citizens to stay indoors and avoid meeting others during epidemics many centuries earlier, but the Wuhan lockdown was unprecedented in its scale, length, and administrative rigor. On January 23, Gauden Galea, the WHO representative in China, called the Wuhan lockdown an extreme intervention that needed to be carefully evaluated: "The lockdown of 11 million people is unprecedented in public health history, so it is certainly not a recommendation the WHO has made" (quoted in Reuters 2020b). Nevertheless, by January many governments had started to issue travel warnings, and some moved to close air traffic with China. Italy, for example, suspended flights to and from China as early as January 31. (Thousands of Chinese tourists then traveled to Italy via Frankfurt instead.) The same day, the US government declared COVID-19 a public health emergency and mandated a fourteen-day quarantine for passengers who had been in Hubei. In many US states, countrywide lockdowns that included closure of businesses and schools and restrictions on all but essential travel came into effect on March 15. In the United Kingdom, similar measures started on March 23. In India, a national lockdown was imposed on March 24, limiting the movement of its entire population of 1.3 billion people. The measures in India were among the strictest in the world (e.g., not even outdoor physical exercise was allowed). Most governments hesitated to impose lockdowns but felt pressured to act by the exponential spread of the virus. On March 6, there were more than one hundred thousand confirmed cases worldwide. Case numbers had doubled by March 17, doubled again by March 23, and doubled again by March 30. By April 15, more than two million people had confirmed infections, and 140,000 people had died from the virus (Center for Systems Science and Engineering 2020). By March 2020, the Wuhan lockdown had become the Great Lockdown of the world (International Monetary Fund 2020). Around three billion people were locked down (Lacina 2020).

Governments in both the United States and the United Kingdom were reluctant to disrupt their national economies by imposing Wuhan-style lockdowns, but by mid-March the exponential spread of the infection threatened to cause hospitals to collapse under a tsunami of people needing intensive care. Until early March, the US and UK governments had declared their countries would "stay open for business"; both denied that COVID-19 was much to worry about, and both failed to prepare their health services for the rise in hospitalizations. British Prime Minister Boris Johnson, referring to the Wuhan lockdown in a speech on February 3, said that Brexit Britain values freedom: "Humanity needs some government somewhere that is willing at least to make the case powerfully for freedom of exchange, some country ready to take off its Clark Kent spectacles and leap into the phone booth and emerge with its cloak flowing as the supercharged champion of the right of the populations of the Earth to buy and sell freely among each other" (quoted in Helm et al. 2020). Dominic Cummings, Johnson's chief adviser, summarized the initial strategy: "Protect the economy, and if that means some pensioners die, too bad" (quoted in Walker 2020). Similar arguments were made in the United States (e.g., Katz 2020). Letting the virus "run its course" while protecting the economy is a typically neoliberal policy response. Free movement and free markets were more important than saving as many lives as possible.

Governments were not meant to disrupt the free market for the sake of population health. Yet even the US and UK governments eventually followed other countries into lockdown, "deliberately inducing one of the most severe recessions ever seen" (Tooze 2020). Governmental attempts to stall the health disaster had to accept that this policy would do unfathomable harm to the economy. The world entered the worst recession in a century. Businesses were going bankrupt, and people were losing their jobs at catastrophic rates. Even countries that did not impose lockdown measures were experiencing an unprecedented economic shock due to the disruption of supply chains, bans on travel, and trillions of dollars in capital flight.

In India, the socioeconomic fallout of the lockdown was far more severe than even in the United States and the United Kingdom. The lockdown hit India's large population of daily wage laborers particularly hard. Some 380 million people in India work in the informal economy; millions of them are rural-to-urban migrants. After the lockdown was imposed, hundreds of thousands of migrant laborers started to walk to rural areas, some of them for hundreds of miles. The government's response strongly discriminated along entrenched social divisions, such as that the majority of casual laborers are from lower castes. The strict measures imposed in India caused extreme economic hardship, with hunger and much collateral damage to people's health and wealth. In turn, the Indian lockdown did not reduce infection rates in the long run and, arguably, cost more lives than it saved: "The national lockdown will delay things, but will not reduce the overall numbers greatly in the long-term. . . . [T]his will cause serious economic damage, increase hunger and reduce the population resilience for handling the infection peak" (Center for Disease Dynamics, Economics and Policy 2020). Another prediction was that the combined effects of the coronavirus pandemic would throw poverty levels back by thirty years; the global number of people living in poverty could increase by 580 million worldwide (Sumner et al. 2020). The Indian government's emergency food relief was stymied by bureaucratic hurdles: to access food relief, people had to be registered with food welfare schemes or have official documents to show that they were entitled, but the majority of people did not have the required documentation (Reuters 2020a).

Coronavirus lockdowns revealed extremely conflicted biocommensurations. To begin with, it was not clear which measures were being compared. Countries adopted a dizzying range of interventions in various constellations, to various degrees, for different lengths of time, and at different points in time. This made it difficult to compare their relative value. The easiest value comparison would be between comprehensive lockdowns and doing nothing, but all governments did something, even if it was just asking citizens to wash their hands. Some countries were able to avoid full lockdowns by using a combination of interventions. Hong Kong, for example, managed to avoid a lockdown by using border restrictions, mandatory quarantine, and physical distancing (Cowling et al. 2020). The coronavirus pandemic was a real-time experiment in biopolitical responses. The research design was extremely messy, and there was no placebo control group. Nevertheless, value comparisons had to be made because millions of lives were at stake.

Biocommensurating coronavirus lockdowns showed vastly different levels of certainty and routinization:

1. What established "similarity" between different policy responses was "number of human lives saved." However, it was not clear whose lives were saved and whether these lives were saved in the short term or in the long term.
2. The degree of similarity was determined by "number of people saved from dying with SARS-CoV-2 infection." How this number could be ascertained, and whether there were not hundreds of *other* criteria for comparison, was uncertain.
3. The "relevance" of valuing different interventions was clear: human lives were at stake at a global scale.
4. *Why* different policy responses might be "similar" was not clear. For example, it was certain that close proximity influenced how fast the virus spread, but it was not clear by how much. How infectious SARS-CoV-2 was and which routes of infection were more likely than others was unclear.
5. To whom the similarities were relevant was clear: anyone who lived on this planet in 2020 or in the near future. One reason why this pandemic was so extraordinary is that no one alive was disconnected from either the virus or the responses to the virus.
6. The pragmatic operation that the comparisons should make possible was deciding whether to start or end various physical distancing measures.

Biocommensurations are context-based negotiations among different actants. Coronavirus lockdowns received a relatively high level of recognition from citizens. Some governments introduced lockdowns almost by popular demand. Countries with high levels of citizens' trust in the government appear to have been more successful in stemming the spread of the infection. (New Zealand is a positive example.) Governments showed various levels of transparency about how the lockdowns would be enforced and what they were meant to achieve. The US government stood out globally for its lack of transparency: government advice was muddled, and President Donald Trump frequently contradicted his own policies (e.g., when he urged US citizens to "liberate" themselves from his own administration's lockdown policies). But no government could be fully transparent about the advantages and disadvantages of the lockdowns, because no one knew what these measures would do.

No one knew how to biocommensurate lockdown effects. One of the deepest shocks of the COVID-19 crisis was the absence of expertise, technological elaboration, and routinization among the agencies in charge of pandemic preparedness.

In hindsight, it is also stunning how unprepared the social sciences were for this pandemic. Before "corona-shock," versions of Foucauldian biopolitics provided a comfortable, almost reassuring frame to describe the work of experts (Caduff 2014; Lakoff 2017). Foucault never doubted that "power" is grounded in "knowledge"; he invariably portrays experts as competent, methodical, and bureaucratically routinized. Social scientists believed that there *were* experts anticipating an outbreak such as this, and they believed that these experts *had* developed a solid grasp of "prevention, precaution, preparedness" (Keck 2020). If anything, social scientists used to believe that pandemic experts went too far in their quest for biosecurity. But when the COVID-19 pandemic unfolded and governments scrambled for a response, it became clear that neither the experts nor the expertise existed. Epidemiologists knew nothing about economic impacts, and economists knew nothing about viruses. Guidance from the WHO was entirely focused on epidemiological interventions such as contact tracing and testing; the organization had little to say about lockdowns and their effects. Institutions such as the World Bank and International Monetary Fund were caught out in cold by the economic shock of the lockdowns. No one knew how to make informed value comparisons between locking down and not locking down. The criteria did not exist; the expertise did not exist; and the technological infrastructure did not exist. The International Monetary Fund (2020: v) opened its 2020 *World Economic Outlook* by admitting that "none of us had a meaningful sense of what [a pandemic] would look like on the ground and what it would mean for the economy." Biocommensurations are most successful when they are routinized and when everyone concerned agrees what should be done. Corona-shock revealed that no one knew what "good practice" in comparing different policy interventions should look like. This was not only a viral pandemic; it was also a pandemic of epistemic unpreparedness. Perhaps "lockdowns" could not even properly be called "measures" because no one knew how to *measure* what they would do.

The five contextual dimensions of biocommensurations came into play in new ways. First, the Great Lockdown was about *power and status differences* through and through. The power of governments over citizens was the most obvious relation. But COVID-19 lockdowns brought to the fore many other significant power imbalances: of gender, ethnicity, type of work, housing, access to food, and countless more.

Second, physical *proximity* among actants was radically devalued: creating spatial distance between people became the key mode of creating life value. At the same time, any kind of social proximity that could be maintained online became more highly valued. The fallout of the lockdown hit different forms of work in radically different ways. Industries that could move work online were hit far less hard by the lockdowns than industries that required physical proximity.

Third, COVID-19 made the question of *in/dividuality* dys-appear in a new way. The pandemic made it clear how difficult it is to maintain individual boundaries and prevent being affected by the aerosols and droplets emitted from others. The lockdowns were meant to prevent identities from getting pathologically coconstituted by exchanges. At the same time, many argued that the term *social distancing* should not be used because it had all kinds of negative connotations, including, in India, caste-based discrimination.

Fourth, COVID-19 lockdowns were as physical as it gets, yet they also made people revalue lives *sub specie aeternitatis*. Revaluations in explicitly religious ways could be heard, especially by Christian evangelicals. But during the lockdown, most places of worship closed down, just like other gathering places (many of which had allowed the "super-spreading" of the virus prior to lockdowns). Transcendence could be found in selfless care for others. *Sacrifice* was the key term in how the deaths of essential workers was understood. People who continued to do "frontline" work outside their homes during the lockdown were "heroes." Anyone who died in the "line of duty" had performed a "sacrifice" for the greater good of the community. Governments communicated the rationale for the lockdown as self-transcendence: citizens had to "sacrifice" economic wealth for the sake of bodily health. Individuals flouting lockdown orders were egotistic traitors and enemies of the common good.

Fifth, among the various factors that changed how lockdowns were biocommensurated, the most important was *time*. Lockdowns were meant to "buy time" to ramp up investments in emergency health care and vaccine development. Lockdowns could not prevent the spread of the virus; they only made it more manageable. Interventions aimed to "flatten the curve" to prevent the collapse of health services, but lockdowns did not make the virus disappear. Expert valuations need to be certain of the criteria used to measure short-term and long-term impacts. But even by late 2020, the experts had only a vague idea of short-term consequences and knew little about the long-term effects of the lockdown measures.

All Bodies Value Living

Biocommensurations draw life into comparisons and exchanges with living and nonliving entities. All commensurations are about life because value springs from life and all valuing is directed toward enhancing life. The shortest expression for this is that *life values living*. Life values what enhances life. In what follows, I flesh out a theory of value that starts with embodiment. What is valuable emerges from a living body in an environment. Biocommensurating is the practice of valuing; embodiment is what makes valuing vital. Embodiment grounds valuing. All of the chapters in this book are about how humans value in practice, but to understand this fully, it helps to realize that valuing is not just something humans do. Valuing is not grounded in "being human" distinct from other forms of life. Valuing is grounded in having a living body, and despite obvious differences among bodies, they are remarkably similar across different species.

Life is both the subject and the object of valuing. That living and valuing are the same processes can be gleaned from their word histories. The word *value* comes from the Latin *valere*, which means to be well and worthy (*valeo*, "I am healthy"). To *wield*, as in "being strong," is directly derived from *valere*. To value means to mean (*verbum valet*, "the word means"). The salutation *vale!* wishes the other to "be well!" Life finds itself worthy of living, and life wants to be as well and as healthy as possible. Life is value, and value is life.

Living means valuing, and what makes people's lives better is valuable. What is valuable improves life, but what, exactly, "improves life"? To say that life values living "still doesn't answer the question of what it means to 'improve people's lives,' and on that, of course, rests everything" (Graeber 2019: 208). So what does it mean to make life "better"? Cognitive scientists argue that all living beings are driven to make life better, and to make life better means to "make the most" of it: "Biological systems (and especially we primates) seem to be specifically designed to constantly search for opportunities to make the most of body and world, checking for what is available, and then . . . integrating new resources very deeply, creating whole new agent-world circuits in the process" (Varela et al. 2016: 42). A theory of value that begins with embodiment goes beyond humans. All life-forms value. Valuing is not a faculty exclusive to humans.

Life is a dynamic state that can range from a small loss of vitality all the way to death. Making "the most" of life can be about survival and reproduction, but it can also be about other valued enhancements. Beauty, truth, and virtue are all enhancements of life. Conflicts of value—for example, when beauty and truth cannot be realized at the same time—are common and often unavoidable. Not all paths can be taken at the same time. Some values can be seen as so vital that they are worth sacrificing one's life for them; others may be of less importance. The path that promises to make the most of life is the one that life will take. Life *is* the highest value. Among different philosophical value theories, those from the phenomenological tradition articulate this point most clearly. Paul Ricoeur ([1950] 1966: 85) writes, "My body is the most basic source of motives, revealing a primordial stratum of values. . . . [A]ll other values assume a serious, dramatic significance through a comparison with the values which enter history through my body."

Any comparison needs to find at least one feature that is common to the possibilities at hand. For any two possibilities, finding a common feature for comparison is easy, because the number of features shared is *infinite*. Possibilities for comparison must be pared down by another criterion: how *relevant* they are to enhancing life. Relevance can be determined only in relation to what brings a good life. *Relevance* comes from the same word as *to relieve*, to bring out of trouble, to rescue. From among endless threats to life, relevance shows which possibility is worthier. For life to maintain life, it cannot remain in a state of indecision. Life must *decide*, and life *must* decide. Living beings "must *decide* what is correct and what is not" (Barnes et al. 1996: 56; Read and Hutchinson 2014). Living beings "*must* decide; they must selectively process the difference between information and utterance if they are to achieve adaptive 'resonance' with their environments" (Wolfe 2010: 23).

Any comparison entails a valuation. Whenever there are two possibilities, one of them will be better than the other. To go *forward* is better than to go *backward*. To feel *uplifted* is better than to feel *down* and depressed. These valuations can be inverted: it can be better to feel *grounded* than to have one's head *up* in the clouds; it can be better to go *back* home than to move *away*. Valuations can be inverted, but the principle of intrinsic embodied valuation remains.

All valuing is embodied. Valuations are grounded in embodied schemata, such as up and down. "More" is usually "up," and "up" is usually "better." As cognitive linguists argue, these "image schemata" are the bodily basis of all perceiving, thinking, and valuing. All comparisons are made relevant through experiencing oneself as a living body in a surrounding sphere. Embodiment affords meaning: "Given the nature of our bodies (how and what we perceive, how we move, *what we value*) and the general dimensions of our surroundings (stable structures in our environment), we will experience regular recurring patterns . . . that afford us possibilities for meaningful interaction with our surroundings, both physical and social" (Johnson 2017: 21, emphasis added). "Being there" in a body means that we are not detached observers but active in the world. Bodies value the outside not through distanced representation but through "functional coupling" (Clark 1998). Loops between body and space create affordances: space starts to lend itself to the body in motion (Gibson 1977).

In embodied experience, the whole world is minimally divided into two: body and non-body. The elementary comparison is between an inside and an outside, a system and its environment (Luhmann 2006). All living beings have a drive to maintain "self-similarity" (Deacon 2011). Self-similarity maintains the difference between inside and outside. Original oneness without a boundary between inside and outside is the most elementary state of being. Life arises "as a singular centre of awareness and agency" (Ingold 2002: 19) by distinguishing between self and other, between system and environment.

Life cannot exist without energy, and any living being must counter the effects of thermodynamic energy dissipation by "minimizing free energy through selectively sampling sensory input" (Friston 2013: 2). External states change internal states through sensory input. In turn, internal states feed back into external states through active states. Internal and external states cause each other reciprocally. This is both the origin of life and the origin of consciousness: "Minimising free energy minimises *surprise*, which can be quantified as the negative logarithm of the probability that 'a creature like me' would sample 'these sensations'" (Veissière et al. 2020: 31).

Humans share the inside-and-outside distinction with all other forms of life. Up-and-down or forward-and-backward valuations come from being a moving human body in an environment. Because of the way that the human body moves through space, humans *value* that their head is "up" and that their feet are "down." We value moving "forward" along a path in the direction of the eyes instead of being "held back" or "moving backward." Different forms of life share some of these values when their bodies are similar. Humans have different values from bats, and bats have different values from trees. Bats orient themselves in space through sonar, which is "not similar in its operation to any sense that we possess, and there is no reason to suppose that it is subjectively like anything we can experience or imagine" (Nagel 1974: 438). Bat bodies are so different from human bodies that they appear to be "a fundamentally alien form of life" (438). However, bats are not dissimilar from humans in *every* way. There are countless similarities. For example, bats have heads, and they move with their heads forward. This means that bat values are not all different from human values. Indeed, bat values are *more similar* to human values than to tree values. Trees have tops but not heads, and they do not move forward on horizontal paths. But even trees share values with humans, because they are alive: "Value . . . is intrinsic to the broader nonhuman living world because it is intrinsic to life. There are things that are good or bad for a living self and its potential for growth" (Kohn 2013: 133).

Valuing is not the same as "thinking," which is an all-body process predominantly located in the brain. There is no need to have a brain to be able to value: to be able to value requires only a living body. There is no need to be a self-conscious, thinking Lockean person to be able to value (see Harris 1985: 15). Georges Canguilhem, writing about life and its milieu, says that "the being of an organism is its meaning" (2001: 21). He also locates value in embodiment: "A meaning, from the biological and psychological point of view, is an appreciation of values in relation to a need" (2001: 28). Exploring "life as value," Ricoeur ([1950] 1966: 94) sees embodiment as the ground of all valuing, long before the emergence of consciousness: "Need is the primordial spontaneity of the body; as such, it originally and initially reveals values which set it apart from all other sources of motives. Through need, values *emerge*. . . . Before I will it, a value already appeals to me solely because I exist in the flesh. . . . The first non-deductible is the body as existing, life as value." All that matters is embodiment, which structures values before language and symbolization. Embodiment comes long before all language and abstraction (Johnson 2017). Thinking can greatly augment life's capacities for valuing, but being able to think is not necessary for being able to value. Even homo sapiens makes most decisions from the gut and not from the head. Thinking, as rational deliberation, is slow and tiring; deciding from habits and gut feelings is far faster and nearly effortless (Kahneman 2011; Spellman and Schnall 2009). Valuing precedes thinking by billions of years. Forests do not "think," but trees value (see Kohn 2013).

Value creation means enhancement of life. *All* creatures are value-creating. All living beings can be compared along a scale of sharing more or less the same values:

> Even lower organisms have needs and active tendencies to fulfil them. These features are also essential parts of what it is for us to have values; so we may say that all living organisms share more or less (some more, some less) of our nature as beings that value. It seems arbitrary to draw the cut off point at any given place on this scale of complexity of living organisms; better to recognise that it *is* a scale—that having values is not an all-or-nothing thing, but a matter of degree. (Collier 1999: 3)

A general theory of value needs to find continuities and similarities *beyond* human life. There need not be any fundamental difference between the life sciences and the social sciences. Value works across the life sciences, both the biological and, to coin a phrase, the social life sciences.

Despite a principal continuity of valuing across all living beings, humans differ from other life forms by their ability to discover new relevant criteria for comparisons. All embodied beings value; hence, all embodied beings biocommensurate. The difference is that humans are able to perform *some* forms of biocommensurations of which non-humans are incapable: not all, not even most, but some. Humans are the only species of being able to represent scales in an abstract way and the only species that developed numerical methods for measuring value. Their abilities in symbolic representation also allows humans to abstract and remove value from immediate embodiment. Humans are the only beings that imagine commensurations without seeing their immediate relevance for embodied value. "Abstraction" is this drawing away from the immediacy of life. Symbolic systems afford humans possibilities of storing and protecting value that other species do not have. Symbols make value transmissible among different actants, across different places, and across different times. The extraction, storage, and accumulation of value is a feat of decontexualization, institutionalization, and technology that cannot be found beyond humans (Bear et al. 2015). Human symbolization allows us to make value convertible among different contexts, something that other animals cannot do as smoothly because they do not have the same technological infrastructure. Mutual recognition, trust, and routinization of action can be found in nonhuman animals as well. Transparency can be found in animal commensurations insofar as deceit can be found among them. What nonhuman value practices lack are institutionalization, expertise, and technological elaboration. From among the five contextual dimensions, many nonhuman animals also display social power differences, proximity, dividuality, and an influence of time. The only dimension that nonhumans do not seem to have is transcendence (Michaels 2015). The idea that value could ever be abstracted, extracted, accrued, and saved for a life beyond this life appears to be exclusively human. Only humans imagine value beyond being-in-*this*-world.

Value is not "outside" lived and embodied reality to be "attached" to it later. The concept that statements about the world are "true" or "false" first, and morally "good" or "bad" second, is misleading. Value is not an abstract assessment of an objectively existing world. "Valuing" is not about ascribing moral attributes to facts. In Indian philosophy, the Sanskrit word *sat* denotes both what is "true" and what is "good" (Müller 1883; see Perrett 2013). The distinction between fact and value, constitutive of Enlightenment ethics since David Hume, is wrong (Bhaskar 2010; Putnam 2002).

Aspiring to "value-free" science (Weber [1922] 2019) is a contradiction in terms: Max Weber clearly valued "value-free" science as *better* than "value-laden" science, which means that the label "value-free" is a valuation (Sedlacek 2011: 7). One cannot not value. Valuing is always already part of any action and any perception of the world. Action is made possible by value. Anything is a "matter of concern" rather than a "matter of fact" (Latour 2004). Truth claims are neither true nor false; they are "appropriate or inappropriate" relative to the "necessity of interests," and these interests "have their basis in the natural history of the human species"—that is, the human body (Habermas 1971: 312).

If there is no difference between fact and value, "value" itself may seem misleading when it is defined by a strict difference between a valuing subject and a valued object. Martin Heidegger (1949: 39) holds that any form of valuing turns what is valued (*das Gewertete*) into a mere "object for man's estimation. . . . Every valuing, even where it values positively, is a subjectivizing (*Subjektivierung*). . . . The bizarre effort to prove the objectivity of values does not know what it is doing." Heidegger rejects the idea that we can look at the world in a value-free way. However, there is no need to dismiss valuing as human subjectivism. What Heidegger ([1927] 1993) calls "care" (*Sorge*) is the same as valuing by relevance. *Dasein*'s being-toward-the-future and choosing between alternatives is careful valuing (Cordero 2018). When valuing is intrinsic to being-in-the-world, valuing does not presuppose an absolute subject-object split.

theory of ethics

Every comparison entails valuing, but not all valuing is about ethics. Valuing one's own life is not yet ethical. Ethics begin where *other* life is valued *as if* it were one's *own* life. Ethics require life to be able to assume an ex-centric positionality to itself (Plessner 1975). Kant's categorical imperative—that one's own actions should be evaluated *as if* their consequences could fall back on oneself—needs looking at the other from the perspective of the other. Whenever philosophers use a "veil of ignorance" argument (e.g., Rawls 1971), they posit that the difference between self and other cannot be known, as if decisions for other lives might be decisions for one's own life. Ethics come full circle when one's own life is reflexively valued *as if* it was another person's life. Reflexive self-Othering as an aesthetics of existence, as the Stoics and others developed it, turns ethics back into a care of the self (Foucault 1984).

what about care + community?

Albert Schweitzer took Kant's categorical imperative two steps further. What Schweitzer calls "reverence for life" (*Ehrfurcht vor dem Leben*) includes *all* living beings, not only humans, and the living Other is sacred because it is living. The self is not separate from other life but fully embedded within it: "I am life that wills to live in the midst of life that wills to live" (*Ich bin Leben, das leben will, inmitten von Leben, das leben will*). For Schweitzer ([1936] 2009: 138), the value of living becomes absolute: "A man is truly ethical only when he obeys the compulsion to help all life that he is able to assist and shrinks from injuring anything that lives. He does not ask how far this or that life deserves one's sympathy as being valuable nor, beyond that, whether and to what degree it is capable of feeling . . . Ethics is responsibility without limit toward all that lives."

Schweitzer's concept of ethics is without limit across species. He is regarded as a medical humanitarian (Redfield 2013: 48–50), but his ethics of life are limited neither to humans nor to medicine. Schweitzer's sources were eclectic, yet Indian philosophies, especially Jainism's principle on *ahimsa* (nonviolence), were most influential (Barsam 2008: 72). Jains acknowledge that life thrives on life and that life must harm life in order to live. Mahatma Gandhi, another proponent of ahimsa, also struggled with the fact that embodiment could never be without any form of violence: "The world is bound in a chain of destruction. . . . *Himsa* is an inherent necessity for life in the body" (Gandhi 1986: 274). Ethical living means doing everything possible to minimize hurt to other living beings and to abstain from any kind of hurt for the sake of hurt. Ethical living cannot avoid all violence, but it can avoid violence that does not sustain life in return (Sharp 2019).

Feeling ethically responsible toward all other lives can be *expected* only of humans. A human may feel responsible toward a tree, but the tree does not feel responsible toward the human. Trees value one another because they cannot live without one another: "If every tree were looking out only for itself, then quite a few of them would never reach old age. . . . Every tree, therefore, is valuable to the community and worth keeping around for as long as possible. And that is why even sick individuals are supported and nourished until they recover" (Wohlleben 2016: 4). Trees value other trees, but it is difficult to say how much trees value non-trees, such as humans. Most likely, trees value certain non-trees, such as mushrooms, more than humans. Valuing is symmetrical across all forms of life, whereas ethics are asymmetrical. Tree ethics might be confined to other trees. Dog ethics reach beyond species boundaries to include humans, because humans have trained dogs to care about humans. Trees might not sense an ethical responsibility toward humans, but humans should not scold them for it. Friedrich Nietzsche ([1886] 1968, 1–2) is right that ethical valuing requires a sense of responsibility that is not naturally given. For a reflexive and self-transcendent ethics to emerge, humans had to domesticate themselves to become "animals entitled to give promises." Ethics require that actions become "calculable" to others and to oneself. The "sovereign individual" is a living being that is "the same only unto itself." Ethics requires a "transvaluation of all values" because valuing comes before ethics.

To create value means to enhance life. To enhance life, possibilities must be weighed against one another. To value means to compare two or more possibilities and to choose what enhances life. Life cannot *not* value. There are only a few moments when life does not seem to value, or when life devalues itself. One of them is the numb indecisiveness of depression. Another is suicidal ideation: deciding that life is not worth living. Disordered moods can be defined by whether they endanger life or diminish the mental, physical, or social life of the sufferer (Heinz 2014). Depressive states of mind and body present the deepest paradox: if living is all about more living, why can life turn against itself? Making sense of depression is a challenge for any theory of value that grounds itself in embodied life.

TWO

Relative Value
Culture, Comparison, Commensurability

Cultural Value Theories

The most sustained efforts to construct coherent value theories come from philosophers and economists. This disciplinary split reflects the two major meanings of "value." In philosophy, value is an expression of what makes life worth living. In economics, value is a measure of relative worth that emerges from exchange. In anthropology, "value" is located somewhere between the philosophical and the economic definitions. Like philosophy, anthropology thinks of value as what makes life worth living. Unlike most of philosophy, anthropology is relativist when it comes to value. Unlike most of economics, anthropology does not quantify value by reducing it to demand and supply in a market; but like economics, anthropology thinks that value is relative. Valuing is a social process, and what is valuable cannot be decided in an absolute way.

Anthropology started out by conjoining "value" and "culture" to the point of making them interchangeable. Beginning in the eighteenth century and continuing well into the twentieth century, anthropologists argued that culture is formed by a unique pattern of values. Some cultures take freedom as the paramount value; others take equality, dignity, or transcendence. All the classic definitions of cultural anthropology include "value" in this way. Ruth Benedict (1934: 1) defined anthropology as the study of human beings that "fastens its attention upon those physical characteristics and industrial techniques, those conventions and values, which distinguish one community from all others that belong to a different tradition." Alfred Kroeber and Clyde Kluckhohn (1952: 35) held that "the essential core of culture consists of traditional (historically derived and selected) ideas and especially their attached values."

"Value" was so integral to "culture" that anthropology did not see the need for a value theory separate from culture theory. Only in the past two decades has the question arisen of whether anthropology can, and should, have its own theory of value. If other disciplines, especially economics and philosophy, have elaborate theories about value, should anthropology not also theorize value beyond culture? One reason that a value theory beyond culture has become necessary is the rise of practice theory since the 1960s (Ortner 1984). Marxian theory pushed anthropology to think of value beyond cultural ethos. The Marxian concept of value, which is focused on labor value, looked utterly different from anthropology's emphasis on cultural patterns. Marx's influence produced a sense of incongruity between culturalism and materialism: are values sets of shared ideas of what makes life worth living, or is value a measure of things and labor in exchange?

David Graeber (2001, 2005, 2013) argues that anthropology should have its own value theory and that such a theory should bridge this gap between idealism and materialism, between ethos and economics. For Graeber (2005: 439), an anthropological value theory should discover "some kind of symbolic system that defines the world in terms of what is important, meaningful, desirable, or worthwhile in it." A theory that does not reduce value to money, labor, or shared ethos must "understand the workings of any system of exchange (including free-market capitalism) as part of larger systems of meaning, one containing conceptions of what the cosmos is ultimately about and what is worth pursuing in it" (443). Graeber challenges proponents of a "great rift" thesis, who hold that "economic value and ethical value are incommensurable" (Lambek 2008: 133–34). Entrenched distinctions between "ethical values" and "economic value" can be overcome.

Graeber distinguishes three types of value theories: *cultural* (what a group holds dear), *linguistic* (differences between signs constitute meaning), and *economic* (price is value). All three theories are united by an assumption of value relativism: nothing is valuable in itself; valuing is a social process (Simmel [1900] 2011: 97). That value is relative is common to all value theories in the social sciences.

Most philosophers and legal theorists do not subscribe to value relativism. Their standard position is value universalism (Renteln 1988). There are rational principles for what should count as the highest good, and these principles are not relative to local practice. A universalist view of what distinguishes the good from the bad undergirds all of the political constitutions of the modern era. The Indian Constitution begins by affirming justice, liberty, equality, and fraternity as incommensurables. Germany's Basic Law (*Grundgesetz*) opens by saying that "human dignity shall be inviolable" (art. 1.1) and continues to list other incommensurables, such as, "Every person shall have the right to free development of his personality" (art. 2.1). The US Declaration of Independence speaks of "self-evident truths": "We hold these truths to be self-evident, that all men are created equal, that they are endowed by their Creator with certain unalienable Rights, that among these are Life, Liberty and the pursuit of Happiness." *If* it had been written from a value-relativist position, the Declaration of Independence might have said, "We are of the opinion, sort of, that these current yet constantly shifting preferences are agreeable to at least a relative majority of citizens"—which, sort of, does not have the same ring to it.

Cultural theories see "values" as collectively shared views of what is good and what is bad. Ideas of what should be desired and what should be rejected rest on culture. Values stand for whatever members of a society hold dear. A society might put collective benefit over individual benefit, or put outerworldly gains over innerworldly gains. Anthropologists such as Clifford Geertz (1973) ask "what makes people tick"—that is, what are the values that drive their thinking and acting. This notion of values builds on Max Weber's ([1922] 2019) sociology, which takes values as a compass that motivates and directs social action.

Two twentieth-century anthropologists stand out for their contributions to value theory: the American Clyde Kluckhohn and the Frenchman Louis Dumont. Kluckhohn (1951: 395) developed the values orientation theory, a systematic framework for comparing cultures. Kluckhohn defines values as "conceptions of the desirable." Values can be studied through symbols, with a hermeneutic method of understanding why some symbols are culturally more salient than others. These notions of the "desirable" can then be systematically compared across cultures. Versions of this approach go back to the nineteenth-century foundations of American anthropology and continue until today. Particular cultural values have to be interpreted in their context and in contrast to other cultures' values. Kluckhohn's particular systematization never became fashionable in anthropology, but it was enthusiastically adopted in psychology, organizational sociology, and business studies. Geert Hofstede's (2001) influential "cultural dimensions" approach is based on Kluckhohn.

Dumont developed a similarly comparative approach. He proposes that cultural "values" form coherent systems or "ideologies." Entire societies can be characterized by which overarching value ideologies they adopt to make sense of the world. Dumont argues that Hindu society subscribes to a holistic ideology of "hierarchy" in which every member is ranked along a scale of purity and impurity. Brahmins are at the top of the hierarchy because they are the purest, and Shudras are the bottom because they are the least pure. Other values, such as worldly power (of which the Kshatriya caste has more than the priestly Brahmins), are "encompassed" by the purity-impurity hierarchy (Dumont 1966). He thinks that modern Westerners fail to comprehend holism because they are fettered to an ideology of "equality" that devalues hierarchy.

Graeber puts Dumont's approach into a different category from Kluckhohn's and calls it "structuralist" because of some overlaps with Saussurean linguistics. According to Ferdinand de Saussure, the "value" of a sign is its contrastive position within a synchronic structure of other signs. For example, the value of the word *dark* lies in its opposition to the word *light*. Dumont ([1980] 2013: 294) distanced himself from Kluckhohn's "pathetic effort," opining that Kluckhohn never understood that values are not individual items but nodes within whole systems. The study of values should be a "solid and thorough comparison . . . between two systems taken as wholes" ([1980] 2013). Following Claude Lévi-Strauss, Dumont puts more emphasis on "structure" than Kluckhohn, but ultimately they share the same relativist assumptions. Dumont's main source is Weber's comparative sociology of religions, which is as focused on "meaning" as Kluckhohn's. Dumontianism is meaning-centered comparative sociology with bits of French structuralism in it. It is not an entirely separate kind of value theory.

That said, Dumont adds a key insight to cultural value theory: binary oppositions always include intrinsic valuations of one side being "better" or "more" than the other. Take, for example, the binary opposition between "right" and "left." When we talk of hands as being "left" and "right," we do not find "that the two poles have equal status" (Dumont [1980] 2013: 298). Instead, we find that "the right hand is felt to be superior to the left hand. . . . Being different parts of a whole, right and left differ in value as well as in nature, for the relation between part and whole is hierarchical, and a different relation means here a different place in the hierarchy" (Dumont [1980] 2013: 298). But Dumont entirely misses the significance of this because he does not have any concept of *embodied value*. For him, valuations are expressions only of "ideologies"; all his values are arbitrary ideas in people's heads. Dumont recognizes left-right differences but overlooks other embodied valuations, such as forward and backward. He also does not realize that "hierarchy" is an embodied up-down image schema.

Few anthropologists follow Kluckhohn and Dumont today (though Dumont has enjoyed a revival [see Hickel and Haynes 2018; Otto and Willerslev 2013; Robbins 2013]). At the same time, the project of cross-cultural comparison is alive and well. The literature on cultural comparison is vast (e.g., Candea 2018; Choy 2011; Fox and Gingrich 2002; van der Veer 2016). But what it means "to compare" different entities to one another *is never even asked* by any of these authors. There is some thinking about "scales" of comparison (e.g., Strathern [1991] 2004), but this never comes back to theorizing either "comparison" or "value." It is ironic that anthropology, which often sees itself as the most comparative of all the social sciences, has never developed any theory of comparison (Otto and Willerslev 2013).

Both Kluckhohn and Dumont argue that there is only a handful of core values, and the only difference between cultures is how they rank these core values relative to one another. Similarly, psychological value theories (by Geert Hofsteede, Milton Rokeach, Shalom H. Schwartz, or Robert S. Hartman) also list "core values" and rank them by salience and relative preference. These core values look "sufficiently similar to suggest that a truly *universal set* of human values does exist" (Hills 2002: 2, emphasis added). Culture neither creates nor adds values, it just "has" them. At best, cultures—or, in the more psychological versions, individual members—can rearrange the order of values by how much they cherish them. Cultures can give more value to one idea or behavior and devalue another. Values can be more or less shared among members of groups, and the valuation of group cohesion itself ("tradition") can go up or down.

Some see in this up and down a "market of values." Sociologists such as Loek Halman and John Gelissen analyze values *as if* they were commodities. Values rise in value through more "demand" for them and fall in value when fewer people want them. This market of values is "liberalized" when individuals, as end consumers of values, can freely pick and choose from values without group constraints: "Because individualized people have been liberated from (traditional) controls and constraints, and given that globalization implies that people can choose from the global cultural marketplace, the likelihood that people will choose the same will decline, and hence the heterogeneity of people's value preferences will increase" (Halman and Gelissen 2019: 539). This transposition of market logics onto cultural values produces all kinds of nonsense questions. Can "consumers" of values also sell values in the market? Does the supply of values go down when demand goes up? If I sell one core value, can I get two lesser values for it? The direct transposition of market logics onto cultural values is a dead end.

Any theory of value should say something about how values are created, how they are enhanced or diminished. But there is no discernible *cultural* theory of value creation and value change. Cultural theories imply that values are not created but merely ranked and that differences can be discerned only in different rankings. Questions of *genealogies*— where values originate and how transvaluations work—are more interesting than relative rankings. Existing cultural value theories do not ask genealogical questions. They ask neither about past changes nor about future possibilities. That is why cultural value theories often feel value conservative.

A recent attempt at a synthesis of anthropological value theory comes from Ton Otto and Rane Willerslev. In their joint introduction to *Value as Theory*, they disagree on whether there can be a general theory of value in anthropology. Otto thinks yes; Willerslev thinks no. Otto believes that a general theory can be reconstructed from ethnographic evidence; Willerslev holds that anthropology is an ethnographic discipline and that ethnography is about discovering cultural incommensurabilities. Otto and Willerslev agree that anthropological value theories fall into two groups. In the first, value is about cultural diversity and incompatibilities between cultures. The second focuses on "how value is created in processes of exchange" (Otto and Willerslev 2013: 1) and how these exchanges create different kinds of social communities. Otto and Willerslev say that the two types of value theory can be merged by "the creation of value through action" (4). Social action provides the most promising direction for developing an anthropological theory of value.

Cross-cultural comparison remains the signature method of anthropology. But what it even means "to compare" different entities defined as "cultural" is never asked. Anthropology, which, again, sees itself as the most comparative of all the social sciences, is taking "comparison" for granted. Otto and Willerslev (2013: 2, 8) argue that "there is not yet a contemporary anthropological theory of value" because there is not yet an anthropological theory of *comparison*: "We have always defined anthropology as a comparative exercise. But very few serious attempts have been made to develop such a theory." So what does it mean "to compare"?

Different Similarities

To understand what it means to compare, we need to understand what "similarity" is. As I argued in chapter 1, the basic distinction is between two entities that are separated by the same boundary (inside and outside, body and space, system and environment). Once there is a distinction, comparisons can be made. Comparisons look for differences and similarities. But what is similarity? What does it mean to find that "x is similar to y"?

A good starting point is how the word *similarity* is used in everyday language. Cognitive linguists explore the semantics of words such as *same*, *similar*, and *different*. In an analysis of English and Hebrew, Tamar Sovran (1992) discovers a wide range of meanings. Similarity can denote likeness in the sense of resemblance. Resemblance can be visual, but it can mobilize any of the other senses, too. Two roses can look similar while their scents are dissimilar. Similarity can mean closeness or nearness. If one item costs $99 and another costs $100, they are similar because the price points are close to each other. Finding equivalent amounts on a scale makes two things similar. Similarity can mean correspondence or symmetry. For example, the left side of a face can be similar to the right side of a face. Similarity can mean counterpart: low tide and high tide are similar to each other by being opposites of each other. Correlations between two effects establishes similarity—for example, psychotherapy is similar to antidepressant use because they have similar effects. Similarity can mean simulation, which can include imitation, deception, and mimicry. Duplication reveals another layer. The photo of a photo is similar to the original photo because it is a copy of the original.

Another type of similarity is "family likeness." This is the type that Ludwig Wittgenstein uses to question the notion of essential properties in classes. For example, many activities are called "games," but there is no essential feature that can be found in all of them. Activities called games have no essence but overlapping and crisscrossing similarities, just like "the various resemblances between members of a family" (Wittgenstein 2017: §67). Sameness, similarity, and difference are language games (*Sprachspiele*) embedded in forms of life (*Lebensformen*) (Cavell 1989). Wittgenstein thought much about similarity (*Ähnlichkeit*), but never asked what it means "to compare" to find similarities and differences. Comparison is taken for granted.

Sovran (1992) argues that "similarity" classifications can be divided by their starting points: either "oneness" or "separateness." Similarity by oneness finds two entities similar because they originated from the same shared substance. Forms of similarity that start from separateness describe things as *different* in substance but *similar* in look or feel. I would add two further dimensions: causality and distinctions between material and form. First, there is different causal reasoning behind classifications by original "oneness" and "separateness." In separateness, we do not need to know any reason for why two separate entities look or feel similar. There can be infinite reasons for similarity or none at all. In oneness, however, we need to know what causes the similarity, and the reason for a similarity must always be that two entities come from the same origin.

Defining similarity by oneness or separateness makes a profound difference to any classification, of both living and nonliving beings. For example, deciding whether two drugs are "similar" changes depending on assumptions of original oneness or separateness. The distinction is even more powerful in classifications of living beings. For instance, animal taxonomies have a different logic depending on whether oneness or separateness is assumed. Carl Linnaeus did not develop his taxonomy with an underlying theory of original oneness of all species. To him, species looked similar, without assumptions that the similarities had to come from shared origins. Even Charles Darwin's *Origin of Species* ([1859] 2008) did not systematically work with the thesis of the oneness of all species. A full theory of evolutionary speciation from original oneness only emerged in the twentieth century (Mayr [1942] 1982; Padian 1999). A few psychiatrists try to emulate evolutionary biology by coming up with classifications of mental disorders that proceed from a principle of original oneness. A "unitary cause" of all disorders is elusive but not unthinkable, and the search for a "single dimension of general psychopathology" continues (Caspi and Moffitt 2018).

Second, Sovran's classification can be made more precise when a difference between "matter" and "form" is added. There is a long history of thinking about form-matter distinctions in Western, Indian, Chinese, and other traditions. I cannot even begin to summarize this here (see Johnston 2006). Suffice it to say that matter-form distinctions also structure perceptions of similarity and difference. Two things can be perceived as similar because they are made of the same *stuff*, or they can be perceived as similar because they are made in the same *form*. For example, two pills can appear to be similar because they look identical, or because they contain the same active ingredient (see chapters 1, 9). Material transmission works differently from form transmission. A "copy" can be similar to the "original" if it is made out of the same material or if it is made in the same form. If it is the "same" material, it is a case of oneness; if it is in the "same" form, it is undecided whether similarity comes from oneness or separateness.

Heraclitus's saying that "you cannot step into the same river twice" depends on the assumption that "sameness" can be ascribed only to things that are made from exactly the same material (Stern 1991). For Heraclitus, one cannot step into the same river twice because (1) the form may be the same but the materiality has changed; and (2) materiality is defined in the narrow sense of "exactly the same" material (a *specific* quantity of water) rather than *any* quantity of water flowing in a river-like form. These questions of similarity also apply to events. If "you cannot step into the river twice" is analyzed as an event, "materiality" drops out as a distinguishing criterion while "form" remains. Even if you cannot step into the same *river* twice, you can *step* into a similar river twice.

Degrees of Similarity

Once we find "similarity," how are *degrees* of similarity decided? Most entities are not *either* similar to *or* different from one another, but they are *more or less similar* to one another. In philosophical value theory, the "trichotomy thesis" holds that the relative value of two items can be defined in three ways: (1) x is better than y; (2) x is worse than y; or (3) x is as good as y (Hirose and Olson 2015; Orsi 2015). Finding more, less, or equal amounts of a property determines relative value.

The usual distinction between "qualitative" and "quantitative" differences is misleading. "Quality" as property, nature, or kind is usually juxtaposed to "quantity" as a numerical amount. Quantitative research must have numbers; qualitative research can do without them. The problem is that both "quality" and "quantity" actually ask how "great" or how "much" something is. Both try to do value comparisons by *more or less*. Both words come from the same root, **kwo*, which is also the root of *question, quibble, quasi, quandary*, and, in Sanskrit, *kah* "who/what." *Quality* is not beyond quantification because it asks about the standard of something as *measured* against other things of similar kind; quality cannot be improved if nothing can be added. *Quality* and *quantity* are not the most useful terms to distinguish different kinds of comparisons. It is better to speak of numerical and nonnumerical value comparisons.

The most basic way to describe degrees is by distinguishing properties as *more or less* similar. This comparison does not have to be numerically specific. It is possible to compare properties that do not lend themselves to numerical metrification. It is also possible to compare two entities by *sets* of different criteria without numerical metrics. For example, one can say that a doctor is a "good" doctor without giving the doctor a score on a numerical scale. It is also possible to compare two doctors and to say that one doctor is "better" than the other doctor without having to make explicit every criterion for comparison that came into play in making this valuation: "There is always a point where we have to recognize that some things are the same as others, without being able to say in what respect they are the same" (Barnes et al. 1996: 52). Nonnumerical metrification (more/less) is a simple form of comparison, but it is more abstract than comparisons between two entities that condition each other, such as self and other or inside and outside.

The next level of abstraction is numerical metrification: two entities do not just have "more" or "less" of something, but this "more" or "less" can be rendered in numbers. Comparing two families to each other, we can say that Family A "has *more* children" than Family B (nonnumerical), or we can say that "Family A has five children and Family B has two children" (numerical).

Stephanie Solt (2016), a linguist, detects subtle forms of nonnumerical quantification in ordinary language. She compares pragmatic uses of "more than half" to "most." In logic and mathematics, "more than half" and "most" have exactly the same meaning. But in ordinary language, they differ. She finds that languages allow value comparisons of "more" or "less" without any reference to numbers. People usually evaluate relations of "greater than" or "less than" between two entities *without* numerical specificity. The word *most*, writes Solt, "places less stringent requirements on measurement" (94) and allows a weaker form of measurement than "more than half." Thus, *most* does not require a number; it requires only the ordering of two entities relative to each other.

The anthropologist Caleb Everett (2017) describes human groups that never adopted numerical comparisons. "Anumeric" people, such as the Pirahã of the Amazon forest, compare quantities but do not use number words beyond *one*, *two*, and *three*. Any number larger than that is not assigned a word. Having no elaborate number terminology works fine for small groups of people:

> We perceive family members as individuals, not as faceless count-able objects. Of course, we can count our family members. But we do not need to in order to recognize their presence or absence. And neither do the Pirahã. There is no evidence that suggests these people require precise quantity differentiation to remember who is missing, or for any other task in their culture. Were that the case, they would no doubt have adopted number words to fa-cilitate such differentiation. A Pirahã child is remembered as an individual, not a number. (Everett 2017: 131)

Nonnumerical comparison can be found in all human societies. Numer-ical comparison, by contrast, is not universal. Anumeric people are *not incapable* of using numbers, but they *do not value* the use of numbers. A similar argument has been made by Lévi-Strauss (1966) about time classifications in societies that think of time as cyclical. People in these "cold" societies are not incapable of reckoning linear, forward-moving, unrepeatable time, but they do not value linear time as much as "hot" societies do.

For Better or Worse (but Never for the Same)

The fuzzy difference between quality and quantity—are they both about amounts or not?—creeps into attempts to distinguish between compar-ison and commensuration. The standard view is that comparisons can be qualitative without any quantification. Comparisons *appear* to be-come commensurations when the relative amounts of a shared feature are measured with a "common metric" (Espeland and Stevens 1998), or when the shared feature can be "put on the same scale of units of value" (Chang 2015: 215). In this view, comparison requires two entities to have at least one feature in common, and commensuration requires that the feature in common can be put on a numerical scale. But if any two items can be compared, and if any comparison entails a valuation of better or worse, then the distinctions between comparison and commensuration by "sharing a common metric" or "same scale of units" does not work. There is *always* a common metric. Metrics can be numerical or nonnumerical, but they are always present in comparisons.

Francesco Orsi (2015) also works with this common metric distinction between comparison and commensuration and adds a distinction between "overall" and *"pro tanto"* incommensurability. Take the question of whether it is "better" to be a psychiatrist or an anthropologist. Overall incommensurability emerges, according to Orsi, when two entities share all the salient features and can be compared point by point for which alternative is doing better or worse. Two entities share all the salient features but have them to various degrees. Yet there is no *"overarching common measure or method to balance their contributions against each other"* (103). Psychiatrists and anthropologists both earn money. One usually earns more than the other, and whoever earns more is doing "better." Psychiatrists and anthropologists both talk to people about how they see the world. Psychiatrists do this in a more clinically applied way than anthropologists. Psychiatrists like to develop structured questionnaires; anthropologists usually work with open-ended questions. Here it is not clear who is doing better: structured and unstructured questions both have advantages and disadvantages without one of them being indisputably "better" than the other. What is better depends on pragmatic contexts. Such differences of degree can be found in endless other features that two entities share. Orsi would say that there is overall incommensurability between being a psychiatrist and being an anthropologist, because the comparison lacks *one* measure that overrules all other measures.

In turn, pro tanto incommensurability emerges when "each career contains some value-making feature that the other simply lacks. . . . [T]he non-evaluative features have not enough in common for their evaluative contributions to be compared with each other" (Orsi 2015: 103). For example, psychiatrists might cherish highly developed skills in scanning brains, whereas anthropologists have no comparable skill. Anthropologists might have highly developed skills in posthumanist theory, whereas psychiatrists have no comparable skill.

Orsi (2015: 103) calls pro tanto incommensurability "more realistic" than overall incommensurability, but the opposite is true: the thesis of pro tanto incommensurability is produced by making the categories for comparison so fine-grained that they look incomparable, when actually they can always be compared as long as the category is more general. For example, instead of juxtaposing brain-scanning skills to posthumanist theory skills, we could compare "highly developed analytic skills." To complicate the picture, there are psychiatrists who cherish highly developed skills in posthumanist theory more than brain-scanning skills. All this means that pro tanto incommensurability does not exist.

What Orsi calls overall incommensurability does not exist, either, because even the most heterogeneous sets of qualities can be compared to each other. An overall valuation can be made. The question is not whether an overall decision of better or worse *can* be made, because it can always be made. The question is whether people *agree* that the valuation is pragmatically useful. True incommensurability never exists. What exists is a lack of consensus about meaningful valuation. This is precisely where commensuration *as a social process* comes in (Espeland and Stevens 1998).

Ruth Chang also draws a distinction between comparability and commensurability. She argues that two entities are *incomparable* when "they fail to stand in an evaluative comparative relation, such as being better than or worse than or equally good as the other"; they are *incommensurable* when they "cannot be put on the same scale of units of value" (Chang 2015: 205). She extends the "trichotomy" of value relations to five and adds algorithms for right choices: (1) if x is better than y, choose x; (2) if x is worse than y, choose y; (3) if x and y are *equally* good, choose either x or y; (4) if x and y are *on a par but not commensurable*, it is not clear what to choose; (5) if x and y are *incomparable*, choose either x or y. Chang holds that incomparability seriously disrupts decision making. Incomparability offers no rational reasons for choosing between alternatives. If two options cannot be valued by which one is better than the other, indecisiveness and inaction strikes: "Incomparability among alternatives, then, leads to a breakdown in practical reason" (206). One of Chang's examples for complete incomparability is how to compare the number "4" to "beauty" in terms of which one is "tastier" than the other. The number 4 and beauty are not just incommensurable, they are not even comparable in terms of tastiness.

There are several problems with Chang's analysis of incomparability and incommensurability. First, comparisons can *always* be made, because a common criterion can *always* be found. This is why neither incomparability nor incommensurability exists. Chang's example for incomparability—the impossibility of comparing the number 4 and beauty in terms of tastiness—is not valid because the criterion for comparison gets switched in between (from something not yet determined that "4" and "beauty" share, to another criterion, "tastiness"). Also, it is hard to imagine any practical reason for comparing "4" and "beauty" for "tastiness." This is a decision problem nobody has ever had. The comparison can be done, but it is hard to see how it would have any pragmatic relevance.

If it is true that anything can be compared with anything else in infinite ways, and that this infinity is constrained only by relevance for a living being (see the next section), it is clear that Chang's additions to the "trichotomy" of better, worse, and equal are wrong. Everything is comparable; hence, the fifth value relation (x and y are *incomparable*) does not exist. And since anything can be put on the same scale as anything else, the fourth value relation (x and y are *on a par but not commensurable*) does not exist, either.

I would go one step further and argue that the third value relation on value equivalence should be set apart from the first two (better and worse). The third relation, "if x and y are *equally* good, choose either x or y," presupposes that two entities *can* be valued as "equally" good. Ever since Heraclitus could not find "the same" river to step into for a second time, it is evident that it is far more difficult to ascertain that two entities have *exactly* the same value than that one entity is better (or worse) than the other. The same applies to Chang's idea of an *on a par* value relation: it is much easier to say that x is *not* on a par with y than that x *is* on a par with y.

When two items are compared, it is in most cases easy to say that x is better than y or that x is worse than y. Finding x better (or worse) than y allows a pragmatic choice between them. But it is much harder to find that x and y are *equal*. In most pragmatic contexts, finding equivalences is not nearly as useful as finding "more" or "less." Even if equivalence is established, it does not make decisions easier most of the time.

There are situations in which establishing equivalence *is* useful. One of these contexts is when quantities of materials are valued in money. Suppose an ounce of gold has a market value of $1,700. If I want to buy an ounce of gold, it makes sense to make sure that *this* quantity of gold I am about to buy is equivalent to any other quantity of gold that *other* people would buy at today's market price. When I put an ounce of gold on a scale, the scale measures whether *this* ounce is equivalent to *other* ounces. The scale does not measure the *equivalent* dollar value of the gold; nor am I putting *this* amount of gold on a scale in order to swap it with an equivalent *other* ounce of gold. The gold is valued in money by establishing equivalent weights.

Another context in which equivalence matters is medicine. Currently the "gold standard" is the randomized controlled trial (RCT). For example, a study on the treatment of depression conducted in the early 1960s by the US Medical Research Council compared the benefits of electroconvulsive therapy, imipramine, phenelzine, and placebo. The study argued that the tricyclic antidepressant imipramine is the most effective treatment based on comparisons of outcomes among these four groups. Subsequently, imipramine became the standard treatment that newer antidepressants had to beat to get licensed (Williams and Garner 2002). Drugs are deemed effective if the treatment group shows a "significant" improvement in symptoms over a control group (Timmermans and Berg 2003). The trials delegated other forms of evidence, such as case studies, to a lower level of significance (Sinclair 2004). Randomized controlled trials rest on the assumption that all of the entities involved in a trial remain "the same," whereas only the treatments are different. It has been argued that it is naive to believe that treatment groups can *ever* be kept "the same" (Worrall 2010). Still, RCTs serve a pragmatic goal when the similarity between test groups is "good enough." In RCTs, equivalence serves to establish a quasi-causal relation between medication and symptom improvement. Establishing "equivalence" of test groups serves an entirely different purpose from establishing equivalence of ounces of gold.

Finding that x is better (or worse) than y works without great precision. In turn, finding x to be of exactly the same value as y requires high levels of precision. Establishing exact equivalence requires precise distinctions, and, in turn, "precise distinctions force comparisons and stratifications" (Espeland and Lom 2015: 17). Try throwing a ball as far as you can. Then throw another ball "less far" than the first. Then throw a third ball *exactly as far as* the first ball. Throwing a ball *exactly* as far as the first is not just a little bit harder than throwing it less far: it is *infinitely* harder. Finding exact equivalence in the world is impossible; it exists only in mathematics. Not even dead objects can be found to be exactly the same. For living beings, exact equivalence is impossible; no two living beings can ever be the same.

The history of measurement scales is a history of attempting to pin down equivalent values. The standard typology of scales comes from S. S. Stevens (1946). He distinguishes four types of scale: nominal, ordinal, interval, and ratio. They are ordered by degrees of numerical exactness, from weak to strong. Nominal scales "do not assign the same numeral to different classes or different numerals in the same class"—for example, running races assign one number to each participant, and no two runners have the same number. "Beyond that, anything goes with the nominal scale" (679). Nominal scales have been called "qualitative measurement" (Bernard 2006: 46–47). Arguably, nominal scales are not even scales because they do not make variables numerically quantifiable. Nominal scales use numbers but only as names and not as scales. Next in the list are "ordinal" scales, which rank items without a defined distance between scale points (e.g., runners crossing the finish line as first, second, third, and so on). An "interval" scale puts measurement points at equal intervals (e.g., a thermometer measuring temperature by regular intervals of degrees Celsius). A "ratio" scale adds a nonarbitrary absolute zero point (e.g., the Kelvin scale measures temperature in reference to the lowest possible temperature, where all motion of atoms ceases). Finding x and y to be of "equal" value requires that a scale be put in place and that the people who use the scale agree on its validity and reliability. It is possible to find x "better" than y *without* a scale, but it is impossible to find x to be "equivalent" to y without a scale. And even with a scale, it is impossible ever to find *perfect* equivalence, because it is impossible to describe any location on a continuous number line. The best one can do is to establish a consensus on how much equivalence is *enough*. Even with the best scales, comparisons can establish only *more or less* equivalence.

Good Comparisons Need Good Practice

In the previous section, I argued that neither incommensurability nor incomparability exists because anything can be compared with anything else. In this section, I develop this further by arguing that there are *infinite* similarities between entities. No two entities can ever be "the same," and yet any two entities share an infinite number of similarities. What limits these infinite possibilities is relevance in a context. Context is always shared with social others.

That there are infinite possibilities for finding similarities is a key insight of the sociology of scientific knowledge. Barry Barnes, David Bloor, and John Henry call this *finitism*. Social conventions, routines, and habits are discovered as the only ground on which similarities rest: "Future use of our conventions of classification is underdetermined and indeterminate. It will emerge as we *decide* how to develop the analogy between the finite number of our existing examples of things and the indefinitive number of things we shall encounter in the future" (Barnes et al. 1996: 54).

The realization of infinite similarities has been of great importance in analytic philosophy. For example, Willard Van Orman Quine ([1975] 2004: 289) thought about the links between sense perceptions and pressures to decide: "Is similarity the mere sharing of many attributes? But any two things share countless attributes—or anyway any two objects share membership in countless classes." Quine tried to resolve the problem through "perceptual similarity"—that is, anything that *looks* similar *is* similar. Natural selection favors living beings that perceive the right kinds of similarities. Perceptions of similarity that "harmonize with trends in the environment" (Quine 2004: 171) maintain and enhance life.

The most compelling argument that similarity is not in individual heads but in distributed practice was developed by Nelson Goodman (1976, 1992), another analytic philosopher. Goodman also realized that any two things can be compared in infinite ways and can be found to be similar in infinite ways. Two things can be in a similar place, be of similar weight, be of similar color, contain a similar number of atoms, and can both be "made on a Tuesday." Similarity is everywhere.

To say that any two things are similar, one needs to know which properties are being compared. Goodman analyzes this through similarities between a sample and the set from which the sample is taken. Whether a sample is a "fair" sample of the whole cannot be answered merely by reference to the properties it possesses. One of Goodman's cases is about a customer who wants to reupholster her sofa. She goes to a tailor and asks to see samples of cloth. She selects her favorite cloth and puts in an order for enough to upholster her sofa. When ordering she insists that the ordered cloth should be "exactly the same" as the cloth in the sample. When the tailor delivers the order, the customer finds a big pile of small cloth pieces, all cut "exactly like" the sample. She is upset and complains that this is not what she had ordered, but the tailor replies that the cloth was cut "exactly like" the sample. For Goodman, the customer is right and the tailor is wrong, not universally but *within* the shared context of "checking cloth samples before ordering cloth for sofas."

Similarity and difference cannot be judged solely by looking at the things compared. There is always another dimension that needs to be considered, and that is context. Meaningful comparisons are always set in contexts of "good practice" (Goodman 1978: 136). Samples make sense only from within habitual practices, and in relation to interests and goals, which determine what is relevant and what is not. Only relevance of certain features in a particular context makes exemplification *possible* in the first place: "We must beware of supposing that similarity constitutes any firm, invariant criterion of realism; for similarity is relative, variable, culture-dependent" (Goodman 1992: 14).

The implications are profound: there are no meaningful differences between reality and how we conceptualize it, or between facts and values: "We cannot find any world-feature independent of all versions. Whatever can be said truly of a world is dependent on the saying—not that whatever we say is true but that whatever we say truly (or otherwise presently rightly) is nevertheless informed by and relative to the language or other symbol system we use. No firm line can be drawn between world-features that are discourse-dependent and those that are not" (Goodman 1984: 41).

We can test the thesis of infinite comparability with a famous example: Jorge Luis Borges's "Chinese encyclopedia" featured in Foucault's *The Order of Things*. The encyclopedia presents a taxonomy of "animal" as consisting of the following subtypes: "(a) belonging to the Emperor, (b) embalmed, (c) tame, (d) suckling pigs, (e) sirens, (f) fabulous, (g) stray dogs, (h) included in the present classification, (i) frenzied, (j) innumerable, (k) drawn with a very fine camelhair brush, (l) et cetera, (m) having just broken the water pitcher, (n) that from a long way off look like flies." For Foucault, what this taxonomy brings to light is not any new understanding of what "animal" means but a sense of radical alterity, "the stark impossibility of thinking *that*" (Foucault [1966] 2005: xvi).

However, with the thesis of infinite similarities reduced by context, this taxonomy of "animal" is *possible but unlikely* in terms of relevance in a context. Human taxonomies of animals *can* distinguish them by either belonging to the emperor or not; by being embalmed or not; etc. But it is unlikely that they would do so. First, the listed criteria do not exclude one another sufficiently. For example, why should there be no animals that are embalmed *and* belong to the emperor? Why should a suckling pig not also look like a fly from far off? It is unlikely but not impossible that humans—or any life form—would find these criteria relevant.

Comparing animals by whether they have mammaries (among several other salient features), as Carl Linnaeus did in the eighteenth century, makes more sense, because this distinction is more relevant (humans use other animals' milk for food). The choice of mammary glands as a relevant criterion for comparison happened within a historical context (Schiebinger 1993). Linnaeus was also the first to put humans *among other animals*. Before him, humans were a divine creation, set apart from all animals. Linnaeus's contemporaries were dismayed at the suggestion that humans are animals. (Incidentally, Linnaeus's comparison of animals by the presence of certain types of glands established another similarity between humans and bats discussed in chapter 1: we are both mammals.) For most people, until quite recently, it was *relevant* that humans had a special status in the divine creation and that undeniable *similarities* between humans and animals would not suffice to make them part of the same class of beings. Yet eventually the context for comparison shifted, and the classification of humans as mammals became the consensus. Taxonomies of living beings keep changing, and whole sets of taxa (domains, kingdoms, phyla, classes, orders, families, genera, species) get added, expanded, and revised. Taxonomies of living beings now look different from Linnaeus's own original classifications, and pre-Linnaean classifications are now nearly as alien as the Chinese encyclopedia.

 If anything is comparable to anything else and only "good practice" allows us to pare down which commensurations are relevant, then all comparisons are *social*. Wendy Espeland and Mitchell Stevens (1998: 313) study comparisons as commensurations and see all commensurations as social processes; for them, commensuration is "the comparison of different entities according to a common metric." Commensuration reveals the relative value of thing, ideas, and actions. The pragmatic goal of commensurations can be to evaluate how an entity can be exchanged for another entity, or how the loss of an entity can be compensated, or how two entities can be deemed to be of similar value. The metrics they describe entail both numerical and nonnumerical valuations. Enormous work in consensus building is required to establish and maintain commensurations as valid (Pigg 2001). All good commensurations are consensual. Even though consensus is never complete, commensurations can be more or less acceptable or "good enough." Commensurations between entities differ by how difficult, routinized and, technologically elaborated they are. Commensurations must be studied empirically because of "the conventional character of classification and the need to understand convention as a collective accomplishment" (Barnes et al. 1996: 55).

One cannot see two entities as "incommensurable" *unless* one has compared them with each other. The first axiom of communication is that "one cannot not communicate" (Watzlawick et al. 2011: 30). The first axiom of embodied living is that one cannot not value. In his *Philosophy of Money*, Georg Simmel overlooks the importance of relevance for life and only sees "embodiment" as a form of materialization of abstract ideas. But Simmel ([1900] 2011: 62) realizes the principle that *living is valuing*: "Our whole life . . . consists in experiencing and judging values, and that it acquires meaning and significance only from the fact that the mechanically unfolding elements of reality possess an infinite variety of values beyond their objective substance. . . . [W]e live in a world of values which arranges the contents of reality in an autonomous order."

Thomas Kuhn, who is supposed to be a champion of incommensurability, actually argued for the impossibility of both incommensurability and incomparability (Sankey 1993). For Kuhn (1982: 670), incommensurability is merely a "metaphor" for situations when specific words from one context cannot be translated into words embedded in other contexts "without residue or loss." Even when strands of meaning are lost in translation, that never amounts to incomparability. Another supposed representative of total incommensurability, Eduardo Viveiros de Castro (2015: 64), says that anthropology is the discipline of "comparing comparisons." He jokes that "it is only worth comparing the incommensurable" (64) to argue that what we call incommensurable is the *result* of comparison.

Espeland and Stevens also say that no two entities are beyond commensuration. *Incommensurability* is a term applied to commensuration processes that have failed to achieve even minimal consensus. "Incommensurables" are not entities that are intrinsically valuable beyond comparison. Instead, incommensurables are things, beings, or dispositions that are *valued* so highly that their value *appears* to be intrinsic: "Defining something as incommensurate is a special valuing" (Espeland and Stevens 1998: 326). People see something as incommensurable when they "deny that the value of two things is comparable" (326). *Life* is valued so highly that it appears to be intrinsically incommensurable. And yet the apparent incommensurability of life is only an effect of its being given such a high value.

Values can be *perceived* by members of a society to have *absolute* validity. Values can cease to be negotiable and become incommensurable *within* a culture. Whatever is valued *ought* never be exchanged. In this way, the highest values can be declared to be incommensurables *by social consensus*. The philosopher Michael Walzer (1983: 97) explored this thesis of consensus-based incommensurability, arguing that anything *can* be commensurated, including life itself: "There is no reason to think that the translations can not be made; indeed, they are made every day. Life itself has a value, and then eventually a price (different conceivably for different lives)—else how could we even think about insurance and compensation?" But not everything *ought to be allowed* to be commensurated. Walzer draws up a list of what should be excluded from exchanges. The first item on his list is human life: "Human beings cannot be bought and sold" (100). Other valued entities include freedom of speech and love. Walzer reasons that each of these entities should not be put up for sale and be commensurated in money. It would have been more precise to say that these entities ought to be excluded from *any* form of commensuration, not just *money-based* commensurations. Consensus-based incommensurability can mean that something valuable ought not to be exchanged for money. It can also mean that *one* incommensurable should not be exchanged for *another* incommensurable. Love should not be exchanged for money, but neither should love be exchanged for freedom of speech, or freedom of speech for life. Love ought not be for sale, but economists argue that, in reality, everything is for sale. The next chapter explores why economists see "life and limb" as fully commensurable.

THREE

Never Enough

Markets in Life

The Price of Life: The Subjective Theory of Value

Most anthropological value theories sense "a great rift between ethical value and economic value" (Lambek 2008: 133–34). Cultural values (in the plural) seem incommensurable with economic value (in the singular). Cultural values are meant to be beyond exchange, whereas in markets, anything can be exchanged. Money appears to make all value commensurable. Oscar Wilde, in *Lady Windermere's Fan*, distinguishes "cynics" from "sentimentalists" by whether they believe that money degrades true value:

> A: "What is a cynic?"
> B: "A man who knows the price of everything, and the value of nothing."
> A: "And a sentimentalist . . . is a man who sees an absurd value in everything and doesn't know the market price of any single thing." (Wilde 1995: 45)

Most anthropologists are sentimentalists, whereas most economists are cynics. Economists want to know the market price of any thing. If there is no market yet, they create one: for carbon emissions, for example (Dalsgaard 2013). On the stock market, derivatives make anything tradeable with anything else. Derivatives proliferate new ways of making anything commensurable and tradable, irrespective of what the underlying assets are (LiPuma and Lee 2004). Economists ask about the value of everything in terms of money (or other currencies) and compare the value of everything by what deal gives the better return on investment. Foucault describes *homo economicus* as someone whose life conduct is steered by profit calculations: "An economic subject is a subject who, in the strict sense, seeks in any case to maximize his profit, to optimize the gain/loss relationship; in the broad sense: the person whose conduct is influenced by the gains and losses associated with it" (Foucault 2008: 259).

In mainstream economics, value is synonymous with market value expressed in price. If the price of an ounce of gold is $1,700, then this quantity of money *is* the value of gold. Market value becomes the only measure of value. Anything can be given a price, and anything can be drawn into exchanges. Human life itself is not "priceless"; instead, its market value can be calculated in many ways (e.g., Baron 2007: 358–60; Hausman 2015). It took economists a while to figure out (lit., put figures on) how human life can be made into a calculable asset. In the first half of the twentieth century, the methodological and ideological work was complete. Life and death became measurable by criteria such as future earning capacity. Once the criteria were established, life could be treated like another type of property (Zelizer 2011: 27).

The website DrugPricingLab.org calculates how much cancer drugs cost in the United States and how much they "actually" enhance life. Users can scale how important certain criteria are: dollars per life year, toxicity, novelty, rarity, population burden of disease, cost of development, prognosis, unmet need. In 2019, the annual spending for cancer drugs in the United States was $32 billion. The website calculates that the value of enhancing life is merely $2.5 billion—a gap of nearly $32 billion. It seems that the drugs are massively overpriced. But they are overpriced only if it is assumed that the value of one year of life is $12,000. If the value of a life year is assumed to be $300,000, the cancer drugs come out as a bargain, because they return a life added value of $62 billion. If the market "novelty" of a drug is seen as highly important, the life added value of the drugs doubles again, to $121 billion. So, are cancer drugs overpriced?

It depends on how much life is worth. Is a life year worth $12,000 or $300,000? That depends on social consensus.

By making the incommensurable commensurable, markets appear to debase all that is valuable. Marxists are especially keen to reveal the value extractions of capitalism. Market capitalism institutionalizes the "shameless, direct, brutal exploitation" of everyone. Capitalism reduces all value to money. All true values are destroyed. The only value cherished in capitalism is "naked self-interest" (Marx and Engels ([1848] 1952).

This is how critics think capitalists think, but not how free-market economists think. For the most radical economists, "economic value" *does not even exist*. Instead, those economists subscribe to a concept of values (in the plural) similar to that of the cultural theorists. For radical free-market economists such as Friedrich Hayek, "values" are changeable estimations of what is important in life. Values are realized and fulfilled by expending scarce economic resources. Economic value theory does not require values to be shared within a cultural collective, and there is no need for values to be permanent over time. By contrast, cultural value theory requires that values be shared and that they stay more or less constant. For economists, the free market does not destroy cultural values; instead, it allows values to change and optimizes their future fulfillment. The market is a mechanism that brings the changing values of individuals into play with one another. The optimal resource allocation under free-market conditions allows the optimal satisfaction of cherished values. Hayek (2011: 87) put changing value orientations together with market liberalization: "We must recognize that even what we regard as good or beautiful is changeable. . . . [W]e do not know what will appear as good or beautiful to another generation. . . . It is not only in his knowledge, but also in his aims and values, that man is the creature of the process of civilization, and in the last resort it is the significance of these individual wishes for the perpetuation of the group or the species that will determine whether they will persist or change." Instead of determining what will count as valuable in the future, the market responds to changing value orientations and allows them to flourish: "Most economists conclude therefore that there is no point in sitting in judgement about what people *should* want; better to just accept that they *do* want" (Graeber 2019: 205). This is the liberal idea of value realization through market exchanges. But it cannot be overemphasized that free-market economics does not "ultimately" value everything in terms of money. Free-market economics is not even an ideology of "capitalism"

because money, as a medium of exchange, can be replaced by other measures of value. It's *not* "the economy, stupid." It's not even the money. It's the "free market as a tool for value realization."

Economists began with the idea that things have intrinsic value. An ounce of gold was considered valuable because its *substance itself* was "precious" metal. Things had a natural price, and natural price was also the morally just price. For Adam Smith ([1776] 1952), markets do not determine the true value of things; rather, free markets let the natural value of things emerge without distortions. In the mid-nineteenth century, economists moved to a "subjective" theory of value: nothing has any intrinsic value; instead, the market determines the value of everything. Markets are constituted by the meeting between supply and demand. Within the individual exchange partner, this meeting between supply and demand is mirrored in a meeting between "sacrifice and gain" (Simmel [1900] 2011: 97), or how much someone is willing to give away in return for something that she wants to gain: "The economic object does not have—as seems at first sight—an absolute value as a result of the demand for it, but the demand, as the basis of a real or imagined exchange, endows the object with value" (97). If demand goes up while supply goes down, value/price increases. If demand goes down while supply goes up, value/price decreases. Natural value is replaced by an ever-shifting point of intersection between supply and demand. "Equilibrium" between supply and demand can never be found: there is always more demand than supply, or more supply than demand. Just as determining equivalence is practically impossible in any comparison, so equilibrium is impossible to achieve in any exchange.

Perhaps the first thinker who formulated a theory of relative value was Thomas Hobbes. In *Leviathan,* Hobbes argues that neither things nor human beings have intrinsic value. Instead, value is entirely dependent on the "need and judgment" of other people: "The value, or WORTH of a man, is as of all other things, his price . . . and therefore is not absolute; but a thing dependent on the need and judgment of another. . . . And as in other things, so in men, not the seller, but the buyer determines the price" (Hobbes [1651] 1998: 59).

Drawing on Aristotle's *Politics* (1952: I.9), Smith ([1776] 1952: 12] distinguishes between "use" and "exchange." Smith first mentions this distinction after saying that money has become "the universal instrument of commerce": money commensurates all things. He wants to find the "rules which men naturally observe" whenever they exchange items. Smith writes: "The word VALUE, it is to be observed, has two different meanings, and sometimes expresses the utility of some particular object, and sometimes the power of purchasing other goods which the possession of that object conveys" (Smith 1952: 12). He then expresses his puzzlement that "things which have the greatest value in use have frequently little or no value in exchange; and, on the contrary, those which have the greatest value in exchange have frequently little or no value in use" (Smith 1952: 12). When Smith then says that "nothing is more useful than water," he defines use value directly by *bodily* needs. Value for *life* determines "use value." In turn, exchange value is free from bodily necessities. Many goods that are exchanged have "scarce any value in use." Smith compares water with diamonds. Water has great use value but no exchange value. Diamonds have no value in use because they do not contribute to the sustenance of life. But diamonds have great value in exchange, because the same quantity of diamonds can be traded for water by a factor of one to billions. This seems paradoxical. Are commodities that sustain life *less* valuable than commodities that have no life-enhancing value?

This so-called paradox of value seemed resolvable through the concept of "diminishing marginal utility" (e.g., Jevons [1871] 2004: 425). When water can be obtained in great quantities at minimal cost, it has low exchange value. Only if water became extremely scarce would its exchange value increase. Exchange value is detached from bodily necessities; hence, it can drive toward infinite accumulation of wealth. The founder of the subjective theory of value (STV), the Austrian economist Carl Menger (1840–1921), defined value as a derivative of embodied wants: "Value is neither inherent to goods nor a property of them, but rather only the meaning that we first attach to the satisfaction of our needs, or our life and well-being, and subsequently transfer them to economic goods as the exclusive causes of them" (Menger 1871: 81, my translation).

This turn to subjective demands is the so-called marginal revolution in economics. Marginal value (*Grenzwert*) is the thin borderline between "still valuable" and "not valuable anymore." The theory is called the subjective theory of value because its core idea is that "subjective valuations of goods depend upon the life situation of their owners" (Coombs and Frawley 2019: 4). Value is not intrinsic to any commodity but pitched as being entirely "in the mind" of the consumer (see Applbaum 2004: 52). The STV assumes that relative scarcity and subjective preferences are the key principles of price fluctuations. In the wake of the marginal revolution of the nineteenth century, economics became defined as the study of how resources are allocated under constraints of scarcity. Eventually, the STV dispensed with the division between use and exchange value and merged them into generalized utility: "Decision makers experience utility from owning or consuming goods" (Glimcher and Fehr 2014: 5).

Different versions of the STV have been proposed since Menger and Jevons invented it in the nineteenth century. A recent formulation, prospect theory (Barberis 2013; Kahneman 2011), analyzes the heuristics that people use to assess value when they do not know all the salient features of the two options and when they may not even know what features to look for. Prospect theory shows that price alone does not determine value. For example, the loss-aversion heuristic makes people prefer "not losing" to "gaining." Exactly "the same" amount of money feels subjectively different depending on expected utility. That does not mean that heuristic decision making always produces the maximum utility. Arriving at the best decision is difficult (Baron 2007). Heuristics can make decisions predictably irrational (Ariely 2009). Prospect theory shows that value parity is never perceived even when two options, by price and risk involved, are exactly "the same." Some choices can be harder than others, but incommensurability and incomparability do not exist. There are only judgments about relative value, with some more straightforward than others. No two things are ever of equal value; there is only better or worse value. Even commodities, which are thought to be fully interchangeable with one another, are all distinct.

Thinking through the proliferation of generic pharmaceuticals that are "the same" and yet are made to look different, the anthropologist Cori Hayden argues that commodities are no longer interchangeable with one another as if they were all the same. Drug regulators use labels such as "biosimilars" or "bioequivalents" to differentiate among different types of similar pharmaceuticals. Dr. Simi, a Mexican chain that sells generic drugs, differentiates its products by saying they are "Lo mismo, pero mas barato!" (The same, but cheaper!). Producers make distinctions by highlighting different properties. Hayden finds that labels for sameness, such as "similar" and "equivalent," are used to make distinctions. Labeling different kinds of sameness introduces *different kinds of difference*: "If 'equivalence' and 'interchangeability' are themselves *forms* of concrete difference and specificity, the very basis for our understandings of the relation between sameness and distinction must be reorganized. Parity situations, no more" (Hayden 2013: 632). I agree with Hayden, except that parity is not "no more," as if parity existed in the past. Instead, it should be "parity situations, *never*." The "commodity" has never been a fully interchangeable thing. Or, to riff on Bruno Latour's *We Have Never*

Been Modern (1995): we have never seen parity. New labels that make the similar different, such as *biosimilars*, do not create difference. Rather, they highlight existing difference and turn it into a marketable asset.

Is Labor the Only Source of Value?

The downside of seeing value as price is that value added outside of markets *cannot* be counted. Measuring all value in market prices means, for example, that whenever people fall sick and have to pay for doctors, medications, and procedures, economic value is *added* rather than lost. In the United States, health-care spending reached $3.5 trillion, or $10,739 per person, in 2017 (Centers for Medicare and Medicaid Services 2018). Health care now makes up 18 percent of the entire US gross domestic product. If by some miracle everyone was cured and became healthy, the US economy would "lose" 18 percent of its value. Value creation should be measured by life enhancement, not by money changing hands.

In her analysis of the economization of life, the historian Michelle Murphy (2017: 27) points out how health is a fatal blind spot of money-based valuations: "The loss of life and world produces no subtractions. . . . [L]ife-sustaining activities of people and the often gendered unwaged work of tending to bodies and communities do not count. They do not register in the calculus but haunt it as zones of life that could not yet be subsumed." The destruction of the natural environment for economic growth is another facet of this flawed calculation. Whatever industrial value creation might be measurable in terms of market exchanges, the destruction of value in the environment is left unaccounted for (Livingston 2019).

With a market-based definition of value, only organizations that sell something for a price are counted as productive and value-creating. This makes the public sector look like a drain on the value-generating private sector. This is particularly galling in the case of pharmaceutical research and development. Corporations draw on publicly funded research to develop products, then reap all the profits: "Taxpayers are now paying twice: first for the research and second for the premium that pharmaceutical companies charge for their drugs" (Mazzucato 2018: 194; Walwyn 2013).

The market concept of value creation is that buyers meet sellers, and whoever gets the better deal out of the transaction gains more value from it. "Value added" can come from charging buyers more than what the product is worth or by reducing production costs to increase profitability. Gaining a dominant position in a market allows one to realize even more gains from transactions. In the pharmaceutical business, one type of market dominance comes from gaining monopolies on patents. Intellectual property rights are legal means of eliminating "the same" products from the market to increase the scarcity (hence, value) of one's own product (Samuelson and Nordhaus 2010: 177).

The Marxian critique of free-market economics remains influential. For Marx, capitalism "fetishizes" relations between commodities instead of recognizing them as relations between human beings. Value appears to be determined by relations between things and things when, "in truth," value is determined by relations between humans. Society is made up of antagonistic classes. In capitalism, the bourgeoisie has gained control of the means of production. This puts them into a position in which they can extract the surplus value created by workers who have nothing to sell but their labor power. Marx proposes a labor theory of value (LTV) holding that all value is created from human labor. Labor is abstract labor time, as in the average amount of time necessary to produce a good (Stiegler 2013: 39). LTV was first conceptualized by John Locke and developed by free-market economists such as Adam Smith and David Ricardo before Marx adopted it for his own theory (Foley 2000). Mainstream economists jettisoned the labor theory of value long ago, but it is still strong in critical theory.

The extraction of the surplus value of labor is the signature biocommensuration of Marxian theory: things are valued by how much bodily effort had to be put into making them. LTV is a form of biocommensuration because labor is a particular mode of being alive as a human being: "Thus has Marx reduced value to embodied social labor-power and social labor-power is reduced to uniform units" (McCracken [1933] 2001: 42–43). "Living" labor as the source of all value is as important in current Marxian theories as it was in Marx's own work. For example, Michael Hardt and Antonio Negri (2017: 118) argue that capitalism extracts the value of productive labor in all its forms; at the same time, all possibilities for resistance against capitalism come from labor, because labor ultimately belongs to the laborers: "Living labor . . . is virtually, and potentially, disposed to affirm its own autonomy."

LTV has also been called an "embodied energy" theory of value (Harvey 2018; Judson 1989). This "embodiment" in LTV is different from embodied life valuing life. In Marxian LTV, the lifeless commodity embodies (*verkörpert*) the human labor spent on it. In embodied value theory (EVT), value is a function of being an embodied living being. Both EVT and the LVT see labor as a source of value creation. In LTV, it is the only source of value; in EVT, it is one of many sources.

The notion of "surplus" value of labor is at the center of the Marxian critique because only the extraction and appropriation of surplus explains the accumulation of capital in the hands of a few. For Marx, the appropriation is bad and must be stopped: "Modern bourgeois private property is the final and most complete expression of the system of producing and appropriating products that is based on class antagonisms, on the exploitation of the many by the few. In this sense the theory of Communists may be summed up in the single sentence: abolition of private property" (Marx and Engels ([1848] 1952).

It is unclear whether Marx saw any cultural or ethical "values" (in the plural) as human universals. In his *Theses on Feuerbach*, Marx ([1845] 2016) says that all social life (*gesellschaftliches Leben*) is "practical" and that all mysteries of the world disappear as soon as we understand human life as human practice (*menschliche Praxis*). Practice would then determine whether a value holds or not. Other parts of Marx's work suggest that the ultimate value of human life is in self-expression through unalienated labor. Marx never resolves the tension between an unchanging, ahistorical species being (*Gattungswesen*) and historically contingent dialectical praxis.

Marx's definition of "surplus" is blurry. He suggests that "surplus" is the remaining quantity of value after what is necessary for bodily reproduction has been subtracted. But the English term *surplus value* and the German word *Mehrwert* imply two different value comparisons. In "surplus," a line is drawn between a quantity of labor necessary to reproduce itself and a quantity of labor *beyond* what is necessary to reproduce itself. In turn, *Mehrwert* simply means *more value*. "More value" is not the same as "surplus." Just as "more than half" is not the same as "most" (Solt 2016), so more value is not the same as value above a threshold. Surplus value implies some kind of numerical scale; *Mehrwert* does not. If we have no idea how much value is created through labor, we cannot know how much of it is "extracted."

The idea that labor time alone can measure value is clearly wrong: ten hours spent building a sandcastle is not valuable in the same way as ten hours spent marking students' essays. To be sure, Marx's arguments about value and labor are more complicated than that. He writes that labor is "*not the source* of all wealth" (Marx 2016: 2784). He also argues that labor produces value only if what is produced is "socially necessary" (Harvey 2018: 450). Yet Marx clearly sees value creation through labor as the key relation between humans and nature. For Marx, the distinction between use and exchange value, and the notion of labor as the true source of all value creation, are universal laws and not historically specific to capitalist modes of production.

The main problem with Marx's value theory is that it is absurdly reductive. Labor time can be a relevant metric for value comparisons, but it *cannot be the only metric*. Human labor is clearly a source of value creation—no one would deny this, not even free-market economists. But Marxists made it an article of faith that human labor is the only source of value creation. Exchanging commodities in the market can never be a source of value, they say. Nor can caring for others be considered value-creating labor (Bear et al. 2015). Marx may be aware of the immense heterogeneity of both use value and concrete forms of labor (Harvey 2018: 43). But Marxian theory still reduces everything to the use-exchange binary and ignores a universe of other forms of value creation. One of the differences between LTV and EVT is that EVT tries to capture the whole universe of ways in which value is created. LVT emphasizes labor as the single source of value creation and assumes that all value can be measured by the kind of labor expended on it. By contrast, EVT sees labor as just one among multiple other forms of value creation and assumes that value can be measured in multiple ways.

Granted, Marx's LTV provides a vantage point for critiquing exploitative relations. In 2020, Jeff Bezos's net worth was $140 billion. At the same moment, Amazon warehouse workers in the United States earned $10 an hour without paid sick leave. If this looks unfair, Marx's labor theory helps see why. If labor were the source of all "real" value, then those who do the work—the laborers—are the ones who should get the credit for value creation. The value gap between Bezos and Amazon workers is obscene. But not even this injustice can be fully explained by LTV because Bezos's "worth" is calculated not by the labor he performs but by his total nonfinancial and financial assets. LTV cannot explain why Bezos's market value is so much higher than his employees'.

Beyond a critical analysis of labor relations, LTV is even less helpful. It creates a semblance of insight by analyzing all processes *as if* they were human/human labor relations and *as if* any surplus was a surplus of labor. LTV is completely inept at analyzing intersections between capitalism and the life sciences. "Labor" is one of the least important factors for pharmaceutical value creation, and "commodity" is not the form that most valued entities take. Most of the value created in the bioeconomy cannot be made sense of within LTV: the total hours spent by pharmaceutical industry employees on developing drugs is a very poor yardstick for measuring the value creation of the industry. And most of what is happening in the bioeconomy is not about commodities but about other forms of assets, such as intellectual property rights. These assets are not commodities and are misconceptualized when treated *as if* they were commodities. Yet Marxian theory forces all assets into the commodity form (Birch and Tyfield 2013). The body and its parts do not intersect with capitalism only when they become commodities. Not everything needs to be a commodity (or get commodified) before it has value. Marxian value theory hangs like a millstone around the neck of critical theory. This is another key difference between LTV and EVT: where LTV gets stuck with commodities as the only type of entity that results from value creation, EVT sees the commodity as just one among many valuable entities.

Marx's theory of surplus extraction has been widely used to analyze bioeconomies. For example, Catherine Waldby (2002: 309) defines "biovalue" as a surplus of vitality exploited by humans, as a "margin of biovalue, a surplus of fragmentary vitality." Waldby assumes that anything valuable has to take the form of a commodity before it can be extracted. In biocapitalism, cells, bodily tissues, plants, and animals are the new laboring proletarians that have their surplus vitality appropriated. Joseph Dumit's (2012) concept of "surplus health" assumes that health is equivalent to labor. Just as earlier capitalists extracted the surplus value of labor, so biocapitalists extract the surplus value of health. This theory rests on the Marxian assumption that health can be reduced to a commodity. Drawing on Dumit, Kaushik Sunder Rajan (2017) looks for the sources of "surplus extraction" in Indian biocapitalism. Marx would have suggested that the capitalist owners of pharmaceutical companies extract surplus value from their employees, but Sunder Rajan does not even see workers as the source of surplus value. White-coated lab assistants in Ahmedabad are unconvincing substitutes for Marx's Manchester factory workers. In his search for the subjects of extraction, Sunder Rajan finds impoverished patients who "labor" by taking part in clinical trials and then have their "surplus health" taken away from them. This reduction of participation in clinical trials to the equivalent of industrial labor obfuscates more than it reveals. Shoshana Zuboff's (2019) analysis of "surveillance capitalism" is right in saying that data (on health or behavior) are turned into resources for profit generation by private corporations. She argues that people become users; users become behavioral data sources;

data are assembled and crunched until a commercial product emerges; and this product is sold to the people who supplied the data. But she also falls back on a Marxian reduction: "We are the sources of surveillance capitalism's crucial surplus: the objects of a technologically advanced and increasingly inescapable raw-material-extraction operation" (Zuboff 2019: 16). Health data allow advanced biocommensurations, many of them for commercial purposes. That does not mean health data are "commodities" produced by "surplus labor" and "extracted" by companies. Rather, digital data are a new type of asset and ill understood as commodities.

Thinking through value when humans meet other species, Donna Haraway (2008) adds "encounter value" as a third value relation beyond exchange and use. Haraway's addition highlights how problematic the original distinction between use and exchange value is. It makes some sense to say that animals add value to human lives by being companions or a source of entertainment (Barua 2016). The problem is that the distinction between use value and exchange value is so reductive that the addition of one extra dimension, "encounter," does not remedy its initial misconception. Is all value really *either* in use *or* in exchange? What about gift value, share value, substitute value, insight value, keep value, borrow value, redistribution value, simplification value, and many more? What about "tending, transforming, reshaping, and rearranging materials and elements that already exist" (Graeber 2019: 228)? It took anthropology a century to realize that sharing is *neither* gift exchange *nor* commodity exchange (Widlok 2017). The notion that things have "biographies" of switching between commodity and gift form (Kopytoff 1986) is trapped in the same reductive gift-commodity binary and wrongly assumes that "gifts" are heterogeneous whereas the commodity is the *only* universally recognizable form of things. The reduction of value to either "exchange value" or "use value" ignores thousands of other ways value is created. The reduction of all value to commodities in either use or exchange is a gob-smacking example of how generations of theorists can be afflicted by a bad case of functional fixedness (Duncker 1945). The realization that "value" cannot be reduced to either use value or exchange value is prevented by a woeful hegemony of thinking of all entities as commodities for use or for exchange. A vital task of a new theory of value is to imagine things beyond commodities and to imagine value creation beyond labor.

Exhausting Too Many Possibilities

What is the relation between free-market economics and poor mental health? Are people who live in capitalism at a higher risk of suffering from depression? One answer is that capitalism increases depression because it overwhelms with its constant pressures to make choices. *LuL* Homo economicus encounters an infinite number of possibilities and has to find the best deal all the time. With scarce resources, utility must be maximized. But when the choosing gets too tiring or fails to give satisfaction, depression increases. Embodied value theory emphasizes the vital importance of decision making for maintaining life (see chapter 1). Life must decide and move forward (Barnes et al. 1996; Read and Hutchinson 2014; Wolfe 2010). Indecisiveness and loss of "resonance" with the environment puts life in peril. As I argue in what follows, the rise of depressive illness goes hand in hand with the deepening presence of capitalist ideology in everyday life.

"Indecisiveness" or "trouble making decisions" appears in all mainstream psychiatric diagnostics as a key symptom of depression. "Indecisiveness" clusters with "feelings of worthlessness," "loss of energy," and "difficulty concentrating." Depressed people find it harder to choose between available options than people without depression. The fifth edition of the American Psychiatric Association's *Diagnostic and Statistical Manual of Mental Disorders* (DSM-5) defines depression by a range of symptoms, including persistent indecisiveness, diminished interest in activities, slowing down of thought, reduction of bodily movement, loss of energy, diminished ability to concentrate, and feelings of worthlessness. The eleventh edition of the World Health Organization's *International Classification of Diseases* (ICD-11) includes diminished interest in activities, difficulty concentrating, feelings of worthlessness, hopelessness, psychomotor retardation (or agitation), reduced energy, and fatigue.

People with depression talk about struggling with decision making in their everyday lives (Leykin and DeRubeis 2010). Just as much as sadness, depression is associated with being numb and without emotional responsiveness. Emotions guide decisions; they literally "move" the person "out" from where they are. The numbing of emotions makes deciding harder, not easier. The common distinction between "fact" and "value" assumes that the best decisions are rational decisions from the head, "without anger and zeal." Indecisiveness in depression shows the opposite: to live is to value, and to value means to *feel* in the body that one thing is better than another. Emotions, as "somatic markers," improve decisiveness (Bechara and Damasio 2005). In turn, affective indifference leads to indecisiveness: "All stages of intellectual enquiry are motivated and guided by emotions of various kinds, such as curiosity, doubt, wonder, surprise, and satisfaction. Given that depression lessens or even extinguishes the capacity for some of these, it surely interferes with belief-forming processes, especially where value judgments are concerned" (Ratcliffe 2014: 273). The German word for affective indifference is *Gleichgültigkeit*, which literally means "being of exactly the same value." When two possibilities appear as exactly equal in value, one perceives them with indifference. Indifference leads to inaction, and inaction leaves the self "stuck."

Feeling hopeless seems to be related to not being able to imagine a better future or to believe that improvement can be possible. Recovering from depression means regaining the ability to see different paths as possible and to regain the emotional salience of why one choice is better than another. Being ill often comes with a state of hopelessness and inflexibility. All forms of therapy try to give people hope that they can heal and that alternatives to the current impasse exist (Csordas 2002; Hinton and Kirmayer 2017).

Psychiatrists say that depressive states make people brood over the smallest decisions. Patients depend on other people to choose among possibilities. Self-reported problems of indecisiveness match psychometric tests that show depressed people's diminished ability to decide. Indecisiveness can, of course, also be a trait of people who are not depressed (Frost and Shows 1993). However, even without depression, severe indecisiveness is strongly correlated with low self-worth (Ferrari 1991). Abstract rumination leads to worse outcomes than rumination focused on concrete tasks. It is better to ask, "How can I fix *this* problem?" than to ask, "What does all this mean for my life?" or "Why is this *always* happening to *me*?" (Di Schiena et al. 2013).

In depression, the ability to choose is diminished; the motivation to choose is diminished; and the energy necessary to choose is diminished. *Devaluing oneself* goes hand in hand with struggling to value anything *outside* oneself. Valuing oneself low, valuing all possibilities of life low, and having no motivation or energy to enhance life all go together in the depressive moods. Feeling sick of life and sick of having to make choices can run together. Some psychotherapies begin by *valuing* clients as worthy individuals so that they in turn might be able to value themselves again. The therapeutic relationship is most effective when it is "marked by one primary value: namely, that this person, this client, has worth. He as a person is valued in his separateness and uniqueness. It is when he senses and realizes that he is prized as a person that he can slowly begin to value the different aspects of himself" (Rogers 1990: 176).

The sociologist Alain Ehrenberg (2010) argues that depressive "weariness of the self" is an effect of capitalism. The hidden link between capitalism and depression is the tiring pressure to make choices. The market economy vastly proliferates the possibilities from which individuals can choose. At the same time, the market increases the pressures on individuals to make good decisions because individual self-worth entirely depends on it: "A society of individual initiative and psychic liberation, insofar as it forces each person to make constant decisions, encourages the practice of self-modification and, in so doing, creates problems with the structuring of the self. . . . [T]he continent of the permitted has been absorbed by the greater domain of the possible" (Ehrenberg 2010: 223).

Ehrenberg retraces French psychiatric discourse across the twentieth century. Between 1900 and 2000, social relations changed from hierarchical to egalitarian, with a more equal distribution of wealth and status. In the 1900s, the prototypical mental conflicts came from struggles with authority and from deviance from social norms. The key pathology of the 1900s was neurosis, produced by the repression of desires. Conflicts lay *between* people. Throughout the twentieth century, flattening social hierarchies reduced neuroses. Desires could be fulfilled more freely. But this openness enhanced inner-psychic conflicts about motivation and decisiveness. Conflicts shifted to *within* people's own selves. All decision making has to be done by oneself, within oneself. One can never do enough; one can never improve enough. Eventually, the self becomes fatigued from having to make so many decisions.

Fatigued indecisiveness is not exclusive to twentieth-century France. The distress associated with "thinking too much" has been described in many places and many different eras (Kaiser et al. 2015). The *Bhagavad-Gītā*, the most important text in Hinduism, revolves around crippling indecisiveness and how to overcome it. Robert Burton's seventeenth-century *The Anatomy of Melancholy* ([1621] 2001: 368) describes how excessive decision making can cause depressive fatigue: "Through our foolish curiosity do we macerate ourselves, tire our souls, and run headlong . . . into many needless cares and troubles, vain expenses, tedious journeys, painful hours." What makes the fatigued self historically specific to the late twentieth century and early twenty-first century is that advanced capitalism cannot tolerate any kind of indecisiveness. When the majority of people still worked in agriculture, excessive choice was hardly a problem anyone had. In the highly routinized factory labor typical of most industrialization, indecisiveness was also still unproblematic. Indecisiveness appears as a serious pathology only in advanced industrialization. When work becomes ever less routinized and ever more demanding of individual creativity and flexibility (Martin 2009), indecisiveness becomes extremely devalued. Only when profit maximization under conditions of extreme complexity rests entirely on assured decision making can indecisiveness become a rampant disorder.

Neoliberalism as Verstimmung

The rise of neoliberalism continues and deepens the demands on flexibility and self-reinvention. Neoliberalism extends market competition into all spheres of life, including the inner self (Brijnath and Antoniades 2016; Hardt and Negri 2017; Rose 1990). In neoliberal selfhood, homo economicus replaces *outside* partners of exchange with his own *inner* self: "In neo-liberalism—and it does not hide this; it proclaims it—there is also a theory of *homo œconomicus*, but he is not at all a partner of the exchange. *Homo œconomicus* is an entrepreneur, an entrepreneur of himself . . . being for himself his own capital, being for himself his own producer, being for himself the source of [his] earnings" (Foucault 2008: 226). The self is turned into a business corporation, and like any corporation it has to be constantly striving, to grow and get better. People either move "up" or they are "out." Standing still is not an option any longer (Rosa 2016). The self takes itself as its own competitor in a market for getting the best deal from every moment of life (Scharff 2016). In the original Protestant ethic that Max Weber ([1904–1905] 2010) describes as the root of capitalism, the goal was not to maximize individual experience but to accumulate capital through strict self-denial. In neoliberalism, however, the goal is not self-denial but self-satisfaction. Foucault (2008: 226) argues that the neoliberal self values the maximization of its own satisfaction. The so-called fear of missing out (FOMO), defined as an anxiety that other people might be having rewarding experiences while oneself does not (Przybylski et al. 2013), can become an existential problem only in highly advanced neoliberalism. In its purest form, neoliberalism teaches that one can never have too many value-adding experiences.

There is no "diminishing marginal utility" to rewarding experiences. In neoliberalism, *one can never live enough*.

It may seem that neoliberalism sets higher *norms* for individual profit maximization through shrewd decision making. But "norms" have a different place in neoliberalism than in earlier regimes. Foucault argues that neoliberalism *displaces* norms as a standard toward which all behavior should be oriented. Neoliberalism designs incentive structures that reward some ways of feeling more than others. It "nudges" people toward some goals and away from others (Thaler 2015). These incentives are *external* to the self, "an environmental type of intervention" (Foucault 2008: 260). It makes decisions easier by setting outside incentives. But neoliberalism also fosters *difference* and maximum diversity. It builds new markets by diversifying demand. Disciplined selves make decisions through shared *internalized* norms. Neoliberal subjects have to decide among a multiplicity of options. The incentives stay on the outside and do not become internalized. Neoliberalism guides "free choice" by setting incentives, yet it diminishes normative expectations. Even when it nudges, neoliberalism puts far more responsibility on individuals to make their own choices than previous regimes. Neoliberal subjects are more prone to tire of decision making, and any difficulty in making decisions is far more noticeable than at any time before.

The self is at risk of getting fatigued when self-worth becomes contingent on market valuations, when the market offers up ever more possibilities, and when demands to "make the most" of one's life become overwhelming. How did self-worth become contingent on maximizing one's own potentials, and can this be traced to a particular point in time?

The philosopher Charles Taylor (1991) traces the concept of a self driven by inner-subjective value orientations back to German Romanticism, especially the works of Johann Gottfried Herder (1744–1803). In feudalism, the measure of worth lay largely outside the inner self: people were born into a position in a hierarchy, and worth depended on the judgment of social others. Herder shifts the locus of valuing away from social others and toward the self. Value now relies on a resonance between inner and outer. Herder calls this congruence a *Stimmung* (attunement) between what the individual self values and what is valued in the cultural and natural environment. Stimmung is the "measure" (*Maß*) of whether inner thinking and feeling resonate with the environment. In Herder's sense of "inner disposition in relation to the outside," Stimmung has been used only since the eighteenth century.

The word *Stimmung* is "untranslatable" (Cassin et al. 2014): it not just the "mood" of an individual or the "atmosphere" surrounding an individual but the alignment between inner and outer (Gumbrecht 2012). It is both inside and outside, a kind of public feeling (Cvetkovich 2012). *Stimmung* comes from "voice" (*Stimme*). When voices are well attuned to one another, they have the right pitch. In German, the same word is used for "true," in the sense of individual opinion being in tune with reality. To say something is true, one says "*stimmt!*" An *Abstimmung* is a group vote toward a consensus decision. If the vote is unanimous, it is *einstimmig*. When two entities are extremely similar, their forms overlap (*übereinstimmen*). *Umstimmen* is to change someone else's opinion. *Bestimmung* can mean "fate," but it can also mean "decision," "conclusion," or "command for action." In the twentieth century, the philosopher Martin Heidegger analyzes Stimmung as the emergence of being-in-the-world. Being-there is always already attuned to being, which allows being-there to orient its action toward and within the world: "Die Stimmung hat je schon das In-der-Welt-sein als Ganzes erschlossen und macht ein Sichrichten auf . . . allererst möglich" (Stimmung has always already opened up the whole of being-in-the-world and allows the self to orient itself *toward*) (Heidegger [1927] 1993: 137, my translation). Another related key word is *Verstimmung*—literally, "being out of tune." *Verstimmung* can mean "discord," as unpleasant disagreement between people. It can mean a lack of congruence or resonance between inner and outer (Rosa 2016). In German-speaking psychiatry, *Verstimmung* used to be the primary term for "mood disorder." *Depressive Verstimmung* continues to be widely used. Affect is the temporary modulation of depressive moods; Stimmung, the long-term disposition (Heinz 2014).

For Herder, Stimmung is the attunement of an individual with its natural and cultural environment. He introduces Stimmung in the context of how humans process sensations from seeing, hearing, and touching. No individual has the same inner disposition to process these sense impressions; everyone experiences the world in a different way. This inner disposition is shaped by culture and natural habitat, without ever being entirely normed into sameness. If an individual's Stimmung becomes too different from that of others, it appears first as oddity and later as mental disorder:

> Every person has his own measure, as it were, his own Stimmung of all sensual feelings to one another. . . . Doctors and philosophers therefore already have entire collections of peculiarly strange

sensations, i.e., idiosyncrasies, which are often as strange as inexplicable. Most of the time we notice this only in diseases and unusual coincidences; we do not notice them in everyday life. . . . [E]very human being speaks and understands only according to his feelings, so different organizations lack a common measure (*gemeinschaftliches Maß*) of their different feelings. (Herder 1965: 278, my translation)

Stimmung has different degrees of similarity within feeling subjects. It is never the same in all feeling beings but tends to be similar enough not to lead to Verstimmung.

Taylor argues that individualized Stimmung and lack of a "common measure" made authenticity and "being true to oneself" a core value of modern selfhood. What is right or wrong cannot be determined in an absolute way but depends on the inner truth in relation to outer environment. If the measure of truth lies in the attunement between self and outside, then losing this inner truth means losing grasp of reality as well. At the same time, every individual has to find his or her own way to truth; there cannot be one truth for everyone: "There is a certain way of being human that is my way. I am called upon to live my life in this way, and not in imitation of anyone else's life. But this notion gives a new importance to being true to myself. If I am not, I miss the point of my life; I miss what being human is for me" (Taylor 1991: 29). Drawing on Taylor, the bioethicist Carl Elliott (2011) sees this high value placed on authenticity as the source of patients' fears of taking psychopharmaceuticals. Can I be true to myself if a psychoactive drug changes how I feel and how I am attuned to the world? If antidepressants change the inner mood, they also change the relation to the outer, and the self risks losing orientation.

Both Taylor and Elliott emphasize the localization of Stimmung within the individual. But in Herder's version, Stimmung not only belongs to individuals; it also belongs to whole collectives. Stimmung is as much about subjective authenticity as about cultural authenticity. The authentic self-determining freedom of cultures, expressed in *Volksgeist* as a kind of collective consciousness, is the main theme of Herder's work. Even when he talks about Stimmung in terms of individual sense perceptions, this is firmly placed within similarities and differences among localized human collectives. Herder's philosophy of authenticity is just as much about individuals as it is about cultures. Stimmung defines cultures, and cultures define individuals. With Herder, valuing becomes relative to cultural consensus. Herder is rightly regarded as one of the pioneers of both cultural anthropology and transcultural psychology (Bunzl 1996; Rodseth 2018). He first described the kind of consensus-based relativism that inspired Franz Boas and the whole American school of anthropology. Boas held that "the strengthening of the viewpoint of the relativity of all *cultivation* and that the evil as well as the value of a person lies in the cultivation of the heart [*Herzensbildung*]" (quoted in Zumwalt 2019: 115). Herder's defense of cultural difference is still the backbone of cultural anthropology today.

Is it a coincidence that cultural value relativism emerged in the same era as the subjective value theory in economics? The great rift thesis (Lambek 2008) suggests that cultural and subjective value theories cannot possibly have the same origin. Herder and the Romantics embraced cultural values as incommensurables; they rejected abstract thought, gross materialism, and cold calculation. They thought that capitalism alienated people from themselves and from culture (Heinz 2014: 167). In turn, economists introduced the STV as a universal model of individual motivations that is valid in all cultures and all contexts. Its founders turned explicitly against historical and cultural approaches, and economics has been looking for law-like cause-and-effect relations ever since. Menger, a nineteenth-century pioneer of the STV, had nothing but scorn for cultural understandings of the economy. For Menger, economics discovers universal laws and steers clear of the morass of historical contexts. Just like biomedicine, economics is a hard science. Whoever thinks that economics can be "a historical science, like ethnography or anthropohistory," should check into a psychiatric hospital (Menger 1884: 63).

And yet Herderian anthropology and subjective value theory agree on some key points. Both see value as radically relative. Both emphasize the subjectivity of valuing. Both emerge from an egalitarian sensibility that it matters more what common people are doing every day than what select members of an elite are doing. Both share a liberal belief that self-determination is better than authoritarian oppression (Zumwalt 2019). While anthropology and the STV share value relativism, each has a different take on what that means. One divergence between them is what "value" is relative *to*. Herder says that every culture is unique in and of itself. Cultural value does not emerge from comparing different communities by a common metric. Every culture has its own pattern, and the value of each culture lies in its authenticity and originality. Herder's era coined the maxim that cultures are similar only when they are compared to themselves (*nur sich selber gleich*) (Fischer 1995: 150). Cultures *can* be compared, but their value remains inestimable: "Cultures are comparable but not commensurable; each is what it is, of literally inestimable value in its own society, and consequently to humanity as a whole" (Berlin 1976: 182). It would have been better to say that "inestimable value" does not come from the impossibility to commensurate cultures by a shared measure. Different cultures *can* be commensurated, but any such commensuration does not add value to them. In economics, making things commensurable always adds value. In cultural anthropology, commensuration subtracts value. Commensurating cultures devalues them because their worth *derives from* their authenticity. For Herder, cultural value is *measured* by degrees of authenticity and originality. Whenever value is measured by uniqueness, the illusion of incommensurability occurs.

Another divergence is the locus of Stimmung: cultural anthropology follows Herder in looking for valuing in the *relation* between an inner individual self and its outer environment. Anthropology has always been more about dividuals than individuals. Valuing belongs into this relational space of Stimmung. In the STV, by contrast, valuing gets localized within individual subjects. Homo economicus makes decisions by responding to outside information, but the decisions are made *within*. Profit maximization is localized in the individual: the decision makers who "experience utility from owning or consuming goods" (Glimcher and Fehr 2014: 5) are always human individuals and never cultural collectives. This is how neoliberal capitalism turned the freedom of "being true to oneself" into an unending demand for self-maximization. For Herder, being authentic means that everyone should be free to unfold their inner potential and seek congruence with the outside. In neoliberal capitalism, being authentic means that everyone is called on to enhance themselves all the time. But whether an individual manages to add value to her life still depends on outside recognition. Only the market can tell the individual whether her value is enhanced or diminished. The individual cannot draw value from within itself; it must seek outside validation. A sense of "inherent self-worth" is displaced by complete dependence on an environment, which is encountered as a market. The self is forced to maximize itself, yet the value added to itself can never be converted into an inalienable possession. In neoliberalism, one can never live enough. This nagging anxiety of "never enough" has been the root of the epidemic of mood disorders since the late twentieth century. The neoliberal demand to self-maximize creates a chronic incongruence between the self and the outside. Verstimmung becomes an inescapable condition in societies under the sway of advanced capitalism. In the next chapters, I return to fieldwork in India to ask whether the same logic of neoliberal economics and neoliberal selfhood can be found there.

FOUR

Making a Difference
Corporate Social Responsibility

Getting Primed for Antidepressants

Pharmaceutical corporations say they want to make a difference in the world. This is corporate social responsibility (CSR), also known as global corporate citizenship (GCC) or corporate sustainability. In this chapter, I explore CSR as a set of strategies that modulate similarity and difference. Corporate social responsibility reworks the boundaries between the inside and the outside of the corporation and moves stakeholders closer to or farther from its boundaries. Outside stakeholders make a difference to the corporation by being *outside yet aligned*. The corporation wants recognition as ethically good and aligns itself with stakeholders to receive this recognition. At the same time, corporations make sure that outside stakeholders do not subtract financial profitability. Corporations need to move stakeholders away whenever they need to protect profitability or reputation. It may seem that through CSR, "social issues get marketized, as opposed to markets getting socialized" (Moon 2014: 112). This misunderstands what CSR performs: it does not "marketize" social issues. It draws a boundary between corporation and society, but it wants to keep this boundary as flexible as possible. It creates new ways of *laying claim to* value generation *beyond* money. Corporate social responsibility first detects and then demands recognition for value generation in spheres outside the generation, in fields such as human rights, ecology, or gender balance.

One day, Dr. Mullick, a psychiatrist, took me with him to a "depression awareness workshop" organized by the world's largest pharmaceutical company, Pfizer Inc. Pfizer had hired Dr. Mullick as its key opinion leader for the event. After a morning shift of seeing patients, we headed to a fancy restaurant at lunchtime. Invited to the workshop were twelve general practitioners (GPs) with private practices in one of South Kolkata's richer areas. After a brief welcome, Pfizer representatives showed a fifteen-minute teaching video. Then lunch was served. Afterward, Dr. Mullick gave a PowerPoint presentation on the epidemiology of depression and the best available treatments. The best available treatment was, unsurprisingly, Pfizer's drug Daxid, the Indian version of Zoloft (sertraline). Dr. Mullick's talk was followed by a group session with diagnostic case studies. Based on patients' answers to questionnaires, the GPs were asked to identify which patients should be labeled "MDD" (major depressive disorder) and given Daxid. Training in diagnostics is a form of applied consensus building, designed to get any two doctors to recognize similar symptoms as belonging to the same condition. Diagnostic training aims to make symptoms commensurable.

The declared goal of the "awareness" workshop was to introduce the GPs to a diagnostic questionnaire called Primary Care Evaluation of Mental Disorders (PRIME-MD) Today. This questionnaire was developed by Robert Spitzer, chairman of the DSM-III task force and the architect of symptoms-based diagnostics (Spitzer et al. 1999). It is meant to be given to patients while they wait for their doctor's appointment. The patient hands the questionnaire to the doctor, and they speak about the results together. Pfizer's teaching video stated that leading American psychiatrists had developed the questionnaire to "enhance the ability of busy physicians to diagnose mental health problems." Because GPs are heavily pressured for time, they needed a "quick, easy to use" diagnostic tool to figure out whether a patient should be given antidepressants. Pfizer's PRIME-MD system promised to give them an "advanced algorithm" with which a diagnosis would not take longer than one or two minutes. The Pfizer material stressed the pivotal role of GPs in the global fight against depression: most patients' first point of contact are general physicians. Yet the GPs overlooked depressive symptoms; hence, the disorder remained heavily undertreated. The video underlined that "depression *should* and *can* be treated by GPS" and called on the doctors to use PRIME-MD daily: "Believe it or not, it is easy to learn, and you can diagnose depression in less than one minute." The video went on to state that PRIME-MD is now also available in eleven Indian languages, including Hindi, Marathi, and Bengali. Translations had been tested with three hundred patients in each language to adjust the questionnaires perfectly to local idioms.

One of the case studies enacted in the video is the story of Mrs. Rao. A GP introduces Mrs. Rao as a patient who is "not well educated." She has to support the whole family because her husband is an unemployed alcoholic. Mrs. Rao complains of backaches and headaches and has previously undergone an operation. When the GP reviews Mrs. Rao's PRIME-MD questionnaire, he detects "underlying depression." The video shows how the doctor and the patient interact (slightly abridged here):

> PATIENT: What is the cause of this?
> DOCTOR: We will come to that. First let's go over some of your answers in the questionnaire. . . . [Y]ou are not feeling so well. . . . [Y]ou are responsible for the whole family. . . . I think your symptoms are caused by depression.
> PATIENT: No, no, no! I just have a headache! I am not going mad!
> DOCTOR: You are not going insane. Depression is treatable. It will take six months to cure.
> PATIENT: Six months! Oh, no! A few days and I will be all right.
> DOCTOR: Depression is a medical condition. You wouldn't let a medical condition go without treatment, would you?

Against her protestations, Mrs. Rao is persuaded to take an antidepressant. Her doctor explains that her problems come not from her dire family situation but from "underlying" depression. The message conveyed by the video is that the GPs' educational mission is much enhanced if an awareness-raising questionnaire such as PRIME-MD is put at the center of the doctor-patient encounter.

By making the questionnaire available "for free," Pfizer says, it is providing a selfless service to the public. Raising awareness is part of the company's effort to be a good citizen. In the teaching video, an off-camera voice states, "Pfizer's commitment goes beyond developing effective therapies. The company works closely with patient groups and opinion leaders to increase awareness, as well as creating disease management programs."

As I enjoyed the buffet lunch with the doctors, I thought I was witnessing a typical moment of "biomedicalization" (Clarke et al. 2003):

patients are turned into flexible, self-caring health consumers who are able and willing to consume the latest pharmaceuticals. What had been called "medicalization" (e.g., Conrad 2005) was driven by the state. Biomedicalization, by contrast, was driven by private capital. In line with neoliberal transformations at large, biomedicalization was shifting the governance of health from the state to corporations and self-maximizing individuals. An imperative to "know and take care of thyself" created new "technoscientific identities."

Biomedicalization is defined, with reference to Michel Foucault, as a form of governmentality: a comprehensive set of techniques aimed at regulating and optimizing both populations and individuals. Biomedical governmentality captures "particular kinds of power often guided by expert knowledge, that seek to monitor, observe, measure, and normalize individuals and populations" (Clarke et al. 2003: 165). Biomedicalization replaces medicalization because national governments do not "claim—or are given—the right, the power, or the obligation to make such judgements in the name of the quality of the population or the health of the gene pool" (Rose 2006: 254). Now each individual citizen is encouraged to take responsibility for their own health, to manage their own lifestyle in a way that will optimize their health. The state is "no longer expected to resolve society's need for health" (Rose 2001: 6).

The PRIME-MD system looks like a good example of biomedicalization. Instead of targeting doctors, Pfizer aims to bring patients to a new level of self-responsibility. Doctors should not just write prescriptions but also raise patients' awareness. The educational mission is driven not by the state but by a private company. Active consumers promise to be better customers than passive patients. Thus, PRIME-MD seems to exemplify an emerging "neo-liberal consumer discourse that promotes being 'proactive' and 'taking charge' of one's health" (Clarke et al. 2003: 181). No doubt, both the incentives to take charge of one's health and the biotechnological possibilities to do so have been massively expanded in the past two decades. Putting "advanced algorithms" into the hands of patients so they can better self-govern is part and parcel of an emerging "algorithmic" governmentality of health (Bucher 2018; Rouvroy and Berns 2013; Ruckenstein and Schüll 2017).

But the message driven by the Pfizer representatives *beyond* the teaching video put the logic of biomedicalization into question. In his lecture, Dr. Mullick told the GPs that giving the questionnaire directly to patients would make them resist the diagnosis. His advice was *not* to hand over the questionnaire. Diagnostics should remain entirely with the doctors.

Patients did not need to know that they were being diagnosed with depression or that the prescribed drugs were antidepressants; PRIME-MD was not about educating patients, but about facilitating treatment.

Dr. Mullick's subversion of PRIME-MD's intended use was encouraged by the Pfizer representatives. His whole performance was put onstage by Pfizer reps: they had supplied the PowerPoint presentation at the venue. During the first part of his talk, Dr. Mullick just read out the prepared bullet points. Pfizer's support of the subversion of patient education was reaffirmed when I asked one of representatives whether he had a Bengali version of PRIME-MD with him. He said that he had not brought any Bengali versions—as if the translating into local languages was useless to begin with. He confirmed that putting the questionnaire into the hands of patients was not the point. Patients might use the questionnaire in irregular ways, misunderstand it, and misdiagnose themselves. The Pfizer representative emphasized that PRIME-MD was "strictly scientific." Thus, it was meant to be used only by doctors. In other words, PRIME-MD was *not* designed to let patients know themselves. Only doctors were allowed to know and govern patients.

Why did Pfizer go through the trouble of commissioning the questionnaire, translating it into Indian languages, and testing it with thousands of Indian patients if it taught doctors *not* to give it to patients? Was it a few rogue representatives in India who sabotaged the strategies of Pfizer's US headquarters? Or was Pfizer's talk of "educating patients" only a façade to cover another strategy? The PRIME-MD system could be criticized as brainwash (of consumers), or whitewash (trying to "look good" in annual reports), or just hogwash (pretending to give something but then not giving it). As I argue in what follows, it is worth taking Pfizer's invocation of "good citizenship" seriously.

Polyspherical Heterarchy

Pfizer says that "patient-focused health information" increases patients' ability to prevent and manage disease. To educate patients—both those currently ill and those potentially ill—about diseases and available drug treatments is part of Pfizer's corporate strategy. Pharmaceutical corporations-as-citizens take responsibility for making citizens responsible for health. Pharmaceutical companies have been changing and diversifying the labels for this over the years: corporate social performance, business citizenship, business ethics, stakeholder relationships.

"Philanthrocapitalism" works with the same principles (McGoey 2015). But corporate social responsibility is the general header under which such activities are grouped. Here I explore both CSR and GCC, the label used by Pfizer.

The most recent move in the industry is toward a unified "values" approach that promises to fully commensurate shareholder value with ethical values. Proponents of the "great rift" thesis say that "economic value and ethical value are incommensurable" (Lambek 2008: 133–34). Practitioners of CSR think that corporate citizenship fully commensurates economic and ethical value. Anthropologists may ask for a theory of value that allows one to "understand the workings of any system of exchange (including free-market capitalism) as part of larger systems of meaning, one containing conceptions of what the cosmos is ultimately about and what is worth pursuing in it" (Graeber 2005: 443). Corporate social responsibility has its own answer to this question in the form of thinking about "integrated" value creation across different spheres. This idea is also known as "shared value" or "blended value" (Aakhus and Bzdak 2012). Many pharmaceutical companies, including Eli Lilly and Sanofi, have stopped reporting CSR activities separately from financial performance (figure 4.1). The new model is an "integrated report" for both. An integrated value-based approach came in the mid-2010s. The promise is that "doing good" ethically does not need to be juxtaposed to "doing well" economically.

Integrated reports work on the principle that "value" is created in different spheres. Value is *irreducible* to financial profits. Ethical, ecological, and social value creation becomes continuous with financial shareholder value by expanding domains of value creation instead of reducing them to finance. Integrated reports square the circle of demonstrating profitability in all spheres without reducing everything to money.

The mobilization of different sources of value *internal* to the organization has been described as *heterarchy*, a form of organization in which the relation of elements to one another is either unranked or open to rearrangement (Crumley 2005; McCulloch 1945). Heterarchy is different from hierarchy, a form of organization in which elements are ranked in relation to one another in a rigid way. *Hierarchy* comes from the Greek word *hierarkhēs* (sacred ruler), reflecting that what is up and what is down within an order cannot be switched around, because the sacred is always up and the profane is always down. In turn, "heterarchy" literally means "rule of *difference*." In heterarchy, all elements can be up or

1.3 Overview of value created by Sanofi

Through the execution of our strategy and daily activities, we contribute to create shared value for both the Company and our stakeholders, always mindful of our impact on the communities in which we operate. The indicators below show the different nature of value created, in terms of economic, financial, access to healthcare, trust, social and environmental value.

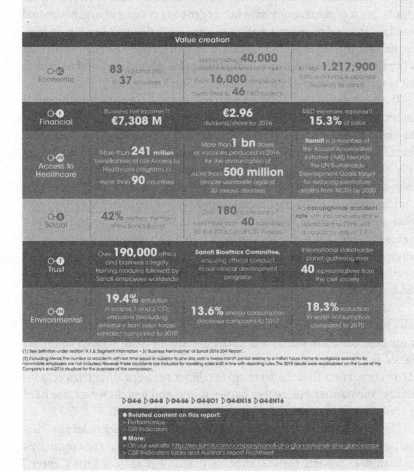

Figure 4.1 | "Value Creation" (Sanofi Integrated Report 2017)

down or alongside one other. Business organizations can be hierarchical or heterarchical.

The sociologist David Stark (2009: 5) describes heterarchical businesses this way: "Instead of enforcing a single principle of evaluation as the only legitimate framework, [corporations] recognize that it is legitimate to articulate conceptions of what is valuable, what is worthy, what counts. Such organizations have heterogeneous criteria of organizational 'goods.'" Instead of reducing all performance indicators to a single metric, heterarchical corporations thrive on difference: "Entrepreneurship is the ability to keep multiple evaluative principles in play and to exploit the resulting friction of their interplay" (Stark 2009: 15).

The new value paradigm in pharmaceutical corporations expands heterarchy beyond the boundaries of the organization. Instead of laying claim to value creation only within the corporation, it lays claim to value creation in spheres outside its own boundaries. Instead of ordering only elements within its boundaries, it also aligns elements outside its boundaries into a new order. This order remains flexible and denies that it is hierarchical. Corporate social responsibility regimes are getting ever more sophisticated at laying claim to value created within and outside, across different spheres. This could be called *polyspherical heterarchy*. In polyspherical heterarchy, the corporation manages to rearrange value-creating elements both within itself and in a multitude of spheres beyond of itself.

Pfizer puts its CSR under the motto "Our Responsibility." Pfizer also calls its CSR program "Global Corporate Citizenship," a term that became established in the 2000s. Chief executives from sixteen countries signed the first agenda for GCC at the World Economic Forum in 2002. Many companies find the term *citizenship* more appealing than *responsibility*. Substantial differences between GCC and CSR, however, are hard to spot. The terms are used more or less synonymously.

Pfizer sees GCC as a dialogic engagement with stakeholders by "listening, understanding and responding" to their needs; the company's 2018 annual report, for instance, is titled "Patients at Our Center." The dialogue takes many forms. Pfizer works with nongovernmental organizations (NGOs) to hear their concerns about its international operations. The Pfizer Medical Humanities Initiative tries to find a "balance between humane care and scientific expertise." Pfizer was the first US-based pharmaceutical company to join the influential United Nations Global Compact, a collaboration of governmental organizations and NGOs that endorse human rights, fair labor relations, environmental sustainability, and corruption-free business. According to Kofi Annan, former secretary-general of the United Nations and the sponsor of the Global Compact, the goal is "to unite the power of the market with the authority of universal ideals" (United Nations 1998). By signing the compact, Pfizer committed itself to ten principles of good citizenship. The first two principles relate to human rights. The first is that the company will "support and respect the protection of internationally proclaimed human rights"; the second is that the company must not be complicit in human rights abuses. The other eight principles relate to good labor standards, the environment, and anticorruption measures.

The UN Global Compact has been extended by other global agendas, such as the UN Sustainable Development Goals (SDGs). Pfizer now emphasizes that its "responsibility" contributes to achieving these goals, especially SDG 3: "Ensure healthy lives and promote wellbeing for all at all ages." The company is also committed to gender equality (SDG 5), clean water and sanitation (SDG 6), sustainable industrialization (SDG 9), sustainable consumption (SDG 12), and working with partners (SDG 17). Being a good corporate citizen means playing a positive role in all of these areas. In 2018, the United Nations issued a new set of guidelines on how corporations can "integrate" SDG attainment into their corporate reporting (Global Reporting Initiative and UN Global Compact 2018).

Pfizer India's CSR focuses on initiatives for "underserved" people: to support patient groups, to foster health literacy, and to build "communities." "Partnering for Health" and "Joy of Giving" are current themes. This includes an annual "festival of philanthropy" that engages people of different ages and backgrounds through "acts of giving." A motto used by the organizers of the festival is "Let's Keep Our Health to Enjoy Our Wealth" (Pfizer 2019).

The corporation as citizen looks like a signature component of neoliberal capitalism. Neoliberalism tries to make individual freedom dependent on market participation and reduce elected governments to an apparatus whose sole mission is to "facilitate conditions for profitable capital accumulation" (Harvey 2005: 7). For pro-business theorists, this is not corporations pushing into areas that belong to the state but, rather, the withdrawal of the state leaving a gap to be filled. In times when states are more reluctant to provide welfare and to ensure social rights, corporations volunteer to assume some of these responsibilities: "As one of the actors most central to globalization . . . corporations have tended to partly take over certain functions with regard to the protection, facilitation and enabling of citizen's rights" (Matten and Crane 2003).

To its critics, CSR is just as selfish as any other corporate activity (McGoey 2015). It is marketing and lobbying in disguise. It undermines democratic decision making (Moon 2014: 112) and is part of a corporate colonization of the public sphere. Corporate citizenship is a way to reconfigure profit maximization through notions of "citizenship" that previously were either neutral or even inimical to free-market capitalism. Being good and asking for something in return is even easier in a language of "citizenship" than in one of "responsibility." Whereas "CSR" emphasizes duties, "GCC" suggests a more balanced give and take. With GCC, pharmaceutical corporations position themselves as the same kind of actant as their primary stakeholders, the patients (who, in turn, get redefined as "pharmaceutical citizens" themselves [see chapter 5]). Defining GCC as "listening" to stakeholders also means that businesses want to be listened to in return. Good citizenship can yield good economic profits. The first return on investment is that a convincing program of GCC inspires consumer loyalty. Interacting with potential critics and pressure groups serves as an early warning system to avoid damage to a company's reputation.

Global corporate citizenship aims to boost the standing of Big Pharma among both citizens and national governments to justify demands for industry-friendly regulations (Abraham and Lewis 2002). The pharmaceutical industry is no different from other industries in pursuing a double strategy of "keeping government interventions away while depending on government to ensure its sustainability" (Ahen 2017: 91). Pharmaceutical lobbies argue that restrictive regulations are blocking innovative drugs from reaching the market. They estimate the cost of developing a new drug to be astronomically high: the full cost of bringing a new drug to market is $2.6 billion, they say, having increased 145 percent between 2003 and 2014 (Mullin 2014). High costs and low success rates undergird demands for more public support for the pharmaceutical industry. Emerging Biopharmaceutical Enterprises (EBE), an association based in Brussels that represents "biopharmaceutical companies of all sizes operating in Europe," is lobbying the European Union for an "improved climate" for private industries. One of the EBE's goals is to win public funding for private companies. Corporate social responsibility makes such requests plausible.

Recent work on rights shifted the focus away from value relativism toward the social lives of laws. The starting point of newer work is that rights have a "conceptual lucidity, simplicity, and universalism" (Goodale 2006: 26) that enables new social justice movements. So far, however, neither legal anthropology nor the anthropology of CSR (e.g., Dolan and Rajak 2016) has thought about what happens when corporations are also laying claim to human rights.

Through CSR, corporations act like rights-bearing citizens. The emergence of the modern corporation came from extending citizens' rights from individual humans to organizations. The corporation was accorded Lockean "personhood" to let it assume a legal standing similar to that of a private individual, with the rights to hold property, enter into contracts, be taxable by the state, and sue and be sued in court. The corporation *as* rights-bearing individual is the origin of the current institutional form (Schane 1986). As a person, the corporation enters into spheres of rights and responsibilities (French 1979). "Corporation" literally means "embodiment," from the Latin *corpus*. By "bringing several bodies together into one body," the concept of "corporation" performs a powerful biocommensuration: separate fleshy bodies merge into "the same" institutional body, which then assumes the status of an individual citizen.

The corporation as citizen can start legal battles for its rights against other citizens (Grear 2007). A striking example of the pharmaceutical corporation as entitled citizen is Novartis's struggle to obtain an Indian patent for Glivec (see chapter 1). One of the company's legal strategies was to lay claim to Indian citizenship rights by arguing that section 3(d) violated article 14 of the Indian Constitution, which guarantees equal protection of all citizens. Novartis, a Swiss corporation, pitched itself as an Indian citizen who defends the rights of all. The corporation declared it its responsibility as a citizen to stand up for the rights of corporations as citizens.

The emphasis on "global" citizenship adds a new dimension to the global aspirations of businesses. Since its institutional inception, the corporation has had ambitions for worldwide reach. It wants to "nestle everywhere, settle everywhere, establish connections everywhere," as Karl Marx and Friedrich Engels ([1848] 1952: 421) wrote. Global corporate citizenship does not reference specific nation-states. It is set on a supranational level; GCC appeals to "local communities" but works across the world. The UN Global Compact and invocation of SDGs are positioned on a global level and not in relation to national governments.

The goal of corporations is to make profits. The right to own property is the most important of all of the rights claimed by corporations. Whether corporations have rights and responsibilities in other areas, including the "social rights" of active and equal participation in the wider community (Marshall [1949] 1991), is not self-evident. Key thinkers of neoliberalism, such as Milton Friedman, believed that corporations should confine themselves strictly to profit making: "There is one and only one responsibility of business—to use its resources and engage in activities designed to increase its profits" (cited in Moon 2014: 102). Friedman's position looks shortsighted now. He had no idea what CSR, redefined as polyspherical heterarchy, could do for corporate value creation.

Implicit in Friedman's rejection of CSR is that corporations have a choice as to whether they want to expand into the sphere of social rights or not. Indeed, CSR had long been maintained as an entirely *voluntary* act of doing good. Until recently, laws detailed how corporations had to behave in the market sphere, but there were no legal obligations for corporations to be good beyond shareholder value. There were, at most, injunctions against firms that signed on to CSR frameworks and then did not stick to them. But apart from being removed from these treaties, there were no legal sanctions.

In recent years, however, many countries have made CSR a mandatory part of business activities. In India, a new Companies Act came into force in 2013. Section 135(3)(c) mandates that larger businesses report their CSR plans and spend a minimum of 2 percent of their profits on CSR. An entire consultancy and auditing business is developing around this new requirement for CSR.

Corporations can be held accountable for abiding by national laws. The legal commitments to being a "global" citizen are lower. This is different from being a citizen in the usual sense of the word, whose rights and duties can be enforced by the state. Being a global citizen carries little legal weight.

Global corporate citizenship aims to be both "global" and "corporate." It is a form of transnational governmentality (Ferguson and Gupta 2002), but without control over a territory. Similar to NGOs and supranational organizations, corporations take over functions for which only national governments previously would have been held responsible. Global corporate citizenship is a form of transnational governmentality through which private corporations fashion themselves as "citizens" to open new fields of government.

It is also a way of governing people *within* the boundaries of the corporation. Global corporate citizenship can be understood as performance indicators set by the top management to govern all levels of the company "through normal corporate-management processes, from individual target setting to performance appraisals to compliance management to auditing to reporting" (Kumra 2006). Defined as actionable conduct of conduct within corporations, GCC compliance becomes a part of individual performance targets. Making salaries and promotions dependent on citizen-like conduct turns GCC into a government internal to business organizations.

While GCC is a mechanism of internal governance, it must always reach beyond corporate boundaries. The inclusion of nonbusiness "stakeholders" is critical for its legitimacy. Those outside of corporations who enter GCC alliances have to agree to many of its forms of governance. At the same time, nonbusiness allies are never subsumed by the corporation. Outside stakeholders add value to the corporation only if their *difference* is maintained. Full cooption would undermine stakeholder legitimacy. The goal of adopting CSR regimes is to make the corporation a citizen *among* other citizens. True recognition can be given by other citizens only from the vantage point of difference.

The requirement for including outside stakeholders makes it impossible to contain CSR strategies within the corporation and creates an openness to changing agendas on the outside. The recent entry of the "sustainability" agenda is an example for how outside ideas enter the corporation through CSR.

In the business literature, the "stakeholder approach" is the most influential way of conceptualizing CSR (Freeman 2010). A company's success rests on alignments with people who are affected by what the company does. Primary stakeholders are customers, employees, suppliers, and investors; secondary stakeholders include NGOs, governments, and the media. Companies strive for a positive alignment of all primary and secondary stakeholders. Managing stakeholders creates "a virtuous circle by which business is best served when the interests and values of all stakeholders are accommodated in company practices" (Moon 2014: 22). Stakeholder management aligns different pragmatic goals with one another.

This necessary openness to the outside is evident in CSR compliance auditing. When CSR moves from voluntary acts to being regulated, CSR auditors become a kind of outsider companies have to let inside. Auditing for CSR is a form of biocommensuration in which life enhancement is measured along defined categories. It biocommensurates the relative value of different actions taken by corporations, and it biocommensurates performance across different corporations.

To commensurate a company's financial bookkeeping, auditors are needed. Corporate social responsibility auditing is still in its beginnings; NGOs usually do not have the necessary auditing capacities and are hesitant to act like a PricewaterhouseCoopers of good corporate citizenship. A few rights institutes have moved into CSR auditing for pharmaceutical companies. For example, Novartis has been working with the Danish Institute for Human Rights to develop a compliance assessment that covers core areas of GCC. The institute's Human Rights Compliance Assessment (HRCA) assesses compliance using thousands of indicators, such as, "Does the company have mechanisms for hearing, processing, and settling the grievances of the local community?" It awards scores for various levels of compliance and prompts corrective actions. Big auditing firms have also developed their CSR portfolios. The Indian branch of the auditing firm KPMG markets a range of auditing services that keep businesses compliant with the Companies Act of 2013 (KPMG 2019). Corporate social responsibility auditing is developing into a competitive and diversified market in and of itself.

With its emphasis on "compliance," CSR aims to establish a uniform code of behavior within corporations and beyond. It appeals to universal values and claims to apply them in all countries. At the same time, as a form of neoliberal governmentality CSR is not about "normalizing" all individuals and populations across the globe. Rather, it is a way to make and maintain *differences.* It is an example of what Aihwa Ong calls neoliberalism "as exception" (Ong 2006). Ong analyzes the emergence of new alignments between business and politics that are "neither state nor market." Corporations use CSR to profit from the credibility of nonbusiness allies and do so most successfully when they do not try to "normalize" stakeholders.

In 1978–79, Foucault delivered a series of lectures on the birth of biopolitics (Foucault 2008). His analysis of neoliberalism as a form of biopolitics is still little known in anthropology because of its delayed publication in French and delayed translation into English. In the lectures, Foucault discusses different liberal and neoliberal forms of government. In the lecture dated March 12, 1979, Foucault asks whether neoliberalism is a form of normalizing discipline and argues that neoliberalism does *not* aim at discipline:

> What appears on the horizon of this kind of analysis is not at all the ideal or project of an exhaustively disciplinary society. . . . On the horizon of this analysis we see instead the image, idea, or theme-program of a society in which there is an *optimization of systems of difference*, in which the field is left open to fluctuating processes, in which minority individuals and practices are

tolerated, in which action is brought to bear on the rules of the game rather than on the players, and finally in which there is an environmental type of intervention (*intervention de type environnemental*) instead of the internal subjugation of individuals (*assujettissement interne*). (Foucault 2008: 259–60, emphasis added)

Foucault argues that neoliberalism does not reform inner selves directly; instead, it regulates the structure of incentives on which actors base their decisions. Neoliberalism replaces forms of *inner* subjectivation with interventions that target actors' *external* environment. It fosters different ways to behave because this is the best way to create new markets and exploit hidden opportunities. For Foucault, neoliberalism fosters minority views and leaves fields of action in a state of oscillation. Because of this, neoliberal society is not a social order in which normalization is either required or desired. This is why Foucault preferred neoliberalism to normalizing forms of power (Dean 2014; Lemke 2001, 2011). If put within the frame of Johann Gottfried Herder's Stimmung, disciplinary power is an outer that wants to transform inner personhood. Neoliberalism is an outer that does not care about the inner so long as the person responds to outside incentives.

Foucault's analysis brings out nuances in neoliberal governance that so far have received little attention. To put even more emphasis on the difference-making power of neoliberalism, I suggest calling it by another name: *near*-liberalism. The term stresses the oscillating form of neoliberalism. Near-liberalism emphasizes that freedom, emancipation, and autonomy are always held out as future goals, even if they are not yet realized in the present. It suggests that neoliberalism is not a uniform practice but tends toward nearness and local differentiation. It also accentuates that neoliberalism can switch back to restrictive modes of governing any time. Near-liberalism is not a program to get rid of the social and political from the sphere of economics. Instead, it seeks to produce new alliances among markets, states, and citizens. These alliances remain flexible to allow moving into new directions and cutting ties to stakeholders that have become liabilities. Near-liberalism allows for the maximization of returns through polyspherical heterarchy. It tends to promote biomedicalization, but it is not shy of suspending patient "awareness" and "self-responsibility" if need be. To show how near-liberalism allows corporations to form flexible alliances with dissimilar outside actors, let us return to Pfizer's PRIME-MD workshop.

Pharmaceutical Near-liberalism in Kolkata

What is Pfizer trying to achieve with its depression awareness workshops? Pfizer has been long established in India, consistently ranking among the country's top twenty firms. For the past two decades, it has been the second largest multinational after GlaxoSmithKline. The drug advertised to the doctors at the Kolkata workshop was Daxid, which, as noted earlier, is the Indian version of Zoloft (sertraline). Pfizer's original patent for Zoloft expired in 2006. In the wake of the expiration and the entry of generic rivals, Pfizer lost its $3 billion-a-year market (Ventimiglia and Kalali 2010). Producers of Indian generics, including Aurobindo, Lupin, Torrent, and Sun, have since captured the majority of the global sertraline market. In India, Pfizer never had a product patent for sertraline. The generic competition for sertraline is fierce: in 2019, there were seventy competing versions of sertraline in the Indian market. Pfizer cannot charge a higher price for Daxid, even though it produced the "original" Zoloft (see chapter 9). In fact, the price competition is so fierce that Daxid is cheaper than many generic brands. Under these conditions, Pfizer struggles to maintain its market share. Inviting doctors to a psychiatric infomercial helps build its brand. Fostering "patient awareness" is at most a welcome side effect. If raising awareness among patients causes a rupture, it becomes a liability.

The conventional story, repeated over and over for the past decades, is that there is a deep treatment gap between developed and less developed countries in regard to mental health treatments (see chapter 10). It is taken as a fact that doctors misdiagnose mental health problems and that they fail to prescribe the right treatments. The public health argument about a treatment gap is heavily promoted by pharmaceutical companies—in India, as elsewhere. As is pointed out in Pfizer's PRIME-MD information pack, general physicians "fail to diagnose and treat 50–75% of patients suffering from common mental disorders" because of their "inadequate knowledge of the diagnostic criteria." This accusation was not repeated in the Kolkata workshop. Yet the implicit suggestion was that the first group that needs better education about depression are the physicians, not (yet) the patients. At stake at Pfizer's workshop was the "global citizenship" of Indian doctors. All information about PRIME-MD—as being developed by cutting-edge American psychiatrists and so on—suggested to the local doctors that they need to prescribe far more antidepressants to catch up with global standards. The PRIME-MD system promises that its algorithm can turn anyone into a "world-class" diagnostician of depression. Pfizer wants to train GPs. Patients are not yet "stakeholders."

If the Pfizer workshop officially aims at aligning its citizenship project to that of Kolkatan doctors, what is the reason for unofficially discouraging them from using PRIME-MD? To answer this question, it helps to separate the views of the psychiatrists from those of the GPs. As the theory of biomedicalization would lead one to expect, it would be in the interest of both the pharmaceutical companies *and* the doctors that patients become cued into mental health problems and more willing to be treated. The psychiatrists do indeed share Pfizer's agenda of patient education, up to a point, but the GPs definitely do not.

Kolkatan psychiatrists are aligned with Pfizer's GCC agenda, especially its drive to raise awareness of disease among patients. When I asked Dr. Roy, one of Kolkata's star psychiatrists, about what should be done most urgently, he stressed the need for more awareness and proactive health seeking: "What has not yet come to India is the transformation from patienthood to personhood," Dr. Roy said. "I would like to see that more and more people come to psychiatry saying, 'I want to function at my best, I want to contribute my best, so tell me: in what way can I make improvements? What nutrition do I require for my brain, and what do I require so I can give the best to my family, my society, my country?'"

Dr. Roy thus envisioned a new alignment among pharmaceutical consumption, citizenship, and Indian nationalism. Taking psychotropics is framed not just as a right, but as every Indian citizen's duty. The low demand for psychotropics in India is turned into a call for a politics of national development and self-development through drugs. Psychotropics should be used like food supplements, not only to treat disease, but also to become "better than well." And the goal should be not just individual betterment but improvement of the whole country.

While none of the other psychiatrists I talked to was as ambitious as Dr. Roy, they all agreed that more mental-health awareness was welcome. This also meant that every patient prescribed antidepressants should be told about depression and why medication is needed. Once patients had made the difficult decision to go to a psychiatrist, no stigma was attached to hearing the diagnosis.

So if the psychiatrists are aligned with Pfizer's "awareness" goals, what do the GPs think? Dr. Mullick told the GPs that using the PRIME-MD questionnaire with patients might cause trouble. But this advice did not teach the GPs anything that they did not already know. Instead, it reaffirmed what they were thinking about the questionnaire all along: that there is no point in using it, as it was designed by Spitzer and Pfizer. Indian GPs would never hand diagnostic questionnaires directly to patients; they leave "education" out of their consultations entirely. In fact, they usually leave patients completely in the dark. When I interviewed GPs, they said that they told their patients *neither* that they had been diagnosed with depression *nor* that the prescribed pills were antidepressants. Patients had too many superstitions about psychiatric disorders ever to talk straight with them. Instead of confronting patients, trying to educate them, or even handing out questionnaires to them, Kolkata doctors avoid mentioning "depression" and "antidepressants." They never liked to confront patients. They did not want to become known as "mental" prescribers. Being seen as a *pagoler daktar* ("madman's doctor" in Bengali) would mean losing precious clients. Private GPs are dependent on patients' fees, paid in cash out of pocket. A doctor who unnecessarily upsets patients loses them to competitors.

To circumvent resistance, GPs have various strategies to prescribe antidepressants without telling patients about them. The most common is to highlight physical symptoms of depression, such as sleeping too much or too little, having too much or too little appetite, and so on, and then telling patients that the pills will help them sleep well or increase their appetites. To quote from one of the GP's replies: "No, I don't tell my patients. They take it very badly. Let's say someone [with depression] is suffering from insomnia. Then I say, 'Take this for insomnia.'" This is exactly how my friend Amit ended up taking generic Prozac to control his "greedy eating" (see the introduction).

When I asked the GPs why they were not telling their patients about antidepressants, they often argued that it was impossible to treat Indians like Europeans or Americans. They said that India is a developing country. Western standards of informed decision making were not applicable, because patients were incapable of making informed decisions.

Another reason for not informing patients is that starting adversarial debates is a waste of the doctors' precious time. They see their role as prescribing drugs, not educating patients. Trying to educate one patient is a disservice to all other patients waiting in line. Everyone has to pay the same fee for a medical consultation. If a doctor spends too much time with one patient, that eats into the time for all of the others. Therefore, not arguing with depressed patients is constructed as the most ethical practice.

A further argument is that relations between GPs and patients are very hierarchical. This hierarchy is constructed in filial terms: just as

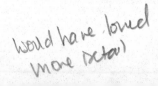
would have loved more detail

parents should treat their children like children *for their own good*, so doctors should treat their patients like children. This was especially true for patients suffering from depression, because they were even more impaired in their capacity to make the right decisions.

Indian GPs gain further financial benefit from telling patients as little as possible while prescribing as many pills as possible because they can directly earn from drug companies. A patient on antidepressants is expected to buy the medicine for several months, if not years. That makes these drugs very profitable for companies. Pharmaceutical companies reward doctors for generating prescriptions. In turn, companies monitor the prescriptions of individual physicians—for example, by quizzing staff at medicine shops (Lakoff 2004). Depending on the kinds of drugs doctors prescribe and how in what quantities, they are classified as "A" (high) or "B" (low) prescribers. Those in the "A" category are rewarded with gifts, conference travel, and consumer commodities. The few regulations that exist to curb such complicity are never enforced.

With more producers going into the psychopharmaceuticals market, there is intense competition for market share, and more money is lavished on doctors than ever before. While the biggest benefits are earned by psychiatrists, GPs are also benefiting. That Pfizer pays so much attention to GPs is one symptom of this. And these marketing efforts have not been in vain: Indian GPs routinely prescribe antidepressants. Selective serotonin reuptake inhibitors (SSRIs) are cash cows for pharmaceutical manufacturers (see chapter 7).

The GPs' idea of citizenship does not entail engaging patients as informed equals. That is why the Pfizer representatives did not bother to bring copies of the PRIME-MD questionnaire to the workshop: they knew that the GPs were not interested in using them. Viewed superficially, PRIME-MD, and, with it, Pfizer's agenda for global corporate citizenship, might look as if it is failing in India. What is happening instead is that Pfizer's representatives are making deliberate exceptions to global standards to accommodate Indian doctors' preference for keeping their relations with patients free of patient awareness. That the marketing representatives exempt GPs from using the PRIME-MD questionnaire shows how GCC, as a flexible regime of governmentality, works on outer incentives rather than inner normalization. It allows adjustments and realignments whenever it sees fit. It can best do so when liability remains with self-responsible "stakeholders" rather than corporations. Near-liberal corporate citizenship suspends biomedicalization and patient empowerment whenever it hurts profits.

FIVE

Pharmaceutical Citizenship, Marketing, and the Global Monoculture of Health

Marketing Demarginalization

People on the margins suffer. Bringing people in from the margins makes them better. Giving drugs to people brings them in. "Marginality as gap": this is the basic problem that all organizations concerned with global public health try to solve. Access to lifesaving pharmaceuticals as demarginalization is propagated by the World Health Organization (WHO), the World Bank, nongovernmental organizations (NGOs), state agencies, and international health and biomedicine at large. Marginality is a form of inequality that must be overcome. Treatment gaps must be closed; barriers to access must be torn down.

To call a person or a group "marginal" implies an ethical mandate to remove the marginality. A World Bank report on the voices of the poor (Narayan et al. 1999) uses the terms *marginal* and *marginalization* to describe social exclusion and the unfair distribution of goods and services. Regarding health care, to be marginal means to be cut off from the circulation of biomedical substances. The marginalized people quoted in the report all speak of being unfairly deprived of medicines (e.g., 87–88, 96, 113). Marginalization, poverty, and the exclusion from social networks become the same: "In explaining poverty, poor men and women very often express a sense of hopelessness, powerlessness, humiliation, and marginalization" (35).

The inclusion of "hopelessness" in this sentence is no coincidence. To be marginalized does not just entail difficulties in obtaining medical care. It is also linked to a greater risk of becoming depressed in the first place. Being depressed is seen as a symptom of being socially marginalized, and untreated depression is seen as a symptom of being marginalized from pharmaceutical networks.

The conclusion is that psychotropics should be made available and affordable to as many marginalized people as possible. A pharmacological promise of demarginalization is evident for most diseases: malaria, tuberculosis, HIV. It is also prominent in the discourse on depression in developing countries. Removing symptoms of depression contributes to removing social marginality, and vice versa. Offering a pharmaceutical substance to those at the margins is defined as the best way to help them. The definition of "marginalization" that the World Bank puts forth is typical of a monoculture of health.

A Dose of Life

The concept of biological citizenship coined by Adriana Petryna (2002) and extended by Nikolas Rose and Carlos Novas (2004) transformed understandings of the relations between biomedical expertise and political recognition. Biological citizenship moved questions of belonging, rights, and duties beyond the dyad of individuals and nation-states. "Citizenship" has become a series of overlapping projects that are not limited to the politico-legal sphere. "Biological" citizenship looks at how citizenship changes through biomedicine and new biotechnologies. Petryna (2002: 4) traced encounters among citizens, state bureaucrats, post-socialist politicians, and biophysical scientists in post–Chernobyl Ukraine to show that "these interactions illustrate how in the modern state, spheres of scientific production and politics are engaged in a constant process of exchange and mutual stabilization." Biological citizenship is focused on biocommensurations between citizens and states in cases where bodily harm is attributed to the state and a commensurate recompensation for the damage is sought from the state. It is a form of mutual validation of citizen and state, with the citizen asking for validation from the state via damaged embodiment.

To think through the political, ethical, and economic dynamics of pharmaceutical exchanges, I coined the concept of pharmaceutical citizenship (Ecks 2005). Pharmaceutical citizenship revolves around two questions. First, how does legal citizenship determine rights of access to pharmaceuticals? This includes the question of whether politico-legal equality between citizens is translated into an equal entitlement to receive drugs. Second, what implications does the taking of pharmaceuticals have for a person's status as a citizen? Questions here include whether the taking of pharmaceuticals impairs one's rights as a full citizen, or whether patients can regain full citizenship only if they undergo pharmacological treatment. Biological citizenship focuses on how bodily suffering is used to demand recompensation. In turn, pharmaceutical citizenship looks at how both citizens and states lay claim to rights and duties in pharmaceutical exchanges. In pharmaceutical citizenship, lives are valued relative to life-enhancing medications.

In India, pharmaceutical citizenship is linked to different postcolonial citizenship projects. This includes the question of who the "citizen" even is. In the discourse on democratic voting rights in India, Dipesh Chakrabarty discerned two rival notions of the citizen. The first is that of the "peasant as citizen," who, despite lacking education, is already a full citizen with all the rights that come with it. The second is the "not-yet-citizen peasant" who still "has to be educated into the citizen" (Chakrabarty 2000: 10). Without proper education, Indian democracy would not fulfill its promise. Pharmaceutical citizenship entails a similar friction between the citizen as patient who is entitled to medicines because she is already a full citizen and the not-yet-citizen patient, for whom taking medicines becomes a practice of becoming a full citizen. In pharmaceutical citizenship, the role of civic education is replaced by marketing in the form of both public health campaigns and corporate marketing of disease awareness.

Pharmaceutical citizenship is particularly poignant in the case of psychopharmaceuticals. Even in developed countries, the message promoted by the pharmaceutical industry is that antidepressants have the power to demarginalize the suffering individual and restore one's "own true self." For example, an American direct-to-consumer campaign for the antidepressant drug Paxil uses the slogan, "I feel like myself again."

Being oneself again means, above all, overcoming the isolating effects of depression and being able to reintegrate oneself into society (Dumit 2012). More than other medicines, psychotropic drugs hold the promise of quick and effective demarginalization. They promise to *restore* authentic selfhood.

The promise of demarginalization through antidepressants is a key theme in the marketing strategies of Indian pharmaceutical companies. In what follows, I discuss a selection of pharmaceutical advertisements (figures 5.1–5.3). The first ad is for the antidepressant Paxidep CR (Symbiosis/Sun Pharma); the second, for the brand Arpizol (Synergy/Sun Pharma); the third, for Firsito (Zydus Neurosciences). All of these advertisements are targeted at doctors. They all feature the brand name, the company logo, and the active substances in various available doses.

The catch phrase for Paxidep CR is "Live . . . Every Moment . . . with Confidence." Its ad gives explicit details of the advantages of the drug: significant improvement of symptoms in the first week of treatment; "56% remission rates" starting in the third week; "unmatched GI [gastrointestinal] tolerability," thanks to a special coating. An image shows a twenty-something couple, a man and a woman, holding hands with a child between them, smiling and dancing.

The ad for Arpizol dubs the drug "The 1st dopamine serotonin system modulator." Instead of describing the properties of the drug, it just shows an image of a smiling young man on all fours on a well-polished wooden floor with a child—presumably his son—riding on his back. Firsito is advertised as "First Choice" and touts its active ingredient: "Escitalopram in the treatment of severe depression." Half of the ad consists of a photo in which a man cheerily spoon-feeds ice cream to his female partner.

All of the people are attractive, smiling, and decidedly fair-skinned. (In India, lighter skin color means higher status; this is the selling point of countless "fairness" creams [Glenn 2008]). They are depicted not as isolated individuals but as cheerfully connected to partners and children. They are all engaged in some sort of play: feeding ice cream to each other, joking, dancing, holding hands. They all wear Western clothes and seem to be well off. None of the pictures show the medicines themselves or the act of ingesting capsules. In each case, it is impossible to tell who is taking the medication: is it the man, the woman, or the child? The medication seems to bring people back into society without stigma

Figures 5.1–5.3 |
Advertisements for
Indian antidepressants

or visible mark. No hint of any "marginal" social status is evident. The only type of person to reappear in all these ads is a male adult. If there is one demographic group in India that is the least marginalized, it is the fair-skinned, educated, middle- or upper-class father. In India, as in many other countries, men are less likely to be depressed than women (Kuehner 2017).

"Reintegrating Lives" is the motto of Zydus Neurosciences. Advertisements for psychotropics contain no trace of marginality (whether on the grounds of class, caste, gender, or stigmatizing mental illness). They suggest that the drug removes both depression and all forms of marginality and promise not just the relief of depressive symptoms, but full mental, physical, and economic integration. The promise of demarginalization is not limited to mental health; it extends to one's social status in general. The message is: take this medicine and you will not only be happy but married with children, rich, and living a Western lifestyle. Being one's own true self in India seems to mean being a middle-class subject clad in Western clothes. Of course, the same message can be found in advertisements for cars, refrigerators, and laundry detergent, which all engage images of happy middle-class selves (Mazzarella 2003). What is special about antidepressants is that there is nothing special about them: antidepressants are like consumer items among thousands of other consumer items. The gray past of suffering has passed, and a new age of middle-class happiness has arrived.

Marketing for psychotropics is full of great promises for the future (Jenkins 2015: 4). One type of this is the "self-test" for mental health. Most self-tests do not advertise a specific product but aim to "grow the market" for antidepressants generally. For example, a leaflet distributed by a Mumbai-based company is titled "The Depression Self Test." On the front, it shows a big "smiley" face encircled by the words: "Defeat Depression—Spread Happiness" and underlines that it is "FREE!" (suggesting that others would pay for a test like this). The back of the leaflet presents a list of ten items for self-diagnosis. If you experience "five or more" of the listed symptoms—"a persistent sad, anxious, or 'empty' mood; sleeping too little or too much; reduced appetite and weight loss or increased appetite and weight gain; loss of interest or pleasure in activities once enjoyed; restlessness or irritability; persistent physical symptoms that don't respond to treatment; difficulty concentrating, remembering or making decisions; fatigue or loss of energy; feeling guilty, hopeless or worthless; recurrent thoughts of death/suicidal attempt"— it says you should "see your doctor." The leaflet was produced and distributed by Ipca Laboratories, a company that produces all available neuropsychiatric drugs. Ipca's special division for "therapy-focused marketing of neuropsychiatric drugs" aims to create consumer awareness of mental-health problems. The Ipca leaflet is based on criteria for depression from the *Diagnostic and Statistical Manual of Mental Disorders* (DSM) but exaggerates the scaling of severity: "five or more" out of these loosely phrased ten criteria were enough to advise patients to go seek medical help. Even people who are not depressed would think they are ill and in need of medicine.

Symptom checklists aimed at patients do not just shift the focus from social marginality to individual pathology. They also suggest that individual pathology can be solved through a kind of globalized pharmaceutical citizenship. First, the language used in the leaflet is English, the global lingua franca. "Your doctor" is someone around the corner in an Indian town doctor and someone who commands the same psychiatric expertise as doctors in Europe or in America. Second, no mention is made of local idioms of distress; nothing is said about an Indian context of diagnosing and treating depression. Third, depression is not associated with "marginal" groups within India who might be more at risk for depression than people at the center. Instead, the "you" of the text could be anyone. Another telling trait of the leaflet is the smiley face, a kind of generic global representation of "face" without any trace of difference— class-based, ethnic, gendered, or other.

The "Depression Self-Test" aims to persuade that depression is a disease; that it is widespread; and that it is largely undiagnosed. Those who are defined as depressed are also defined as marginal to society so long as they do not go to see a doctor and get medicated. The promise of demarginalization comes in the form of "your doctor."

The blurring of boundaries between the normal and the pathological through antidepressants takes on a new spin in relation to marginality. The aim of the leaflet is to make as many people feel "depressed"—and, hence, "marginal" to society—as possible. It does so by reclassifying symptoms from normal to pathological. These diagnostics effectively shift the *measure* for symptoms from the healthy range to the disordered range. Reentry into society, in turn, is possible only with the help of medicine. But the "society" that one will reenter is not just any society but mainstream middle-class consumer society in tune with the global monoculture of happiness.

Two kinds of biocommensurations are evident. The first is the suggestion that "you" are depressed *like* so many other people. The second is that "you" can become free from *both* depression *and* socioeconomic marginality *like* so many other happy customers. What is going to be exchanged is not only a pharmaceutical. It is also an all-round enhancement of life. Ipca Laboratories' corporate motto, "A Dose of Life," captures this well.

Beyond Sociocentrism

Social scientists distrust pharmacological fixes for health because they present a pernicious reductionism. What has been described as "pharmaceuticalization" is a series of reductions. The initial meaning of "pharmaceuticalization," as coined by the health activist Mira Shiva (1985), was double reduction. First, health and well-being are reduced to biomedicine. All hopes are placed not on changing self-care, nutrition, the environment, or the workplace, but on biomedical therapy. Non-biomedical possibilities are sidelined. Second, biomedical therapies are reduced to doctors' prescribing the products of profit-oriented pharmaceutical corporations. Mark Nichter and Mimi Nichter (1996) also defined pharmaceuticalization as a reduction of human problems to medical prescribing. The difference between pharmaceuticalization and medicalization is that the reduction to drug prescriptions enhances the profit margins of companies, whereas the reduction to biomedical interventions enhances the professional power of doctors. John Abraham (2010: 605) also argued that pharmaceuticalization bypasses medicalization: "Pharmaceuticalization can grow without expansion of medicalization, because some drugs are increasingly used to treat an established medical condition involving no transformation of a non-medical problem into a medical one." João Biehl (2007) highlights a reduction—not the reduction of (individual) health to commodities but a reduction of (public) health to "vertical" interventions focused on supplying specific medications instead of tackling the underlying problems. A comprehensive approach to health is difficult; a targeted approach to supplying selected pills is relatively easy. This is why "pharmaceutical fixes of diseases often constitute the path of least resistance in contexts of underdevelopment" (Nichter and Vuckovic 1994: 1512).

Drugs seem like an inauthentic solution to problems of marginality. Giving drugs is a quick fix, at best, and a new form of exploitation by pharmaceutical companies, at worst. Marxian critiques of pharmaceuticals usually speak of drugs as "fetishized commodities" that divert attention away from unequal relations among humans while disguising them as relations between things and humans. This suspicion of commodity fetishism runs deep (e.g., Cohen 2016: 31; Downey et al. 1995). It would seem that, in the debate about psychotropics as a means of demarginalization, we are left with two positions. On the one side, most biomedical practitioners, the pharmaceutical companies, and public-health organizations subscribe to psychotropics as a cost-effective and logistically efficient way to reduce marginality. On the other side, social critics see psychotropics as fetishized commodities that create a false consciousness and stand in the way of solving the "true" problems of marginality and exploitation.

Bruno Latour rightly suggests that these dichotomies are not useful. Concerned by reactionary appropriations of sociological views of science as "constructed," Latour asked whether critical social theory of science should rethink what it is doing. For him, the social-constructivist critique of "commodity fetishism" itself worked *like* a "potent euphoric drug" (Latour 2004: 163) because it could never be falsified. Any object that the critic politically dislikes can be branded a "fetish" and discarded as useless: "When naive believers are clinging forcefully to their objects, claiming that they are made to do things . . . you can turn all of those attachments into so many fetishes and humiliate all the believers by showing that it is nothing but their own projection" (163). In the case of psychotropics, the easy social critique is to call them fetishes of biomedicine or of development. Instead of dividing the world into false fetishes and true underlying causes, we can see pharmaceuticals as matters of concern and not as matters of fact. We should find a way to think about psychiatric problems that neither reduces them to a logistical challenge of distributing best evidence therapies nor simply reject all psychotropics in all circumstances as commodity fetishes.

Medical anthropologists should not be too quick to separate human actors from nonhuman actors (e.g., pharmaceuticals). Instead, it is more fruitful to follow pharmaceuticals around and study their power not only to transform the bodies and moods of individuals but to transform social relations, as well (Ecks 2013; Hardon and Sanabria 2017; Whyte et al. 2002). Before returning to India, I want to illustrate this point with an analysis of one seminal North American text on psychopharmaceuticals: the *Beyond Therapy* report (President's Council on Bioethics 2003). A close reading of the report highlights patterns of sociocentric thought. The main idea of the report—that depression can be "truly" healed only through social reintegration—serves as a point of comparison with examples from India.

True Happiness   *⌐I skipped this*

Beyond Therapy: Biotechnology and the Pursuit of Happiness, published by the US American President's Council on Bioethics in 2003, remains the most comprehensive bioethical engagement on widening psycho-pharmaceutical uses to date. Also known as the Kass Report (after the council's chairman, Leon Kass), it presents a nuanced discussion of bio-medical enhancement technologies that promised to make people not just well, but "better than well." The starting point of the Kass Report is an idea from the American Declaration of Independence: "We hold these truths to be self-evident, that all men are created equal, that they are endowed by their Creator with certain unalienable Rights, that among these are Life, Liberty and the pursuit of Happiness." The Kass Report defines the pursuit of happiness as an inalienable right of all citizens. The right to individual authenticity is taken as universal. Happiness is an "overarching interest in our complete and comprehensive well-being" (President's Council on Bioethics 2003: 203). What "life" might mean, however, is never brought into focus or defined.

Along with "Better Children," "Superior Performance," and "Ageless Bodies," the problem of "Happy Souls" is a main concern of the report. The report, drawing on various sources, repeats standard epidemiological data finding that up to 29 percent of all US Americans suffer from "some form of depression" (President's Council on Bioethics 2003: 240). It also cites a constant rise in the number of depressed people and calls this a *true* increase in suffering. In other words, according to the report, rising disease rates were neither an artificial outcome of changing diagnostics (especially the widening of the "depression" classification) nor an outcome of different statistical methods. Although the number of people who were receiving antidepressant medication had increased dramatically, depression was still undertreated (240). Placing faith in future advances in pharmacological treatments, the Kass Report predicts a rapid further spreading of prescriptions for antidepressants.

By itself, the expansion of the use of psychotropics is not an ethical problem. The report suggests that psychotropic uses cannot be reduced to an artificial "commodification" of health. Rose (2010: 80) finds that the Kass Report criticizes neither "commodification" nor "pharmaceuticalization": "The critics are wrong in saying what is promised here is a shallow, illusory happiness in a pill. . . . [W]hat is involved here cannot be divided according to a binary logic of treatment versus enhancement." The bioethical problem is not that drugs may either relieve "true" suffering or facilitate "true" enhancement. What emerges instead is a neoliberal citizenship project that forces one "to manage one's self as a kind of enterprise of itself—a continuous work of modulation of the self in relation to an idea" (80).

The Kass Report separates the normal from the pathological and the enhanced. Low moods, sadness, and feelings of hopelessness are all part of "normal" life and should be accepted as such. These crises reflect the truth of human existence. Suppressing them through the use of antidepressants entails the risk of "undermining our true identity" (President's Council on Bioethics 2003: 225). The ethical difficulty is how to distinguish between true (objective, clinically evidenced) suffering and inauthentic suffering. Drawing this distinction is difficult, as the report acknowledges: "How can one tell the difference between true and false happiness, between the real thing and the mere likeness?" (209).

The term *true* is pivotal to the report's line of argument. Being able to distinguish truth from falsehood is a key concern of life. Only the authentic life is a good life: "In human affairs, we care a great deal about the difference between 'the real' and 'the mere appearing.' We care about 'living truly'" (President's Council on Bioethics 2003: 251). The report aspires to rediscover "the true meaning of our founding ideals" (xiv) while still savoring the fruits of biomedicine.

If "living truly" is so essential, how should we live truly? The answer that the report develops is that a true life is a life lived with other people, a deeply committed social life. The route to authentic happiness is to live one's life engaged with other humans. The report states that "we" want to be happy not because of pills but only because of "real loves, attachments, and achievements that are essential for true human flourishing" (President's Council on Bioethics 2003: xiii). True happiness can flow only from "the ties that bind and that ultimately give the individual's identity its true shape" (265).

Human lives are authentic when they are tied to one another. For the authors of the Kass Report, this close interweaving never poses problems of inequality. Disease is the sole reason for marginality. Class, race, and gender inequalities do not feature. In the Kass Report, being marginalized consists only of not being tied closely to others, and the reason for not being tied closely is depression. That is why antidepressant medications cannot bring back authentic happiness. Authentic happiness can come only from rebuilding and strengthening social ties. Only after social integration has failed to alleviate depression is it justifiable to draw on pharmaceuticals. If one does not strengthen social ties first, taking pharmaceuticals will *deepen* marginality; otherwise, drugs give only a "semblance" of authentic happiness. A life lived with things is a bad copy of a life lived with humans. True health is to be realized through social (re)integration. Taking psychotropics is inauthentic if building authentic social ties gets substituted by the taking of neurochemical substances. For the report, inauthenticity is the most serious threat to "living truly." The eerie *similarities* between happy states induced by social ties and happy states induced by drugs must be disambiguated. An inauthentic *substitution* of true social ties for fake pharmacological fixes must be avoided. There is one kind of biocommensuration that scares the authors of the Kass Report more than any other: the illegitimate substitution of social ties with drugs.

Even if most social scientists would shy away from such a frequent use of the term *true*, I suppose that they would readily agree with the report's conclusion. This argument about inauthentic substitution does not reflect enough what constitutes "true" or "authentic" happiness in the first place. In the Kass Report, the distinction between "authentic" and "inauthentic" forms comes down to a distinction between the true happiness that is achieved on a human level and the false happiness won through ingesting nonhuman substances such as antidepressants. In this perspective, reintegration through pharmaceuticals is ambiguous because it is not purely social.

What gets overlooked is that this definition of "authentic" happiness is *already* mediated by the *absence* of mood-altering drugs. It may seem obvious that "authentic happiness" is rooted in "true" social ties. But the concept of "social ties" is based on a *previous exclusion* of drugs from human relations. The grounding of authentic happiness in true social ties rests on what Jacques Derrida (2016) describes as logocentrism. The Kass Report puts "authentic" against its opposite, "inauthentic." It then privileges the primary term, *authentic*, and subordinates the secondary term, *inauthentic*. By the same logic, "social" ties are grounded in a subordination of "non-social ties"—in this case, ties mediated or created by pharmaceuticals. "Social" ties emerge as "social" only after nonhuman substances are prohibited from entering into a relation. Human relations produce "authentic" happiness, whereas relations between humans and nonhumans can produce only a poor and inauthentic copy of it. Humans can be truly reintegrated only when nonhuman substances are marginalized from human society. The Kass Report's definition of true happiness relies on the crossing out of pharmaceuticals as inauthentic nonhumans. This could be called *sociologocentrism* (see Halton 1995: 273).

The next question is whether this type of sociologocentrism is quite as universal as the Kass Report assumes it is. The report is looking only at the United States; it never takes a wider transcultural perspective. In fact, it does not even ask whether this insistence on authentic social ties is found as strongly elsewhere. In what follows, I look at how "true happiness" is defined in a different way in Hindu thought.

Untying the Ties That Bind

Achieving control over one's mind through meditative practices is a central element in all strands of Hinduism (Michaels 1998: 347–77; Rodrigues 2018). Virtually all of the major figures of modern Hinduism, including Ramakrishna, Vivekananda, Aurobindo, and Mohandas K. Gandhi, emphasized mind-control as a path to enlightenment, freedom, and "true happiness." The same notion is strong in popular Bengali Hinduism (e.g., McDaniel 2004; Östor 2004; Sarbadhikary 2018; Sarkar 1992). For Bengalis, the path to true happiness leads through controlling one's mind. A mind at peace, a "cool" mind, is a precondition for a truly healthy life. When the mind is not worried about anything, when the mind is concentrated, the body will also be healthy. The symptoms of a cool mind are a shiny, radiant face; success in any sphere of life where one chooses to excel; and the ability to transcend petty worldliness. In turn, when the mind is disturbed, the body will be disturbed—or, as the saying has it, "Mon kharap lagle, sharir kharap lage" (If the mind is bad, the body is ill). A jumbled mind can be the source of any disease: fever, headache, high blood pressure, diabetes, obesity, deranged hormones, heart attack, drug addiction. For true health, the lower body must not be allowed to rule the mind. An aphorism attributed to the nineteenth-century saint Ramakrishna lists belly, anus, and sexual organs as the three constituents of a *tribhumi* (tripartite land) from which all desires spring. For Ramakrishna, most people's thoughts never rise to the divine, never get beyond the borders of these "three lands" governed by the gross desires of eating, sex, and excretion.

I once asked Sarbani Ma, a female guru in the Kriya tradition, which reaches back to Mahavatar Babaji Maharaj, about the relation between true happiness and psychotropics (Ecks 2013: 23). Sarbani Ma said that drugs could only ever act for a short time. True happiness could come only from changing one's *inner* view of the outside world: "Depressed people are misguided. They don't know the other side of life. They go with the material life." The mind must rise upward: "All ego problems come from the lower self. The lower self rules the mind when the mind becomes attached to it. But when the mind is attached to the higher self, then it washes the lower self, and all good qualities come when a person practices yoga, all diseases will go, insomnia and mental disorders." Sarbani Ma's views—on mind over matter and on inner self over outside attachments—are representative of all traditions of Hindu monism.

The same notion of mind over matter appears in the works of Ramakrishna's most famous disciple, Swami Vivekananda. Once while accompanying psychiatrists on a hospital round, I encountered a Ramakrishna Mission monk who had been admitted with a severe episode of manic depression (Ecks 2013: 4). According to the psychiatrists, the monk had fallen back into severe episodes because he refused to take prescribed psychotropics (a mix of Prozac and lithium) regularly. The monk wore his saffron robes and was sitting upright in his bed, reading *Lessons in Raja-Yoga* by Vivekananda, when the psychiatrists arrived. The head psychiatrist asked the monk how he was feeling, and the monk replied that he was better and wanted to leave the hospital. Challenged by the psychiatrist over why he was not taking his medications regularly, the monk read out a passage from the book. For Vivekananda, the "force of thought" holds the key to physical health. Sensory perception makes "the particles of the brain fall into a certain position like the mosaics of a kaleidoscope." Conjuring memories of past perceptions means "resetting these particles." As in perception, a state of bodily and mental health is a constellation of particles, while disease comes from the particles in disarray. Similar to an act of remembering, powerful thought can rearrange these particles into a healthy order: "In case of illness the memory of the ideal of health may be roused and the particles re-arranged in the position into which they fell when healthy." Once the mental work is done, the body will "follow the brain" and get well again. From this supremacy of the mind over the body, Vivekananda extrapolates that medicines, as gross substances ingested from the outside, can never cure the body on their own. Drug action always needs support from the mind. All drugs do is to prop up the internal healing process that is ruled by the mind. The best medicines stir up this inner healing force: "There is only one power to cure the body, and that is in every man. Medicine only rouses this power."

This passage is emblematic of Vivekananda's philosophical thought. Similar quotations can be found in all of the best-selling religious self-care literature in India. Vivekananda's ideas are invoked to endorse all sorts of commercial, political, and social activities. Sayings by Vivekananda even feature in pharmaceutical advertising. For example, in one of its marketing posters, the Kolkata company Pharmagen's corporate logo is placed alongside an image of Vivekananda in meditation and a quotation from his works: "The world is in need of those whose life is one of burning love, selfless."

Vivekananda reformulated Hindu teachings in relation to the capitalist transformation of India in the nineteenth century. More than most other Hindu thinkers, he stressed the importance of working with, and for, other people. Yet just like other Hindu thinkers, Vivekananda saw the path to true happiness in *detachment* from ties to other people:

> We are attached to our friends, to our relatives. . . . What . . . brings misery but this very attachment? We have to detach ourselves to earn joy. . . . We get caught. How? Not by what we give, but by what we expect. We get misery in return for our love. . . . Desire, want, is the father of all misery. Desires are bound by the laws of success and failure. Desires must bring misery. The great secret of true success, of true happiness, then, is this: the man who asks for no return, the perfectly unselfish man, is the most successful. (Vivekananda [1907] 2003: 3–5)

Any form of being close with others ultimately leads to suffering and misery, because there will always be expectations of reciprocity. Being with others means being in an exchange relation, and whenever there are exchanges, there are disappointments. True happiness consists in doing work without expecting anything in return. Doing work and getting involved in the world should only be a practice of overcoming selfishness. Ultimately, happiness cannot be derived from social ties; it can be derived only from unraveling the ties that bind. Hindu philosophy emphasizes that there is no substitute for inner calm. It shares this point with Buddhism, which also understands mental suffering as an essential aspect of embodied being-in-the-world with other people rather than as an individual pathology in urgent need of medical treatment (Kitanaka 2011: 14; Obeyesekere 1985).

Among the different forms of biocommensuration, Hinduism finds *exchanges* most problematic: exchanges create dependence on outside others, and dependence stands in the way of true liberation. While Herder's Stimmung conceptualizes authentic selfhood as a *relation* between inner and outer, Vivekananda sees concrete others as a hindrance to liberation. Stimmung is based on a deeply dualist cosmology (God and man, I and thou). Vivekananda's philosophy is based on a monism of self and cosmos: both are already of one substance; it is only the concrete form, the embodiment, that creates an illusion of separation.

In my research on what Bengalis see as a good way to alleviate low moods, I found that they often cite social support as a source of getting better (Ecks 2013). Talking to friends and family clearly looks like a sociocentric strategy of health seeking. Indeed, India is always described, in both the psychiatric and the social-science literature, as a culture that values strong social ties (Markus and Kitayama 1991). Strong social ties are considered the reason that Indians with mental disorders seem to have better recovery rates than people in the West (Halliburton 2021).

Yet it also holds true that Hindu thought sees social ties as transitory, deceptive, and inauthentic. Social ties are part of the world of *maya*—the concrete form that the universe takes but ultimately a transitory illusion. In all of the monist streams of Hinduism (especially Advaita Vedanta), the true shape of the self can emerge only when social ties are severed and the soul (*atma*) is released from the world into blissful union with Brahma. Brahma is like a Superliving Body, alive and yet immortal at the same time. Brahma endows living beings with life.

In Hindu cosmogeneses, the space enfolding the living body is not an environment devoid of life but a timeless Body with endless energy. The difference between *atman* (self) and *Brahman* (the All) is a temporary illusion. The realization of the *Upanishads* is *tat tvam asi* (You are *that*), which means that the particular self is always already one with the universal All. A person's true shape is the transcendence of all shapes. Such experience of oneness, of a body identical with an All-body, can never be described and never be grasped, because all grasping needs minimal difference. In Hinduism, life is ever-trans*forming* (*samsara*). It never falls into inert emptiness. The soul (*atman*) can achieve liberation from the cycle of death and rebirth through merging with the super-alive All (Michaels 2015: 200). This is *jivanmukti*, which means "life released," as if relieved of a burden or a debt. In Hinduism, releasing life is the highest value, overriding the other life goals: pleasure (*kama*), worldly power (*artha*), and righteousness (*dharma*) (Rodrigues 2018). *Jivanmukti* is not the end of life; it is the *elevation* of life. Transcendent life is life relieved of the necessity to draw distinctions.

Social ties give only a temporary semblance of happiness. True bliss can be had only when there are no "ties" at all, when the boundaries between self and other are dissolved. Secular thought expects living beings to dissolve back into lifeless matter after death. Hindu thought also expects living beings to dissolve their fleshy form after death, but to carry on living in a higher form. There are two kinds of death: one that returns life to a no-energy state (the secular version) and one that makes life part of an eternal living All (the Hindu version). Transcendence, which is the essential element of religion, is the continuation of life in a *super*human form. Hindus believe that transcendence of the human leads to a super-alive state rather than to a state of cold emptiness.

The crucial distinction between Hinduism and the Abrahamic traditions lies in whether relations with other human beings are a necessary precondition for release from life and for entry into the Superliving Body. The Abrahamic religions are all strictly dualist. In Abrahamic cosmogeneses, a superalive and supremely powerful other is God. The Hebrew word *elohiym*—translated as "God"—literally means "strength" or "power." Drawing *distinctions* is a primordial act that brings everything into being: "Creation is nothing but the injunction: 'Draw a distinction!' Heaven and earth are thereby distinguished, then man, and finally Eve. Creation is thus the imposition of a mode of distinguishing, if God himself is beyond all distinction" (Luhmann 2006: 43). Once distinguished, beings can then be compared for similarity. God creates humans "in his own image" (Genesis 1.27)—that is, as *more similar* to divinity than any other living being (Eilberg-Schwartz 1986). Abrahamic cosmologies *start* with primordial oneness but do not *end* in oneness: a distinction between God and humans is maintained—even after the death of the individual living body, in what the New Testament calls eternal life (*aiónia zoí* in Greek). Humans may get closer to God and even share eternal life in God's heaven, but they cannot become *one* with God. This dualistic cosmology makes all humans *the same kind of fallen being* opposite God. In turn, salvation cannot be gained through individual efforts alone; the salvation of one human depends on the salvation of all humans. The same condition creates a *Heilsgemeinschaft* (salvation through fellowship). In the Jewish tradition, being part of the people of Israel is necessary to be in relation with God. In the Christian tradition, the Church is the body of Christ, and every member is a member of Christ's body. Resurrection and eternal life are possible only for members of this body. The Christian tradition takes life as the highest value. The anthropologist Didier Fassin (2018: 176–77) argues, along with Hannah Arendt, that the Christian concept of the "sacredness of life" is the source of biological citizenship. But the sacred life in question is not the mortal human body but the human body sanctified by communion with the body of Christ. Only as members of Christ's body can humans transcend biological death.

In Hindu philosophy, however, social ties are not a source of bliss. Nor is truth based in what society considers true or false. Society undergoes historical transformations, but social changes do not move humans closer to or farther from an eschatological end (Dumont 1975: 51; Trautmann 1995: 189). Salvation is not a communal affair; it can be achieved only by the individual soul (*antaratman*). An idea of linking different humans into one salvational body is alien to Hindu thought. Independence overrules solidarity with others. Hinduism has a principal disdain of the social, *including* social hierarchy:

> [Hinduism] devalorizes society and disregards power. The ideal is not hierarchical interdependence but the individual break with society. The ultimate value is release from the world. And this cannot be realized in a hierarchical way, but only by the abrupt break of renunciation. Indian society and its ideal are separated by a chasm and cannot be united. Nor are they intended to be united. The chasm is intentional. . . . Above the Indian world, rejecting and at the same time informing it, the renouncer stands out as the exemplar of ultimate value and authority. (Heesterman 1985: 192–93)

One can take this one step further to argue that Hindu thought does not just devalorize society. It does not see society as a significant category for salvation. The embodied Other is an illusion, just as much as the embodied Self is an illusion. The highest level of spiritual attainment in Hinduism is to become a *sannyasin* (renouncer). To some extent, the sannyasin leaves "social" ties behind through the act of renunciation. He is no longer a part of a family or a householder. But renunciation is not reducible to severing social ties. Renunciation radically supersedes the realm of communal life. Hinduism has no concept of salvation through fellowship.

Independence became the encompassing value of Hinduism through the interiorization of sacrifice (Heesterman 1993; Michaels 2015). In Vedic religion, sacrifice always referenced several human others apart from the sacrificer. In the post-Vedic era, the person who performs the sacrifice, the beneficiary of the sacrifice, and the sacrificial being itself all became one. The supreme sacrifice was then performed *by* the single Brahmin *for* the single Brahmin, and "relative superiority implies relative autonomy" (Fuller 1988; Parry 1994: 266). The force of this value of autonomy is still evident in the relative inferiority of Brahmins who performs sacrifices for others (Fuller 1984: 49–71). A Brahmin who receives gifts from sacrificial patrons also receives their inauspiciousness (Raheja 1988) and impurity (Parry 1994: 119–48). Only those who stay detached from others can maintain purity.

Hindu society never strives toward "normal" belonging to the community so that all "members" will behave and think in a uniform way. A homogeneous space of values is an ideal of the Abrahamic religions, but not of Hinduism. In the Abrahamic traditions, salvation is bound up with the fellowship of other believers. In the Hindu tradition, salvation can be achieved only by breaking away from the realms of the communal, the family, of exchange and mutual dependence. "Society" as fellowship for salvation is a key category in Abrahamic streams, but nothing commensurate can be identified in Hindu philosophies. This is not to say that Hindus would not acknowledge the existence and value of human-to-human relations. The point is that Hinduism radically devalues social relations. Social ties are nothing but a hindrance on the path to freedom.

The bioethical notion of true happiness emerging only from "ties that bind" is not a value that is shared by Bengali Hindus. Any promise of demarginalization—whether by means of stronger social ties or by means of psychotropics—might not be perceived as a path to ultimate happiness. The global monoculture of happiness does not ride only on the back of objects such as psychotropic medications. It also rides on the back of sociocentric ideologies that propagate social ties as the only authentic source of happiness. The promise of demarginalization through pharmaceutical citizenship is emblematic of this ideology. Marxian critiques of pharmaceuticalization as commodity fetishism and calls to find authenticity in social ties instead perpetuate rather than subvert this global monoculture of happiness.

The global spread of psychotropics is changing the parameters of what "true happiness" ought to mean. Giving pharmaceuticals as a quick way out of marginality is a concept so obvious as to be beyond questioning. In this chapter, I showed what underpins the politics of demarginalization and argued that strengthening social ties can be a source of happiness only in a dualist cosmology in which fellowship with an embodied Other is necessary for salvation. It cannot be the source of all true happiness in all places. In Hinduism, detachment is more highly valued than any promise of pharmaceutical demarginalization.

SIX

What Drugs Do in Different Spaces

Global Spread and Local Bubbles

Polyspherical Psychotropics

Psychotropics seem to have no spatial presence. They are tiny things that travel lightly from production to consumption. Their sole purpose is to be dissolved in the human digestive tract so that the active ingredient can find its way through the blood-brain barrier (Wilson 2015). But as I argue in this chapter, psychotropics are not without spatial presence. Instead, psychotropics can be powerful agents in the creation of pathological spaces. At the same time, the spatial relations between patients and prescribers can matter greatly for how different treatment options are evaluated. Relative social proximity makes a difference to how drugs are valued. The ethnographic cases from Indian clinics I unfold here show that social proximity between doctors and patients is better than distancing. I also show how face-to-face interactions in the clinic are deeply entangled with the capitalist globalization of psychopharmaceuticals.

The first clinical encounter took place in the outpatient psychiatric department (OPD) of a large Hindu charitable hospital in south-central

Kolkata. The hospital caters to low-income patients, but richer people also come because of the good reputation of its staff. Most psychiatric clients are seen in the general outpatient department on the ground floor of one of the hospital's wings. In the middle of a large hall are wooden benches where patients can sit while waiting to see a doctor. Cubicles for consultation line each side of the hall. A pool of psychiatrists gives a few hours per week of free service (*seva*) while maintaining for-profit practices elsewhere in the city. The doctors practice separately from one another and leave right after their shift ends.

While shadowing psychiatrists in the OPD, I observed around one hundred encounters. One of them was between the psychiatrist Dr. Mullick and Mrs. Saha, with her son Neel. Mrs. Saha was around forty years old at the time; her son, twelve; she had been bringing her son to Dr. Mullick for the past six years. Initially, Mrs. Saha sought the help of a psychiatrist because her son struggled in school. Dr. Mullick diagnosed Neel with attention deficit hyperactivity disorder (ADHD) and gave him methylphenidate (Ritalin). On the day I met them, Dr. Mullick first asked Mrs. Saha how Neel was doing. She replied that, on the whole, he was fine. Whenever he started to lose his temper, she was giving him the prescribed drugs. The discussion then shifted into a different direction: I learned that Mrs. Saha was *also* in treatment with Dr. Mullick. Four years after diagnosing Neel, Dr. Mullick diagnosed Mrs. Saha with manic depressive psychosis (MDP).

Mrs. Saha's goal in seeing Dr. Mullick that day was to get his authorizing signature for a brain scan that she wanted to have done in another department of the hospital. It had not been Dr. Mullick's idea to send Mrs. Saha for diagnostic tests, and they got into a lengthy discussion about why she felt that she needed a brain scan. During this dialogue, it emerged that Mrs. Saha had already had several blood tests and X-rays. She was desperate to find a biophysiological reason for her disturbed state. But Dr. Mullick was not convinced that a brain scan would bring up any relevant findings.

Dr. Mullick later explained how Mrs. Saha's suffering had unfolded. When she first brought her son to the outpatient clinic, her husband and in-laws were terribly upset. In the family's opinion, there was nothing wrong with the child. The boy was certainly not "mad." If someone was mad in the family, it was her, and if anyone was responsible for the boy's troubles in school, it was her. They pushed Mrs. Saha to seek psychiatric treatment herself. As Dr. Mullick explained, "They are blaming her, that she is responsible. On her own initiative she brought the child. The child was very much aggressive . . . , but they said that no treatment is required for the child. [They told her,] 'You are the patient. You go to the doctor. You are responsible for this.'"

This is how Mrs. Saha became a psychiatric patient after her son had become a psychiatric patient. At the same time, Mrs. Saha's status in the family home deteriorated: her husband and her husband's brother started to beat her, and eventually she was exiled from the inner part of the house, to sleep alone under the stairway, like a dog.

When Dr. Mullick asked Mrs. Saha during the consultation whether she was feeling better with the drugs she had been prescribed during her previous visit, she said that she was not taking them regularly. The pills did not help. "I'm having this fear [bhoi] all the time," she said. "I am not able to talk properly with other people." Mrs. Saha was fully aware of the family tensions that made her suffer, yet she was also convinced that what she really needed from the hospital was a thorough biomedical examination. She pressed Dr. Mullick to authorize the brain scan because she craved recognition that her symptoms came from the body and not from the mind. After more discussion, Dr. Mullick gave in and signed the form, saying, "Come back with the results."

The second case is set in the small practice of Dr. Sen, a general practitioner (GP) in Kolkata. Dr. Sen's chamber was only a short walk away from the Hindu hospital, right at the edge of a slum amid legally built houses. Dr. Sen told me that almost all of his patients came from the slum. His own home was close by. When I asked him how he diagnosed and treated mental illness, he said that he did not like to prescribe antidepressants to poor people. His main consideration was the financial burden of paying for drugs out of pocket for a long time. Another reason was the stigmatization of depression as a form of madness. By way of example, he mentioned one of his female patients from the local slum: she was severely depressed, but Dr. Sen did *not* prescribe antidepressants. Her husband was an unemployed alcoholic, and she had to maintain the whole family on her own. For Dr. Sen, giving the woman antidepressants would be irresponsible. "I cannot give her antidepressants," he said. "She would just go to sleep. But she must get up in the morning to go to work. The economic problem is more of a burden than psychiatric depression. So she has to suffer. . . . It is better that sooner or later she realizes that this is her fate. . . . I think that is a better solution than me giving her some medication. . . . [Pills] would . . . bring down the house." Thus, for Dr. Sen, psychotropics were not the right response to the problems in the woman's life: they would be too costly; they would end her husband's alcohol addiction; and they would cause her to lose any motivation to change her situation. On balance, drugs could not enhance her life.

In the two cases of psychotropic uses described here, it would not be enough to say that pills had only symbolic significance or were limited to subjective experiences. In Mrs. Saha's case, the introduction of psychotropics into her son's and her own life changed her *place* in the family. No doubt, stigmatization is a serious problem—specifically, stigmatization *within* the intrafamily space. Stigmatization is usually described as a feature of the public sphere (Goffman 2009; Marcks et al. 2005). Yet some of the worst stigmatization happens within the family sphere (Bradley and Ecks 2018). Stigma is "located in the intersubjective space—in the interpersonal actions and communications that signal recognition of shame—between patients and their closest family members" (Yang et al. 2007: 1532). Stigma is a Verstimmung between self and Others that can be as bad in proximal relations as in wider, more anonymous relations. Intrafamily stigmatization has had, in Mrs. Saha's case, appalling consequences. But stigma is not a concern in the case of Dr. Sen's patient. Dr. Sen was not worried about the woman being labeled "mad." He worried about the economic burden of a drug regimen and about how the woman's household sphere might change.

In both cases, the drug effects in question relate to changes in social spaces. They could therefore be called *sociotopic* drug effects. The most obvious sociotopic impact of the drugs that Mrs. Saha received from Dr. Mullick is that she was thrown out of the inner space of the house and moved into a marginalized corner, a bed alone under the stairs. A less obvious spatial effect is that Mrs. Saha sought to compensate for the loss of her household space with a kind of secondary home in medical institutions: her desire to get a brain scan might be, at least partly, an attempt to stay out of her own house and within the hospital space as much as possible. In turn, the spatial effect that Dr. Sen tried to avoid by not prescribing antidepressants was that drugs would split the household sphere. For him, pills could not be allowed to "bring down the house." For Mrs. Saha, the impact of the drugs exceeded any inner experience. In the case of Dr. Sen's refusal to prescribe antidepressants to poor patients, the social dynamics are more prominent than considerations of how patients might feel subjectively after taking drugs. In each of these two stories, transformations of social spaces are more important than transformations of subjective experiences. In the terminology of public health services, these two encounters are located in the same space; they are both instances of "care in the community." That is, both doctors deal with mental illness beyond the walls of psychiatric institutions. How is this space usually delineated?

Deinstitutionalization and Market Liberalization

Deinstitutionalization, as a strategy of closing psychiatric hospitals and shifting care into the community, has been a key policy for several decades. The confined spaces of total institutions are said to be detrimental to long-term recovery. Hospital closures improve care and quality of life (Patel et al. 2018: 32). Drugs are credited with making this spatial shift possible. Psychotropics made the *space* of treatment open and flexible. When drugs became widely available, asylum walls could be broken down. Care in the community set people free from the shackles of asylums and ensured a true "empowerment of people" (World Health Organization 2001: 50). Drugs allowed people to overcome the pathological effects of closed psychiatric spaces.

There were millions of psychiatric hospital beds in the global North in the first half of the twentieth century. Numbers were expected to rise even further in the 1950s. But instead of increasing, asylum-based care reduced dramatically. Deinstitutionalization began in the 1950s and continued until the 1980s. It was a complex process that came about through the confluence of changing national health-care provisioning (associated with the privatization of health care) and the availability of new psychotropic drugs, especially antipsychotics, during this time.

The role of drugs in the history of psychiatric deinstitutionalization has long been debated. One argument is that drugs did not cause deinstitutionalization but accelerated it (e.g., Gronfein 1985). Another argument is that psychotropics allowed doctors to leave the asylums and work privately. This was a "deinstitutionalization of psychiatry and psychiatrists rather than patients" (Healy 2008: 428). The most plausible reason for deinstitutionalization was a political drive to save money: asylums were deemed to be very expensive. In most countries (with a few notable exceptions, such as Japan), care in the community is seen as more cost-effective. Letting patients be supported in the community looked like the better economic value proposition.

This reimagination of therapeutic spaces is supplemented by a reimagination of economic spaces. For the past two decades, global mental health policies assume that there is a "vicious cycle" of poverty, mental illness, and macroeconomic impacts (see chapter 10). Poverty leads to a higher prevalence of mental disorders. In turn, higher prevalence, lack of care, and more severe course of disease had negative consequences on the whole economy: people could not work or were less productive, which led to decreased economic performance. This also made it more expensive to treat people, which further depressed gross economic income. To turn this situation into a virtuous cycle, investments in best-evidence therapies become investments in global economic growth. By the same logic, global economic growth promises to decrease the incidence of mental illness.

How global mental health links pharmaceuticals, economic growth, and spatial flexibility is eerily similar to perceptions of globalization as a process that squeezes space up to a point where distance vanishes and the world becomes "flat" (Castells 1996; Friedman 2005). In a globalizing world, space disappears, and time becomes immediate presence: "Space has lost its constraining quality and is easily traversed in both its 'real' and 'virtual' renditions. . . . The shrinking of space abolishes the flow of time" (Beck 2009: 56). Any event can be broadcast instantly to a global audience. The surface of the globe is mapped by satellites down to the last millimeter, and transport reaches any spot. In the twenty-first century, inaccessible terrain and unpacific oceans are relics from the past. There are no more explorations of unknown distances, only congested streets and delayed flights.

By generating economic growth, globalization is meant to eradicate poverty. That global market growth will lead to better mental health for all has become the credo of the movement for global mental health as well. Drugs, in turn, eliminate treatment differences between the rich and the poor. The spatial dynamics seem to be the same, too. Globalization breaks down boundaries and reduces spatial distance, while psychopharmaceuticals set people free from the bounds of institutional treatments. "Space disappears, and for the better of it" is the master narrative of both global psychiatry and global capitalism. Shrinking space becomes a signature value creation of capitalism: maximum speed, maximum proximity of all to all. Stigma is a barrier to access and must be eliminated. Mental illness is a barrier to productive participation and must be eliminated, too. Neither capitalism nor psychiatry sees market participation as an anonymous, distant, and alienating experience. Instead, a market becomes a "body of persons who are in intimate business relations and carry on extensive transactions in any commodity" (Jevons [1871] 2004: 427).

And yet sociospatial distances refuse to go away. Neither deinstitutionalization nor economic globalization have made them disappear.
Shifting treatments out of publicly funded institutions and into the private
sphere is a mere displacement of problems. The retreat of psychiatric institutions often means declining care or a pathological substitution with
other closed spaces. In the United States, ten times more people with
serious mental health problems are locked up in prisons than are in psychiatric hospitals (Patel et al. 2018: 32). As João Biehl (2005: 145) argues
for Brazil, deinstitutionalization is symbiotic with neoliberal transformations of health care. These two processes worked together to unburden
the state of unwanted people. Deinstitutionalization is a smoke screen
for letting people suffer on their own. To shift suffering "into the community" does not make it disappear; it only makes it invisible. Neoliberal psychiatry often replaces the *inclusive* violence of institutions with
the *exclusive* violence of abandonment.

Before the coemergence of neoliberal economics and psychiatric
deinstitutionalization was possible, psychiatry had to be brought into
the fold of global capitalism. This merger of capitalism and psychiatry
would have never been possible without the sociotopic effects of psychiatric drugs.

Three Shapes of the Globe

Peter Sloterdijk's *Sphären* (*Spheres*) presents a sprawling philosophical
analysis of globalization. He suggests that the world is getting rounder,
not flatter. Sloterdijk (1998, 1999, 2004, 2005) describes three modes of
globalization: metaphysical, terrestrial, and communicative. "Metaphysical" includes all forms of philosophical and religious reasoning about
the shape of the world. Metaphysical globalization is by far the oldest
mode of globalization; metaphysical reflections are part of all religious
and mythical accounts of how the world came into being. Some early
cosmogeneses describe the world as shaped like a globe. According to
Plato's *Timaeus*, a Creator compounded the world from a harmonious
mixture of four elements (fire, water, air, and earth) and chose to form
the world in the shape of a globe because it is the *perfect* form: "He
made the world in the form of a globe . . . a body entire and perfect"
(Plato 1952: 33b). This world body is a *living* being, a "Living Creature
which is designed to embrace within itself all living creatures" (33b).
Plato adds a "world soul" located at the center of this globe (Ecks 2020).

The soul maintains the structures within the world body. The Creator shaped the world as a sphere because this shape maintains perfect self-similarity: "He wrought it into a round, in the shape of a sphere, equidistant in all directions from the center to the extremities, which of all shapes is the most perfect and the most self-similar, since He deemed that the similar is infinitely fairer than the dissimilar" (Plato 1952: 33b).

Sloterdijk calls the second form of globalization "terrestrial." He dates the beginnings of terrestrial globalization to the voyages of Christopher Columbus in the late fifteenth century and its end to about the middle of the twentieth century, when most of the former European colonies achieved political independence. Terrestrial globalization has been driven by an alliance of merchants, missionaries, and aristocracies since the fifteenth century. "World" history began with terrestrial globalization: it was only when every last inch of the world's surface had been explored, named, taken into possession, and settled that people everywhere started to share the same historical time frame—Greenwich Mean Time for everyone. "World time" achieved a startling commensuration of all beings. Two entities could be said to be both made on "Wednesday, August 28, 2021" *before* world time was *put in place* at Greenwich. The globalization of a uniform pattern of time measurement was a monumental act of biocommensuration.

Cross-ocean navigation scaled up terrestrial globalization. As Adam Smith noted in *The Wealth of Nations* ([1776] 1952: 271): "The discovery of America, and that of a passage to the East Indies by the Cape of Good Hope, are the two greatest and most important events recorded in the history of mankind . . . uniting, in some measure, the most distant parts of the world." Smith's "*in* some measure" should have been "by giving a *measure*." Shipping also changed constitutions of the self, making them more uncertain and shifting. Philosophy never fully engaged with trans-ocean selfhood. For Sloterdijk, philosophical thought remained firmly land-bound. Its "ego," in its various formulations, never left terra firma, never took to ship.

The third and current type of globalization Sloterdijk calls "communicative." While metaphysical globalization is not bound to any particular era, terrestrial globalization ends where communicative globalization begins. During communicative globalization, historical transformations gradually stop being driven by Northern powers. Within the one-sided worldview that came with terrestrial globalization it seemed plausible to divide the world into "developed" and "developing" parts, with the developed ones charting the future of the developing ones. As Sloterdijk holds, this terminology is obsolete. Looking toward the developed countries does not reveal anything about the future of developing countries. Terrestrial globalization has moved into a phase of global interconnectedness, or "density," where it is impossible to say where the world is moving, what is "before" and what is "after." Once the world is circumnavigated and all points are connected, the origins of these links do not determine their future. In times of communicative globalization, world history is coauthored. Continuing global inequalities do not contradict this. In fact, the very notion of "global inequalities" presupposes a globalized relation among points on the same sphere.

Sloterdijk's polyspherology presents a new perspective on globalization, but how does it help make sense of psychopharmaceutical uses in India? Are there psychiatric equivalents to metaphysical, terrestrial, and communicative globalization?

A Polyspherology of Psychotropic Drugs

Psychiatry's spatial move from "the era of the asylum to the age of Prozac" (Shorter 1997) began in the eighteenth century, when the old madhouses were gradually abolished and new buildings for therapy were introduced. Before the advent of psychotropics in the 1950s, psychiatry first came into its own through a reform of its spaces. Reforms of closed institutions from the late eighteenth century onward consisted in making the space of the asylum progressively more open. Philippe Pinel's (1745–1826) unchaining of patients at the Bicêtre Hospital and William Tuke's (1732–1822) designs for the York Retreat are emblematic moments in this history. During the nineteenth century, a large number of asylums were built in industrializing countries. They were ideally located in airy and elevated places, removed from the disquiet of the old cities. Throughout the nineteenth and early twentieth centuries, psychiatric institutions grew greatly in their number of patients (Braslow 1997). One of the world's largest, the Central State Hospital in Milledgeville, Georgia, was founded in 1837 and, at its peak in the early 1960s, housed nearly twelve thousand patients (Cranford 1981). From the 1950s onward, this trend was reversed through deinstitutionalization. Closed psychiatric wards and hospitals for long-term treatment have been disappearing rapidly over the past fifty years in all the parts of the world.

There were many reasons that psychiatry moved out of closed spaces, but the introduction of more effective drug therapies was certainly important. In 1952, chlorpromazine was found to have a calming effect on psychotic patients. In the late 1950s, imipramine was launched as the first tricyclic antidepressant and remained the "gold standard" for clinical trials for decades afterward (see chapter 2). The drugs did not just improve treatment options; they also shifted the locus of psychiatry from closed to open spaces. This shift was welcomed by both psychiatrists and policy makers. Asylum-based psychiatry had many downsides, with poor living conditions and chronic human rights violations. Care in "the community" became the preferred option. In a message to the US Congress, President John F. Kennedy argued that psychotropic "breakthroughs have rendered obsolete the traditional methods of treatment which imposed upon the mentally ill a social quarantine, a prolonged or permanent confinement in huge, unhappy mental hospitals where they were out of sight and forgotten" (cited in Whooley 2019: 147). To be sure, the extent to which psychiatric spaces were transformed was not visible at the time the drugs were introduced, and the drug discovery process was not propelled by a desire for deinstitutionalization. There is good evidence that the main reason for the closing of institutions was a cost-saving drive by governments (Scull 2015). However, deinstitutionalization during the second half of the twentieth century would not have been possible without the promise that drugs could manage patients beyond asylum walls.

The building of asylums around the world can be described as the first stage of psychiatry's terrestrial globalization. Roughly at the same time that mental asylums were built in Europe between the eighteenth century and the twentieth century, such institutions were also erected in the European colonies. In India, the first asylums were built in the late eighteenth century under the rule of the British East India Company, the earliest one at Calcutta in 1787 (Sharma 2004). These asylums were meant to care for personnel of the East India Company, both Britons and Indians in British service. For the Britons among the patient population, asylums aimed less at therapy than at repatriation to the United Kingdom (Ernst 1997). After the Indian Mutiny of 1857 and the subsequent strengthening of British rule, a few asylums were built that functioned more or less like prisons or as "refuges and temporary receptacles" (Ernst 1991: 166).

It is not surprising, then, that almost all the colonial asylums were based in the maritime port cities (Calcutta, Madras, and Bombay). This also holds true for those institutions that were built in India's interior regions, partly with an idea of providing patients with cool air and a calm atmosphere. Two of these institutions that continued into post–Independence India were built in Bangalore and Ranchi. Despite their distance from the port cities, both were also built for Europeans, not for Indians. The Bangalore institution, which became the National Institute of Mental Health and Neurosciences (NIMHANS), originated from a lunatic asylum built when the city was the British military headquarters in the Mysore region. What is now the Central Institute of Psychiatry at Ranchi was founded in 1918 as the Ranchi European Lunatic Asylum.

In his work on disciplinary biopower, Michel Foucault (1975) argued that society had taken on carceral forms and that the swarming of disciplinary techniques made diverse institutions, such as hospitals, schools, and prisons, all *similar* to one another. All of them served the production of "knowledge," and all knowledge produced and sustained (capitalist) power. Foucault's "swarming" of institutional form is an example of biocommensuration through architectural forms. The buildings look "the same"; hence, the subjects meant to be produced in and through them should look "the same," as well.

But this biocommensuration through built spaces remained patchy and never reached around the globe. These forms did not swarm from Europe to European colonies. Gyan Prakash (1999: 125–27) argues that European institutions either were not introduced in the colonies or were introduced only in a scaled-down version. Indians were not constituted as "modern subjects" but as a population in subordination. The European colonizers did not think South Asians had the "same" bodies and minds as them. This is why there was never a swarming of psychiatric institutions in colonial India and why there was never any serious effort to include Indians among the inmate population.

Indian asylums remained scattered and small, even when, from the nineteenth century to the middle of the twentieth century, asylum populations in Europe and North America expanded (Mills 2006). In 1865, a few years after India was made a Crown Colony, the number of inmates in asylums of the Bengal Presidency was 627. This number peaked at 1,147 patients in 1875 and then declined. The numbers rose again in the first decades of the twentieth century but only hovered around the 1,200 patient mark. Similarly, small figures can be found in the Bombay and Madras presidencies. The costs involved in running asylums had always been a concern for the British, as is evident from several committee reports and from the closure of asylums in Moydapore and Hazaribagh in the late 1870s due to tight budgets (Mills 2006).

At the beginning of the twentieth century, critiques of asylums as pathogenic institutions were increasing in India, as well (Pinto 2014). During the 1930s, the first psychiatric outpatient services were opened at R. G. Kar Medical College in Calcutta and at the J. J. Hospital in Bombay (Sharma 2004). The demise of the asylum and the rise of outpatient care evolved in India in the second half of the twentieth century. The main reason for this, in India as elsewhere, was the availability of psychotropics, which made it possible to treat patients in general hospitals and private chambers (Kapur 2004). For example, Ranchi's Central Institute of Psychiatry started to use lithium in 1952 and chlorpromazine in 1953. To be sure, asylum staff had always used psychotropic substances, among them chloral hydrate, opiates, and alcohol: "A little wine or arrack at that time induces a quiet sleep, and I do not consider the use of opiates desirable when simple means can be employed to effect the desired result" (*Annual Report of the Three Lunatic Asylums in the Madras Presidency during the Year 1873–1874*, cited in Mills 2006: 338). However, these substances succeeded only in subduing restless patients within the walls of institutions. Whatever medicines were available before the 1950s, they did not lend themselves to outpatient treatments.

Psychopharmaceuticals first allowed "community care" for mental illnesses, and psychiatry in post–Independence India has been moving in this direction ever since. In 1983, the Indian government launched the National Mental Health Program (NMHP), a scheme that pushes for the further deinstitutionalization of psychiatry and for the extension of community care. The program's tenth five-year plan (2003–8) had a budget allocation of $42 million, which was seven times more than the budget for the ninth five-year plan ($6 million). Destigmatization of mental illness through public education is a key objective of the NMHP (Agarwal 2004). In practice, however, the program contains few psychosocial components and is focused mostly on making psychopharmaceuticals more widely available in state hospitals and health posts (Bayetti et al. 2019; Jain and Jadhav 2009).

Sloterdijk's distinction between metaphysical and terrestrial forms of globalization helps us understand this. Like other subfields of medicine, psychiatry has been complicit with projects of terrestrial colonialism, seeking to show how minds of colonial subjects were substantially different from those of the Europeans. But psychiatry has never been a tool for extending colonial power (Vaughan 2007), especially not in an area as vast and diverse as British India (Mills and Jain 2007).

Far more important than any involvement in terrestrial globalization was that psychiatry moved toward a form of "metaphysical" globalization that believes that all humans in all societies have essentially the same minds. This metaphysical decision made it possible to construct disease classifications and treatments that apply to every human on the globe. Psychiatry's universalist claims, as they are embodied in manuals such as the *International Classification of Diseases* (ICD) and the *Diagnostic and Statistical Manual of Mental Disorders* (DSM), are the flip side of the field's lack of interest in cultural and regional variability. If sociospatial specificity is allowed into the discipline at all, it is allowed only into the antechamber of transcultural psychiatry. Variations are only local dialects of the same universal symptom language. Transcultural psychiatry, which is psychiatry's initial form of terrestrial exploration, remains an exotic footnote to the discipline's universalistic core (Kirmayer and Jarvis 2007). Psychiatry *thinks* globally; *therefore*, it does not see the need to physically travel far and wide. In this sense, the assumption of universal categories is a form of metaphysical globalization. The first and foremost biocommensuration enacted by psychiatry is that all minds are essentially the same. The brains of people in any culture or context are interchangeable; hence, they can be diagnosed with the same criteria and be treated with the same therapies.

To be sure, anthropology's notion of a "psychic unity of mankind," on which the paradigm of "many cultures/one nature" rests (see Kohn 2013), is the same kind of metaphysical globalization. Since this principle was formulated in the nineteenth century by Adolf Bastian, Franz Boas, and E. B. Tylor, anthropologists have held that all human beings share the same mind, irrespective of cultural, regional, or genetic differences. Neither insights on brain plasticity (Rees 2016) nor on epigenetics (Lock et al. 2015) ever question the biocommensuration of all humans having the *same* mind.

The building of asylums beyond Europe and America was a limited form of psychiatry's terrestrial globalization. Full terrestrial globalization began only with the easy availability and transportability of drugs. Drugs allow a far-reaching flexibilization of space: they enable treatment beyond institutional walls, and they carry psychiatric disease classifications and therapeutics around the world. That is why there are such similarities between psychiatric deinstitutionalization as a flexibilization of therapeutic spaces, on the one hand, and globalization as a process of economic, political, and cultural flexibilization, on the other. It is not a coincidental similarity between two independent chains of events but, rather, the transposition of the dynamics of one field onto the other. Psychotropics sucked psychiatry into capitalism's inherent drive to go global.

In contrast to psychiatry, capitalist modes of economic production and consumption were terrestrially global from the start. Capitalism is essentially about investing money in the hope of getting more money in the future. This temporal reach for the future always contains ambitions for an expanded spatial reach. Capitalism seeks out all the places in the world where consumers can be found and from where riches can be brought back. The so-called discovery of the New World in 1492 by the seafaring entrepreneur Christopher Columbus was motivated by the search for a faster trading route between Europe and India. The language of capital, with terms such as *revenue* and *return on investment*, conjures up images of ships stacked with possessions returning from risky journeys to foreign shores. Karl Marx and Friedrich Engels ([1848] 1952: 421) were right in saying that "the need of a constantly expanding market for its products chases the bourgeoisie over the entire surface of the globe."

For capitalism, global exploration always carried hopes of reaping rich rewards. By contrast, psychiatrists did not have an inherent drive to expand their reach around the globe until global mental health was formed in the 1990s (see chapter 10). Traveling to India promises profitable business to the entrepreneur, but for a psychiatrist it is more of an interesting distraction from the main job back home. It was only the development of profitable pharmaceuticals in the 1950s that turned psychiatry into a global enterprise. Only when psychiatry became based on mobile commodities that could be produced, distributed, prescribed, sold, and consumed everywhere did the discipline become fully enmeshed with terrestrial globalization. Long before neoliberal reforms, psychiatric treatments *had* to become based on pharmaceuticals (see Biehl 2005: 22, 49). Drugs merged capitalism's terrestrial globalization with psychiatry's universalistic claim to be relevant for all people in all places.

This link does still not require European and American psychiatrists to travel to foreign areas themselves because the drugs are supposed to work in the same manner for anyone in the world. The industry for clinical trials in India is built on the assumption that Indian bodies (including brains) are the same as those of people elsewhere, even if Indian people are not accorded the same social status (Petryna 2007). But the alliance between psychiatry and a profit-driven drug industry opened up new spaces for both of them: drugs allowed treatment to leave the confines of asylums and potentially enter every household in the world. Capitalism accounts for the massive increase in prescriptions for psychopharmaceuticals in India over the past three decades. That psychotropics are now widely used has little to do with public health programs for mental health. The Indian market for psychotropics is driven almost entirely by private-sector prescriptions.

Psychiatry has undergone both a metaphysical and a terrestrial globalization, but "communicative" globalization is still rare. Psychiatric therapies come to India but are not changed and then reexported to Europe or North America. A "global monoculture of happiness" promises that everyone can be "pain free, completely comfortable, and ready and able to acquire and consume the greatest quantity and variety of the newest goods and fashions" (Kirmayer 2002: 316). Participation in this homogeneous space is defined through the ability to pay for medical goods and services. Those who can afford it are on the inside of this sheltered place; those who cannot are left outside. Through cheap generics and public health efforts to close treatment gaps, the size of this sphere is expanding.

While psychiatry's "metaphysical" core is still firmly based in Europe and America, the beginnings of its communicative globalization are evident in the international psychopharmaceuticals market. Even if these drugs came originally from the United States and Europe, they are now also imported as generics from countries such as India. As the world's leading producer of generic drugs by volume, India is a key importer of psychotropics in European and American markets.

A notable case of such a globally reversed flow of psychopharmaceuticals is the success of Dr. Reddy's Laboratories (DRL) with exporting fluoxetine to the United States. Founded in 1984, DRL is now one of India's chief pharmaceutical companies (Dr. Reddy's Limited 2006). From 2001 onward, a large part of DRL's profits came from its fluoxetine exports to North America. In 2001, DRL challenged Eli Lilly's patent for Prozac in a US court and won 180 days of exclusive marketing rights for fluoxetine 40 mg. This was a historic event for the Indian industry: no other company had ever achieved this. Over the 180-day period, DRL earned almost $70 million, while Eli Lilly's Prozac lost 80 percent of its US market. In 2004, fluoxetine was by far DRL's best-selling product, contributing more than 40 percent to its annual revenues ($45 million out of $107 million). Since then, DRL's fluoxetine sales have declined, down to $21 million in

2005 and further down to $9 million in 2006. The reason for this was not renewed strength of US producers but increased generic competition from other Indian companies.

That India has become a key exporter of psychotropics to North America and Europe is an ironic fulfillment of Smith's ([1776] 1952: 271) prediction that globally connected commerce would enable "the most distant parts of the world . . . to relieve one another's wants, to increase one another's enjoyments, and to encourage one another's industry." The globalization of psychopharmaceutical markets may, in the long run, also have an effect on the kinds of drugs developed and marketed.

Pharma Foam

To think about globalization in terms of three modes seems to imply homogeneity. As Robert Frank (2004: 16) shows in his analysis of medical globalization, most theorists have predicted a process of homogenization, or "McDonaldization": once every corner of the world was mapped and linked with all others, it would be inevitable that the same Euro-American monoculture would spread everywhere. Local cultures would be unable to withstand homogenizing pressures and vanish. Applied to medicine, the analysis presumed that biomedicine would eventually displace all other forms of healing. Later theories made alarmist claims about increasing polarization: the aggressive advance of Euro-American capitalism produces resistance in various forms. In the realm of medicine, the boom in alternative medicine—as a revolt against biomedicine—seemed to be an equivalent process. Current globalization theories highlight complexity and heterogeneity: the world is multipolar; the local and the global are intertwined in complicated ways; and not one way of life dominates all others. Particular forms are universalized, and universal forms are particularized (Sloterdijk 1999: 1002–3).

Sloterdijk (2005) also presents arguments in favor of homogenization, as certain spheres appear as emergent across the world. One of them is defined by the increasing tendency to see human beings as consumers and to tie rights of access to purchasing power (see chapter 5). Capitalism divides the world into an "inside"—an air-conditioned mall where access to commodities is dependent on buying power—and an "outside" that is still exposed to harsh weather. Sustainable development and universal health coverage (Patel et al. 2018) are the latest labels of a project that aims to extend the world interior of capital far enough to bring everyone inside. The rich and the poor are still divided by their ability—or inability—to access commodities, but now the poor *know* what they do not have. To be a "have-not" does not mean to be a "know-not" anymore. This notion of air-conditioned capitalist interiors as the emblematic space of the current era applies not only to countries of the North but also to India. Since the mid-2000s, Indian cities have been transformed by three types of built structures: ever-larger shopping malls, high-rise residential enclaves shielded from the chaos and pollution of the rest of the city, and "fly-over" car routes constructed above older streets.

Yet in communicative globalization, homogeneity is the exception rather than the rule. Compared with terrestrial globalization, communicative globalization produces amorphous spaces. Sloterdijk deepens this argument with Heideggerian phenomenology. For Sloterdijk, terrestrial globalization only conceals what communicative globalization brings to light: that the spheres humans inhabit are oriented toward *being close*. Being *takes place* by creating and re-creating the space in which it unfolds from within itself (Sloterdijk 2004: 24). Grounded in bodily experience, these spaces bend toward spatial proximity. Heterogeneity is far more likely than homogeneity. The space of the Stimmung between the inner and the outer is centered on the embodied self, which makes its radius relatively small. Stretching the notion of inhabited spheres further, Sloterdijk describes "society" as an ephemeral, amorphous, polyspherical heap of foam: "an aggregate of micro-spheres (couples, households, companies, associations) of different formats, which border on each other like individual bubbles in a heap of foam, building layers above and below each other, without being in touch with all others, but also without being separable from others" (59).

Sloterdijk proposes that *foam* is a better word for the shape of society than *networks* (Castells 1996; Latour 2005; van Dijk 2012). *Foam* foregrounds that being-in-the-world tends toward closeness and roundedness: "However much [spheres] pretend to be connected with the Other and the Outer, they seek to *round* themselves first and foremost *within themselves*" (Sloterdijk 2004: 59, emphasis added). The network metaphor stresses mutual coconstitution and symmetries among participating elements. It overestimates interconnectedness and underestimates asymmetries. "Network" highlights the links between beings in favor of the elements themselves. Foam, by contrast, emphasizes the unpredictable and unique forms of distinctive spheres, their *Eigenräumigkeit* (being of/in one's own space): "The notion of foamy co-isolation allows to correct the strained metaphor of the network. . . . [I]nstead of emphasizing the *Eigenräumigkeit* of the communicating communicators, the image of the network knows only dots without inner depth, mere intersections of lines" (257). Sloterdijk's distancing from the network image has found favor even among actor-network theorists. Bruno Latour (2009: 139) says he was "born a Sloterdijkian" and agrees that "what is usually called networks is an 'anemic' conjunction of two intersecting lines." His own concept of "network" is meant to be as spherical as Sloterdijk's.

The moment that Mrs. Saha brought psychotropics into her house, a new, pathogenic bubble appeared and started to expand within. Instead of reintegrating her son through drugs, she found herself exiled to an isolated spot in the house. She was pushed into a pathological *Eigenräumigkeit* that separated her from her family.

Mrs. Saha's bubble was cocreated by the bubble in which Dr. Mullick lives. Dr. Mullick seems as networked as it gets: he is part of a globalized elite of medical doctors. He travels several hours every day across the city to practice in different clinics. His encounter with Mrs. Saha took place in the transitory space of an outpatient clinic that he visits for only a few hours each week. Even though Mrs. Saha had been going to see him for several years in the same place, the space for Dr. Mullick remained coincidental and interchangeable. The commensurability of the spaces he inhabits translated into a commensurability of the patients he treats: they are all equal by their symptoms and all get the same "best evidence" treatment. Dr. Mullick does not live close to where his patients live, and he does not know other family members unless they come to the consultations. He realizes the social side effects that the medication causes—after all, I learned about Mrs. Saha's history from him. But for Dr. Mullick, the main consideration is that whatever patient comes to him with a symptom profile that fits into the classifications of psychiatry, he will prescribe the recommended pills.

Dr. Sen, by contrast, practices only in his local office. The patients he sees all come to this stable point. Because he is located right next to where many of his patients live, he knows much about their family histories and tends to treat several members of the same families. As a general practitioner, Dr. Sen is only weakly linked to globalized professional networks. The view that antidepressants cause drowsiness and inhibit patients from resuming work is derived more from his own experience than from evidence-based guidelines. He allows the social side effects of pills, such as financial strains and family tensions, to override clinical judgments about depression. Dr. Sen's refusal to give antidepressants is a refusal to treat all patients using one-size-fits-all best evidence, irrespective of patients' life circumstances. Dr. Mullick compares patients by symptoms only. Dr. Sen uses wider criteria for comparison to include socioeconomic and intrafamily circumstances. He lets sociospatial proximity change how he values antidepressants. Dr. Sen's revaluation of treatments also reveals an important link between two of the contextual value criteria: proximity and in/dividuality. Dr. Sen's relative proximity to his patient allows him to see her "dividuality" in relation to her family and spatial contexts much more clearly. Proximity makes these contexts of valuing become part of his own valuing context.

These different spaces change how each of the doctors perceives the sociotopic effects of drugs. Dr. Sen does not want to interfere with the minds of individual patients if doing so creates divisive spaces. He believes that there can be no health for individual patients if the household sphere is disrupted. Dr. Mullick, by contrast, uses pills to target the inner spaces of individual patients and excludes the social impact of his practice from treatment decisions. Dr. Sen wants to leave patients in the bubble they already inhabit, while Dr. Mullick is ready to bring patients into the biomedical sphere, no matter if this destroys the space they lived in before. The GP's local connectedness makes him shy away from what global biomedicine would define as best treatment, while the psychiatrist's global connectedness isolates him from the spheres his patients inhabit. I doubt that Mrs. Saha's inclusion in a global psychiatric bubble was better than leaving her untreated.

SEVEN

Acting through Other (Prescribing) Habits

Habit

Is Depression Rising?

This chapter analyzes the prescribing habits of doctors in Kolkata. Writing about other people's habits is not "ethnography," it is *habitography*. Habit, as I argue here, is an immensely useful but strangely neglected concept. In what follows, I define habit as the ground of creativity and show why anthropologists should make habit a central concern of study.

Habit is a beautiful word. It congeals many layers of meanings that are equally about humans and nonhumans, about interiority and exteriority, as well as about affecting and being affected. It comes from the root **ghabh*, "to take, hold, have, give, receive," stemming from "hand" or "forearm" (Pfeifer 1995). The "hand" image of giving/receiving/keeping motivates the meaning of practical ability, "to be able to" and "make able again." Therapeutic "rehabilitation" literally means "to en*able* to grasp again." The idea of "keeping" and "holding" enfolds the idea of habit as "dwelling," as in "staying in one place." The spatial meaning is contained in words such as "to inhabit," "habitat," and "habitation." Habit can mean "physical appearance." Habit in the sense of "dress characteristic of a particular group" was the dominant meaning in the English language until the seventeenth century. (Dafoe's Robinson Crusoe—clearly someone who had to make his own habitation and change his habits in tune with his habitat—uses "habit" only in the sense of clothing; the word *garb* comes from the root **ghabh*.) Habit also means a mental and bodily disposition, a posture, and a kind of demeanor. This has become its primary meaning in English today. As "routine pattern of behaving or feeling," habit signals extended temporality—repeated patterns rather than one-off events.

Habit links up with commensuration in three ways. First, habit commensurates a set of actions as "similar" to one another across time. Habit says that a diverse set of actions occurring at different time points are all similar in form. This makes habit the core of any "form of life," or *Lebensform* (Helmreich 2015: 23; Wittgenstein 2017: §19; see also chapter 2 in this volume). Forms of life are made up of patterns and regularities. Second, habit comes from a group of words that belong to commensurative practices such as giving, receiving, and keeping. Third, habit is a mode of commensurating different possibilities for action in an instantaneous and nonreflected way. Habit is an embodied and swift mode of valuing. Working through key ideas about habit, from Marcel Mauss's *habitus* to Thinking through Other Minds (TTOM), I argue that habitography describes "acting through other people's habits."

I ground this exploration of habitography in an *empirical* question that has long haunted my work in India: is depression increasing, and if it is, what causes its increase? Over years of fieldwork in Kolkata and the rural districts of West Bengal (Ecks 2013), I was struck by how utterly sure general physicians were that depression is rising rapidly and that the reason for the rise are socioeconomic changes related to "globalization" and "capitalism." Allopathic practitioners of different specializations are sure that they now see many more patients with low moods, indecisiveness, hopelessness, loss of joy in daily activities, withdrawal, and a range of unexplained chronic pains. The doctors say that depression is rising relative to other disorders (e.g., an epidemiological transition from acute to chronic conditions). They also think that depression is rising in absolute numbers, meaning that a far higher proportion of all patients are now experiencing symptoms of depression.

Many of the psychiatrists I interviewed thought that the rise of depression is real. As one of the psychiatrists said, "I think there is a real increase. I believe that the Indian mindset is undergoing a very big change because of globalization. . . . Indians used to be very fatalistic, 'It's all in our karma.' But now these people are questioning that." The "exit from fatalism" described here is not a switch from religious fatalism ("It's all fate") into neurobiological fatalism ("It's all in the brain"). Rather, it is a cultural change from accepting one's socioeconomic position as decreed by fate toward a hungry aspiration for a wealthier future. A cultural belief in karma and fate kept people in a suppressed state, but it also reduced their anxieties about the future.

Psychiatrists tended to be less sure about the rise of depression, saying that the statistical evidence was too poor to make such a claim (Ecks 2008). However, all of the nonspecialists, and especially the general practitioners (GPs), firmly believed that depression was rising rapidly. They were also quick to establish a clear causal link between depression and India's socioeconomic transformation. The GPs said that people felt economically more insecure than ever before, that competition for education and jobs had increased tremendously, and that the joint family system—the bedrock of traditional life—was crumbling. There was often a slippage in the GPs' statements between actual socioeconomic changes and changes in people's perceptions of them. Put simply, even if life was harder for previous generations in absolute terms, public perceptions had changed so that life now seems *relatively* harder. Bollywood movies and television programs showing affluent lifestyles created great expectations that could only be disappointed by harsh realities. One of the GPs, Dr. Mukherjee, had many patients from a nearby slum: "Their aspirations are higher. Earlier, people would say, 'OK, I am in the slum. I remain in the slum. My aspirations are not high.' But nowadays, with all these electronic media, the coverage and all that, the younger generation has a higher aspiration. If someone was a rickshaw puller, his son wouldn't mind being a rickshaw puller, but now the son doesn't want to become a rickshaw puller. He wants a motorcycle. That is the basic problem. They are more prone to depression."

Dr. Mukherjee expressed a view of depression as a multidimensional problem that could not be reduced to genetics or neurotransmitters. He mentioned no fewer than four factors that caused depression: (1) social inequality (the slum and beyond); (2) intergenerational change (grandfather, father, and son); (3) consumer desires (the motorcycle); and (4) the ambiguous impact of the mass media. For this GP, to suffer from depression is not reducible to physical pathology; it is a form of *social* suffering. Specifically, depression is a disorder of having many more lifestyle and consumption *choices* than before. That made people experience many more *disappointments* than before when the desired choices get frustrated. Depression is a disorder of excessive choice and disappointed hopes. Dr. Mukherjee's analysis of depression affirms Alain Ehrenberg's (2010) thesis of the "weariness of the self" (see chapter 3).

Other GPs made similar assumptions about a rise of depression. Dr. Chanda explained the typical groups of patients whom he diagnoses as depressed and in need of antidepressant drugs. Older people, Dr. Chanda said, were most affected: "Suppose someone suffers from a chronic ailment. There I prescribe antidepressants routinely, for at least six months. Or if someone suffers from a cardiac problem. Anyone who suffers from chronic health problems, it is routinely prescribed. Previously in Bengali families, they would look after their elders, but not so much anymore, they suffer from loneliness. When they come to me, routinely I prescribe antidepressants, almost always. Previously that was not there. . . . But now depression is increasing by leaps and bounds." Older people were likely to have chronic health problems, including heart disease. Dr. Chanda explained how the mental health of elderly people had deteriorated. Parents expected their children—specifically, their sons, who traditionally stayed with them in a joint family setup—to look after them in old age. Now, however, the children want to set up their own, separate households away from their parents. Many of them migrate to other places within India or go abroad.

Biomedical quacks, known in West Bengal as rural medical practitioners (RMPs), were also convinced that depression is rising. Similar to the GPs, the RMPs saw a clear causal connection between depression and socioeconomic changes over the past decade. Not one RMP I talked to thought that people were more troubled in the past than they are now. Today's life was unequivocally perceived as more depressing and stressful than earlier days. Depression was identified as a side effect of modernization. People were depressed about their economic situation. "Anxiety, depression is increasing," RMP Sasumal told me. "It is mainly because of the economic situation. This is our analysis, and we are sure of this conclusion. In my fifteen years' experience, I have seen the number of patients coming with such problems has increased." Several RMPs saw a correlation between poverty and depression, with depression hitting the poorest the hardest.

Similar to the trained GPs, the RMPs also reasoned about the question of rising numbers of depressed people in India in relation to prescription practices. While they all agreed that the roots of depression were socioeconomic, they had more reservations against prescribing antidepressant drugs quite as easily and as routinely as Dr. Chanda. The RMPs generally regarded depression as an illness that needs treatment, but many of them were not certain what treatment might be successful. "One cannot do much about depression patients," according to RMP Alam. Nevertheless, RMPs said that antidepressants could alleviate depression caused by socioeconomic strains at least over a short period. "I don't think this problem [depression] can be solved with medicines. The cause is socioeconomic. But we use medicines to take care of the symptoms," according to RMP Ghosh.

The RMPs are acutely aware of their quasi-illegal standing and are careful to show that their prescription patterns are the same as those of the licensed doctors. As one of them explained, patients prescribed with antidepressants by licensed doctors who come to them are an invaluable source of insight into professional doctors' prescription routines: "Psychiatric patients come to us who are already on psychiatric drugs that have been prescribed by some specialist. They start the medicine and then come to us to know what it is all about, or they may have stopped the medicine and then come to us for the problems that arise after stopping the medicine. [Or] they may come for other health problems and in the process show us the prescriptions from where we can learn what they are taking."

The perceived rise of depression does not come from epidemiological data but from learning patients' medication histories. The RMPs get access to prescriptions when patients are unsure about treatments advised by licensed doctors. Patients come with prescriptions that they do not fully understand to ask the RMPs, to whom they have a less distanced relation, "what it is all about." They come with prescriptions that they discontinued without supervision by a licensed doctor. Through "floating prescriptions," the RMPs learn about psychiatric treatments through doctor-shopping patients, and they deduce from a noticeable increase in psychotropic prescriptions by licensed doctors that mental illnesses are rising.

When these three types of practitioners—specialist psychiatrists, GPs, and RMPs—are compared in how they make sense of rising depression, we get a better sense of the empirical puzzle at hand. How good is the evidence for the argument that depression is rising? For the psychiatrists, a rise of depression was a plausible assumption, but the epidemiological data to support it seemed weak. For the GPs and the RMPs, the rise of depression was an obvious fact. They thought that depression was rising because of a systematic change in people's daily lives and routines. Globalization and market liberalization appear as plausible causes for an increase of depression rates: people have more life choices and higher aspirations. Poverty was due not to fate and karma but their own responsibility. The doctors' reflections on the question were also tied up with changes in their own prescription practices: the rise of depressive suffering goes hand in hand with a rise of antidepressant prescriptions. More *need* for drugs generates more *demand* for drugs.

The question remains: why do the doctors think they *know* all this? Where is the evidence? There have not read any studies that correlate rising depression with intensifying globalization or the weariness of the self. And why should social change be so depressing? Were people's lives not stressful before? Poverty and deprivation were worse in the past, so should rates of depression not *fall*? The doctors' idea that "rapid socioeconomic change is leading to rising depression" cannot be taken at face value.

Before Indian doctors could claim that socioeconomic change made depression rates rise, they needed to make a series of comparisons. The first comparison is between "depression" as a distinct disorder and other health problems. The second comparison concerns changes over time: are there more depressed patients now than in the past? The third comparison is about the time-bound changes in the "socioeconomic situation": what is different in society and economics now as compared with the past? Once these comparisons are made, the doctors commensurate them into a causal relation: "depression" is caused by changes in people's socioeconomic environment. Another comparison, about the time-bound changes in prescription patterns, is not factored into their explanation of causes. Herein lies, I think, the flaw in the GPs' reasoning: their reflections are all about changes in *other* people's lives but not enough about changes in their *own* lives. If anything has evidently changed, it is the doctors' own prescription patterns, yet the doctors do not recognize this change as having any explanatory power.

Beyond Norms

It is conceivable that more people get treated for depression because of changing social *norms*. Norms about perceiving symptoms of depression or norms about health-seeking may have changed, so that more people are diagnosed. However, I argue that norm changes are not the reason; habit changes are. Norm and habit do different conceptual work, but habit is a more useful concept than norm.

What is the difference between norm and habit? In much of the literature, norms and habits are used interchangeably. For example, Michael

Tomasello (2009: 105) argues that human habits are based on normed behavior: "[They] form with others joint goals to which both parties are normatively committed, they establish with others domains of joint attention and common conceptual ground, and they create with others symbolic, institutional realities." Norms also feature in the philosophical literature on value, in the form of distinctions between truth and value. The norm is a value that solidifies into an agreed standard of what *ought* to be by social convention (Orsi 2015).

A norm is a commensuration that sets one kind of thought or action as standard, then measures distance from the standard by degrees and sanctions by how far away an action departs from the norm. The scale of deviance can be numerical or nonnumerical. The simplest definition of social norms goes back to the etymology of the term, the Latin word *norma*, which is a measuring device for building walls in perfectly straight lines. If the wall is not straight, it will fall. A *norma* distinguishes objectively right forms from objectively wrong forms. Deviations become measurable by how close or far they are from the norm; deviations can be close to the norm or very far from the norm. This simple definition captures that norms are about creating conformity in stuff, people, and actions. For the concept of the norm to be useful, there must be at least a partial consensus within a group about which norms are valid and which are not. That makes norms habitual.

Norming is different from punishing. Deviation from the norm can be sanctioned, but sanctioning is not essential for the definition of a norm. For a norm to make sense, it must be clear if a deviation has occurred or not. It does not have to be clear what *sanctions* a deviation might entail. Social norms are always at play in evaluations of wrongdoing (Astuti and Bloch 2015), but how wrongdoing gets negatively sanctioned is a separate issue. Defining norms is one form of commensuration; defining sanctions for violating norms is another form of commensuration.

An influential definition of norms comes from the sociologist George Homans (1974: 76): "A norm is a statement specifying how a person is, or persons of a particular sort are, expected to behave in given circumstances—expected, in the first instance, by the person that utters the norm. What I expect of you is what you ought to do." Homans's "norm" includes several assumptions. The first is the "oughtness" of norms: a norm sets an expectation that a certain kind of social action should be, or should not be, performed. In the case of rising depression in India, this "oughtness" condition is not immediately evident. The socioeconomic changes that the doctors worry about are not changes in social norms. A clearer version of a social norm change is, "You should go see a doctor if you have low moods." But according to the doctors, this is not the case: patients come with problems that they themselves did not usually identify as psychological. That someone tells someone else they "ought" to go to the doctor is less common than people wanting to go to the doctor themselves. Even with these tweaks, the concept of "norm" does not help explain why doctors are so convinced that depression is rising and why more prescriptions need to be written. We need a different concept: habit.

Habitography

Among anthropological concepts, habit is like Edgar Allan Poe's *The Purloined Letter*: it is right before our eyes yet hidden because no one *pays attention* to it. Edward Burnett Tylor's (1871: 1:1) definition of culture is typical for forgetting habit after mentioning it: "Culture or Civilization, taken in its wide ethnographic sense, is that complex whole which includes knowledge, belief, art, morals, law, custom, and any other capabilities and habits acquired by man as a member of society. The condition of culture among the various societies of mankind, in so far as it is capable of being investigated on general principles, is a subject apt for the study of laws of human thought and action."

Habit is introduced only to fade immediately into the background. It is as if habit is such an obvious category that it needs no further thinking. As far as I am aware, no one in anthropology has ever written a genealogy of habit or raised the question of what habit might bring to anthropology. (Pierre Bourdieu's "habitus" concept is, as I show later, one of the reasons anthropologists have *not* seen the significance of habit.)

There has been an upsurge of interest in habit in a wide range of disciplines in the past decade. Philosophy, psychology, economics, neurosciences, and literature studies have seen a renewed interest in habit, both in the history of the concept and in a multitude of empirical applications (e.g., Barandiaran et al. 2014; Malabou 2008; Ringmar 2016; Sparrow and Hutchinson 2013). Drawing on recent philosophical works on habit (Carlisle 2014), I want to highlight seven aspects of habit that are particularly relevant to anthropology.

First, habit oscillates between individual and collective ascriptions. Habit is sometimes reduced to the traits of individuals and opposed to the "customs" shared by larger groups of people. But there is no clear distinction between habit and custom. Habits can be shared among people living together, be transmitted from generation to generation, and imitated across group boundaries. Habit is never purely individual or purely social.

Second, habits wavers between active and passive habituation. A habit can be acquired actively and consciously, through repeated action, and a habit can be acquired passively and unconsciously through repeated sensation and experience.

Third, habit can be the source of action or the result of repeated action. Many habits are born from repeated action and are then the source of repeated action. "We first make our habits, and then our habits make us," as the saying goes.

Fourth, habits have different degrees of how changeable they are. Some habits can be changed with a little effort and some practice. For example, to swim while exhaling under water rather than above water is a habit that can be learned quickly. Some other habits can be extremely difficult to change—for example, one's native accent while speaking a second language.

Fifth, there is a difference between habit as an *ability* to act in a certain way and habit as a *disposition* to act in a certain way. As a skill, a habit does not immediately propel one to act in a certain way, whereas as a disposition, habit makes one primed to act in a certain way. Thomas Reid, an Enlightenment philosopher, explains this difference by comparing it to river swimming: one can swim against the stream or one can swim by letting the river carry one forward. "We are carried by habit as by a stream of swimming, if we make no resistance" (Reid [1778] 2011, cited in Carlisle 2014: 9).

Sixth, habit is located both within individual beings *and* within their environments. Reid's reference to swimming is interesting because he shifts imperceptibly from habit as a property of an individual being to habit as an affordance of the surroundings (Gibson 1977; Veissière et al. 2020). The habits that carry us through life are as much *within* as *outside* the self. What makes habit such a powerful concept is that the distinction between subjectivity and objectivity, and between the inner and the outer, is always already blurred.

Seventh, the "double law" of habit (proposed by Maine de Biran and elaborated by Félix Ravaisson), holds that there is a dual process at work in the development of habits. The repetition of sensation weakens it, whereas the repetition of action strengthens it: "Prolonged or repeated sensation diminishes gradually. Prolonged or repeated movement becomes gradually easier, quicker and more assured" (Ravaisson 2008: 49). The double law captures that repeated passive exposure to a sensation gradually weakens it and may even make it fade from consciousness entirely, whereas repetition of an action strengthens effortless performance. Habituation can mean both becoming accustomed to a repeated sensation and becoming skilled at doing something. Habit is an embodied form of decision making. Habituation is just as much about outward action as about affect. Repeated affects create a habituation of living *Stimmung* between inner and outer (*habituell gewordenes Stimmungsleben*) (Bollnow 2009: 120).

Lived-in Habituation

I called the rise of depression an "empirical" puzzle because I wanted to avoid the term *ethnographic*. I am not the first to say that there is something wrong with how the term *ethnography* is used today and that it is useful to distinguish between anthropology and ethnography (Rees 2018). The word *ethnography* contains two concepts: "ethnos," in the sense of specific human people, groups, and societies, on the one hand, and "graphos" in the sense of writing. Hence, an ethnographer is someone who writes about other people. As such, ethnography contains the assumptions that the object of study are differences among groups of humans and that what we do with these humans is write about them. In most definitions of ethnography as a practice, it is said that ethnography always entails moments of comparison (what is different about these people?) and moments of contextualization (e.g., why are people doing what they are doing?) (Sanjek 2009). In this way, "methodology" and "theory" are difficult to separate. Arguably, all ethnography is a kind of "ethnographic theory" (Da Col and Graeber 2011) because ethnography always makes an argument about people studied.

What is not to like about this definition of ethnography? Tim Ingold (2014) argues that "ethnography" is an overused and overextended concept. It wants to capture the entirety of what is done in anthropology when actually it is only a limited mode of working. For Ingold, the term *ethnography* should be reserved strictly for writing up what people are saying and doing. Ethnography is not the same as anthropology, which he defines as a form of participant observation that "join[s] in correspondence with those with whom we learn or among whom we study, in a movement that goes forward rather than back in time" (Ingold 2014:

390). Ethnography is reportage and not engagement; it is description and not correspondence; it is an account of the past rather than a co-imagining of futures.

Ingold points to the temporality, ontology, and ethics of the "writing" aspects of ethnography. In turn, I am more bothered by the "ethnos" aspect of the word *ethnography*. Few anthropologists are working on bounded "ethnic" groups, and whether anthropology's bounded ethnic groups ever existed is questionable (Laidlaw 2014: 30). The emphasis on "ethnos" does not reflect that most anthropologists are studying complex assemblages of humans, nonhumans, and things in several sites and across several time frames that are irreducible to the past, the present, or the future (e.g., Marcus 1995). Anthropologists are still grappling to find a conceptual language for the matters of concern that emerge only through being both dispersed and connected beyond bounded human groups. We gesture beyond the human but have no good words for it (Haraway 2016). "Anthropology" is just as human-centric as "ethnography." The *ethnos* part of ethnography is clinging on only for want of a better term. The *anthropos* part of anthropology is also clinging on only for want of a better term.

An alternative term was suggested by Annemarie Mol: *praxiography*. Her idea to "write about practice" came from hospital fieldwork on how multiple sclerosis is "enacted" across different sites and different kinds of experts. Praxiography "locates knowledge primarily in activities, events, buildings, instruments, procedures" (Mol 2002: 32). The emphasis on practice rather than on ethnic grouping makes sense, not just for multiple sclerosis, but for most topics at which anthropologists are looking. Practice theory has a long-standing place in anthropological and social theory. Sherry Ortner's (1984) point that anthropological theory since the 1960s can be summarized by a turn to "practice" still seems right decades later. Most anthropologists want to study what people are actually doing.

Replacing *ethnos* with *praxis* is a good move, and *praxiography* is clearly a better term for what anthropologists are doing than *ethnography*. Yet practice, and praxiography as a form of writing about practices, also entails layers of meaning that are constraining. Practice implies an emphasis on human agency over nonhumans. Nonhuman agents may "make a difference" (Latour 1995) to how humans do their practices, but they themselves do not "practice." If value is life, and if all creatures create value, ethnographies of humans can never be the basis of a general theory of value (see Otto and Willerslev 2013). Practice carries within it a dualistic opposition between mind and body, between idealism and materialism, and between the imagined and the real that practice theorists try to overcome. Practice also tends to emphasize action in particular places and times rather than actions that are more stable, more enduring, and less particular.

Another term might be even better: *habitography* (Ecks and Kupfer 2014). Habit is not bound up with *ethnos*. Nor is habit confined to human practice. Habitography does not make a cardinal distinction between primary data from fieldwork and secondary data that have been collected by methods other than participant observation. Thus, it does not get stuck in a polar opposition between ethnography and theory. Habitography is a comparative study of habits as localized somewhere between humans and nonhumans, between the inside and the outside, between consciousness and unconsciousness.

The standard sociological work on the history of habit was written by Charles Camic (1986, 2015). According to Camic, habit was an important category in sociology up to the 1920s. Then it disappeared for four decades and reappeared in Bourdieu's habitus concept. Habit featured prominently in the works of Émile Durkheim and Max Weber. For Durkheim, education instills dispositions that provide the basis of all practice. Habit is the opposite of consciousness, and it is more important than consciousness: "It is not enough to direct our attention to the superficial portion of our consciousness; for the sentiments, the ideas which come to the surface are not, by far, those which have the most influence in our conduct. What must be reached are the habits—these are the real forces which govern us" (Durkheim 1905–1906, cited in Camic 1986: 1052).

Weber used "habit" to make sense of the endurance of dispositions, such as the innerworldly asceticism that led from Protestantism to capitalism. Weber also conceived of habitual action as one of the four cardinal forms of social action. Social action could be characterized as instrumental, value-driven, affective, or traditional, in the sense of "established habit." Weber (2002: 112) calls this *eingelebte Gewohnheit*, which literally means "lived-in habituation." Weber saw habitual action as a borderline category of "meaningful" social action, because it was a "dull reacting to habitual stimuli toward an established disposition" (Weber 1984: 46, my translation).

According to Camic, habit disappeared from sociological theory when it became the central concept of behaviorist psychology. For the behaviorists, social action could be reduced to stimulus and response, which is better studied by the biological life sciences. Instead of sharpening a social-science definition of habit, sociologists rejected habit as the opposite of meaningful social action: "Social scientists simply dispensed with the concept, opting to conceive all human action as though it were a reflective process of selecting means to ends in accord with normative standards" (Camic 2015: 478).

Whether the same *Begriffsgeschichte* of habit can be written for anthropology is hard to tell. If anthropologists work with habit, they do so only in a communitarian line that stretches from Aristotle to Alasdair MacIntyre (Laidlaw 2014). A history of the habit concept in anthropology would also need more work to relate habit to terms that have some overlaps, such as *culture, custom, tradition,* and *structure.* At least one difference between anthropology and sociology is clear: a challenge from behaviorism, which Camic sees as central for sociology, cannot account for anthropology's silence on habit. Behaviorism has never had much influence in anthropology.

Sociology and anthropology intersect in the works of Mauss and Bourdieu. In his essay on the techniques of the body, Mauss (1973) foregrounds habit but does not develop a systematic definition of it. He uses different swimming styles as examples for habit differences. Ways of swimming are specific to societies. For example, he describes how the French swim differently from other people. These styles were changing with time: earlier, French swimmers used to swallow water and spit it out again, "like a steamboat," but not any longer (Mauss 1973: 71). These changes were happening both through conscious education and unconscious transformations. The French Navy had not required all of its sailors to learn to swim but later made swimming skills mandatory.

For Mauss (1973: 73), habit becomes a topic only when it is socially shared: "These 'habits' do not just vary with individuals and their imitations, they vary especially between societies, educations, proprieties and fashions, prestiges." For the social nature of habit, Mauss (1973: 73) introduces the term *habitus.* The social nature of habit is what leads to different levels of how reflected or unreflected habits are and how much habits are instilled to "inhibit disorderly movements" (Mauss 1973: 86) of the body.

Turning against Aristotle's "psychological" view of habit as belonging to individual souls, Mauss (1973: 73) emphasizes the "techniques and work of collective and individual practical reason." He also foregrounds the embodied aspects of habitual action over mental or psychological states. Even meditative exercises and the "mystical states" of the mind, as practiced in India and China, could be brought back to techniques of the body. At the same time, he maintains habit as a "sociopsychobiological" (Mauss 1973: 87) phenomenon.

The moment that habit appears to make a full return to social theory was when Bourdieu (1990) introduced his version of *habitus*. Bourdieu draws not only on Mauss, but also on Durkheim, Weber, and Claude Lévi-Strauss. All these authors have a concept of habit that is focused on fixity, inertia, and unreflexive tradition. Lévi-Strauss (1963: 19), for example, thinks of habit as unconscious and inert: "We act and think according to habit, and the extraordinary resistance offered to even minimal departures from custom is due more to inertia than to any conscious desire to maintain usages which have a clear function."

Habitus, in Bourdieu's definition, is a system of durable dispositions that generate and structure perception, emotion, thought, and action of an agent: "systems of durable, transposable dispositions, structured structures predisposed to function as structuring structures, that is, as principles which generate and organize practices and representations that can be objectively adapted to their outcomes without presupposing a conscious aiming at ends or an express mastery of the operations necessary in order to attain them" (Bourdieu 1990: 53). This definition of habitus entails four assumptions. The first is that the social world becomes incorporated by the agent as a "permanent disposition, as a durable way of standing, speaking, walking, and thereby of feeling and thinking" (69–70). Incorporation of the social world becomes synonymous with the process of socialization. Socialization consists in the acquisition of "motor schemes and bodily automatisms" (Bourdieu 1990: 69). Through the notion of embodiment, Bourdieu's theory of socialization is anti-mentalistic. The social world is acquired not as a set of mentally represented rules and beliefs, but as a "technique of the body" (69). It is the concrete physical body that functions as "a living memory pad, an automaton that 'leads the mind unconsciously along with it'" (68).

"Technique of the body" is taken from Mauss (1973), yet Bourdieu says he goes beyond Mauss, who was unable to explain why social structures and structures of individual perception and classification are homologous to each other (Bourdieu and Wacquant 1992: 13). The assumption of incorporation is important to Bourdieu's claim that there is an "immediate adherence" (Bourdieu 1990: 68) between habitus and social structures, which produces the illusion that the incorporated social relations are "natural" and beyond critical question. Moreover, the dispositions of agents show a high degree of regularity because the agents' experiences that instill the habitus are similar to each other.

The social world does not become incorporated by the subject in its totality, but subjects acquire dispositions that "fit" each particular "field" in which they are acting. Each field (economics, religion, education, and so on) is relatively autonomous and distinguishable from other fields as a specific "network, or configuration, of objective relations between positions" (Bourdieu and Wacquant 1992: 97). Each has its own implicit and unconscious "regularities" of what is "at stake" and what can be "invested" in it. In other words, each field has its own contexts for what is valuable and what is not. Although all fields are related to one another, the subject has to incorporate the structure of each field separately to succeed in it. What is valued in one field does not translate immediately into what is valued in another field. Bourdieu is a value pluralist. To say that Bourdieu reduces all action to "ultimately commensurable transformations of *the same* social 'capital'" (Laidlaw 2014: 53, emphasis added) is wrong. *Different* forms of capital are commensurable (with transaction costs), but these forms of capital are not all "the same." For Bourdieu, one form of value does not subsume all other forms of value. Bourdieu's vision of value is one of ever "more" through capital conversions from one field to another. His concern is not value creation but how the loss of value through friction in the conversions is minimized. "Ideology" in Bourdieu's sense is a form of reducing frictions in value conversions. However, Bourdieu's value pluralism is masked by his unfortunate choice of the word *capital* for *all* of these different forms of value. The word *capital* suggests that all forms of valuing can ultimately be commensurated in one particular form—that of economic capital.

Second, Bourdieu claims that the incorporation of social structures by the subject makes any principal distinction between habitus and field difficult, or even impossible. They are "the two states of the social world" (Bourdieu 1990: 56) and stand in a relation of mutual production. Through embodiment the structure of a field becomes ingrained in the subjects as a *habitus*, a set of durable dispositions. With their actions thus oriented, the subjects reproduce the social field by acting in it: "Through the *habitus*, the structure of which it is the product governs practice, not along the paths of a mechanical determinism, but within the constraints and limits initially set on its inventions" (55). Strategies of practice are generated by the fit between habitus and field. The agents' strategies can be successful because the incorporation of the field does generate them as adjusted to the "objective potentialities" (53) of each particular field. Thus, neither does the subject determine the objective relations, nor do these relations determine the subject, but habitus and field stand in a relation of codetermination.

Third, Bourdieu's concept of habitus holds that the subject is unaware of the strategies governing its actions—that is, the subject is unaware of its position in a field, as well as of the history of the field. Both the adjustment of a habitus to a particular field and the permanent reproduction of the field through practice produce *doxa* as "uncontested acceptance of the daily lifeworld" (Bourdieu and Wacquant 1992: 73). The more an agent's habitus is adjusted to a field, the more unconscious is the generation of successful practices. Only when the intimacy between habitus and field breaks down does conscious reflection on the implicit conditions become possible.

Fourth, habitus is always at risk of becoming maladjusted to the field by which it was produced in the first place. Habitus can adjust to new conditions, but only within limits and only with delay. If the habitus is not adjusted to the field any longer, the subject's practical sense fails to lead its action to success. Similar to the implicitness of the habitus, its durability (or inertia) becomes visible when a gap opens between habitus and field. This disjuncture is called *hysteresis*.

There have been many criticisms of Bourdieu's habitus theory. The most common is that Bourdieu emphasizes "structure" over "agency," that individuals are mere pawns on fields of action, a field that they did not select and that they cannot change. Habitus and field establish a closed circle of mutual production and reproduction (Jenkins 1982: 273) and a "combined determinism that makes significant social transformation seem impossible" (Sewell 1992: 15). Habitus presents a "relentlessly watertight explanation of a world in which it would be a miracle if anything were ever to change" (Laidlaw 2014: 9). Even scholars such as Loïc Wacquant, who work within Bourdieu's paradigm, diagnose a "strong tension, perhaps contradiction, between [Bourdieu's] will to provide instruments for increasing consciousness and freedom and the demobilization that an overly acute awareness of the pervasiveness of social determinisms threatens to produce" (Bourdieu and Wacquant 1992: 194).

The problem of agency in Bourdieu's theory is hard to deny, but the problem is falsely located in the closed circuit between habitus and field (e.g., Laidlaw 2014: 5). The real flaw of Bourdieu's theory is not a determinism of habitus and field but the alleged *coherence* of individual habits *within* an all-encompassing habitus. Bourdieu never asks whether habitus can be separated into distinct habits and whether these different habits might have different shapes, temporalities, and levels of salience. Bourdieu's theory hinges on a totalizing version of manifold dispositions congealing into a recognizable whole. Not one of the authors of an interdisciplinary history of habit (Sparrow and Hutchinson 2013) notices that Bourdieu talks only about *habitus* but not about habit. What Bourdieu lacks is not a theory of change and agency but a concept of habit that does not melt everything together into a homogeneous habitus. Bourdieu's habitus is not a rediscovery of habit in social theory. Rather, habitus pushes habit even deeper into the background. One of the benefits of Mauss's habitus over Bourdieu's habitus is that Mauss allows that habits are studied individually and are not reduced to a "structured" set of dispositions.

Bourdieu's habitus concept has been further developed by other theorists. A recent addition is the TTOM theory (Veissière et al. 2020), which combines neurobiological, evolutionary, psychological, and sociological perspectives. The TTOM theory argues that human minds are fine-tuned to understand what other human minds are thinking and expecting. Understanding the intentions and experiences of others saves vital energy and hence becomes an evolutionary advantage.

Bourdieu is one of TTOM's sources. An equivalent to Bourdieu's "field" is "affordance" (Gibson 1977). Affordances enable practices: "An affordance is a relation between an agent's abilities and the physical states of its environment. . . . Affordances are defined in terms of physical properties of the thing in the world (e.g., being graspable, being able to support the weight of a person) and in terms of the abilities or expectations of the agent (e.g., knowing how to sit straight). Abilities can be described in terms of the spectrum of expectations with which the agent is endowed" (Veissière et al. 2020: 20). An affordance forms a nexus with habitual action, just like a field forms a nexus with a habitus. Water affords drinking; a cup affords holding drinking water; a house affords dwelling; a path affords forward movement: "The affordances of the environment and the capacities of an individual are inextricably interwoven, and co-determining" (Veissière et al. 2020: 27–28).

Thinking through other minds captures how "shared habits, norms and expectations [are] learned and maintained with precision and reliability across large-scale sociocultural ensembles" (Veissière et al. 2020: 1). It presents a synthesis of habitual thinking and acting within an environment and across social groups. However, TTOM overemphasizes "thinking," which, on balance, is a less powerful driver than embodied, habitual practice. For life to value, it needs a body but not a brain. Hence, I suggest renaming this approach "acting through other habits" (ATOH). The crucial idea in Bourdieu's habitus/field, TTOM, and embodied value theory is that habitual action saves time-consuming reflexivity and enables swift and precise responses. Habituation allows practical virtuosity. Learning other habits and acting through those other habits frees up energy that does not need to be used for critical thinking. If reflexive thinking and habitual acting are biocommensurated in terms of how much energy they save, habitual acting will come out as clear winner. Acting through other habits outdoes thinking through other minds.

Prescription Habits

Let me bring the work on habit back to the puzzle of why Indian general physicians (both licensed and unlicensed) are convinced that depression is rising. What they are arguing is that there is a series of macro- and micro-level changes that are causally related to one another. First, the lifeworld of Indians changes, and the causes for the change are globalization, capitalism, and market liberalization. These changes lead to changes in the life of communities, families, and individuals. People are more stressed; they do not have as much time for one another, and social support is weakening. They compete with one another for limited resources. They change their consumer aspirations and are not content with what their parents were able to afford. Their time horizon expands, and they are more worried about the future than they used to be. People are also less willing to believe in the same philosophies of fate and karma than were earlier generations. The changes on the macroeconomic level are coming together to change people's social lives, and social life changes individuals' experiences, increasing the risk of depression. Since more and more people are falling prey to depression, more and more people are going to the doctors to get treated. Basically, the doctors describe a monumental and multi-leveled transformation of habits that is bad for mental well-being.

By foregrounding habit changes in the lifeworlds of patients, the GPS deflect attention away from their *own* habit changes. While the doctors lament socioeconomic change, they applaud the changed availability of antidepressant treatments. The effectiveness and ease of use of new antidepressants brought a change in their prescribing habits, and they are now prescribing these drugs more commonly than in previous years.

The introduction of selective serotonin reuptake inhibitors (SSRIS) has, in their opinion, made it possible to take the treatment of depression out of the domain of specialized psychiatry and into general practice. While they find older types of antidepressants too hard to handle, new antidepressants are "easy" to prescribe and "safe" to use. When the GPS were asked how many of their patients they were giving antidepressants to, they said that they "routinely" prescribed antidepressants. One estimated that half of his patients had received a prescription for an SSRI. The GPS also admitted that they never told their patients about either their diagnosis of "depression" or about the nature of the medicines to avoid hostile reactions from them. The reason for this is that the patients were too steeped in old ideas and mental habits of thinking of psychiatric drugs as drugs for "mad" people that they were too difficult to educate or convince. Instead of confronting patients, they preferred to tell them that the drugs were for "better sleep" or "better appetite."

If we do not accept the doctors' story of how the habits of their patients had changed but instead look at how the prescribing habits of the doctors have changed, a different explanation for the "rise of depression" becomes more plausible than socioeconomic change. The rise of depression is less about patients *thinking* through other minds differently; the rise of depression comes from GPS *acting* through other prescribers' habits.

The treatment of depression was of marginal importance in Indian GPS' practice before the late 1980s. A few GPS had treated symptoms of depression before, mostly with tricyclics. The market launch of "safe and easy" SSRIS since the 1990s massively expanded the reach of depression treatments to nonspecialized doctors. Pharmaceutical companies' marketing efforts are playing an important role in this. With these pills at hand, the GPS started to diagnose more and more patients with "depression," all made possible by the actual presence of drugs that they themselves could prescribe. The formation of new prescribing practices that began to rely on the routine uses of antidepressants was made possible only by the arrival of newer and affordable drugs since the 1990s. The prescribing habits for new antidepressants were first established by psychiatrists, then became established among GPS, and then trickled down to unlicensed prescribers by way of floating prescriptions carried around by patients to different doctors (Ecks 2013).

If we start with material habits of prescribing rather than with changing socioeconomic conditions, the doctors' conviction that depression is actually rising looks more like an unreflected justification for their increasing uses of antidepressants. The "affordance" that has clearly changed is the ready availability of psychotropics. What I find so striking about the doctors is their honest conviction that depression is rising and that depression is truly caused by social changes. There are social changes that increase the risk of suffering from depression: flatter hierarchies and (neo)liberalism are indeed in evidence. However, in the Indian context, the material affordance of psychotropics is a more proximate factor. The belief that depression is rising is formed by their own changed prescription habits, but it is systematically misrecognized as a change of habits among patients. The GPs are making up epidemiological evidence through their prescription patterns.

This is a case for the advantages of habitography, as opposed to ethnography. The GPs are not differentiated by ethnicity, and almost no aspect of Bengali or Indian ethnic identity has any bearing on what is going on. In fact, ethnography tends to conceal what is actually happening and conspires with the doctors' deflection of attention away from their own habit changes and toward blaming social change for a rise in depression. Habitography can redirect our attention away from what people say they do toward embodied valuing practices.

EIGHT

Culture, Context, and Consensus
Comparing Symptoms and Things

Symptom-based Commensuration

In 2013, the American Psychiatric Association (APA) published the fifth edition of its *Diagnostic and Statistical Manual of Mental Disorders* (DSM-5). The DSM is dubbed the "bible" of psychiatry. The DSM-5 replaced the DSM-IV, first published in 1994 and again, in a revised form (DSM-IV-TR), in 2000. The DSM-5 continues the format used by previous editions, defining disease labels by symptoms and grouping them into larger areas, such as mood disorders. The manual focuses on describing and ordering symptoms, not on etiology. The DSM rules what, for example, "depression" looks like. It does not define what causes depression. It also does not contain any therapeutic advice. There are no algorithms for treatment in the main manual.

The place of culture in psychopathology received a substantial reformulation in the DSM-5 (APA 2013). In this chapter, I explore what the DSM-5 says about culture, as well as what it does *not* say about culture. The DSM-5 says lots about culture, but it says nothing about how the use of things is part of culture. The manual makes no mention of any treatments, either in the chapters on disease classifications or in the culture sections.

There are reasons for not letting these pesky things into the rules for diagnosis. One of them is that the DSM-5 continues the "atheoretical" approach that the DSM-III initiated. The third edition of the manual tried to construct a consistent classification of disorders by leaving aside both etiology and therapy (Frances and Cooper 1981; Horwitz and Wakefield 2007: 165). In the 1980s, this was seen as a necessary move to get the many warring schools of psychiatry to agree at least on what disorders look like. The different schools would have never come to a consensus on what causes problems and on what therapy should be given. Freudians would have never agreed with neo-Kraepelinians on either etiology or therapy. Atheoretical symptom classification was the softest target for building consensus across a fractured discipline (Decker 2007). With the DSM-III, psychiatry tried to bring its different practices together by focusing on a *partial commensuration*. The hope was that, sometime in the future, etiological and therapeutic models could be fully commensurated. In chapter 11, I analyze the failure of psychiatry to commensurate biological markers with DSM symptoms. In this chapter, I describe psychiatry's double failure to commensurate symptoms with the use of psychotropics and to commensurate symptoms across different cultural settings.

Anthropological engagements with psychiatry often stop at "revealing" that psychiatric diagnostics are not universal, objective, and scientific; they are regarded as cultural artifacts like any other belief or practice. Critics have shown that the disease labels listed in the DSM are historical and cultural through and through. It is not hard to prove that the DSM is "more a cultural than a scientific document" (Shorter 2013: 17), that the DSM is a "historical document with a complicated pedigree" (Mezzich et al. 1999), or that the DSM itself has become a "cultural icon" (Sadler 2013: 21). A constructivist argument can be made about any scientific text. Bruno Latour's (2005) point that we should not stop at a cultural constructivist critique of science still holds.

Instead of yet another critique of the DSM as cultural construct, I develop a take on "culture" that goes beyond a reduction of the DSM to an arbitrary convention. I will do this by putting some things back that the DSM-5 strains not to mention: psychotropics. I return to this focus on drugs as matters of concern after showing why all the criticisms of the DSM so far have been versions of cultural constructivism.

complicate the cultural construction argument w/ an analysis of pharmaceuticals

Two Critiques, One Culture

The long-winded preparation and final publication of the DSM-5 in 2013 provoked severe criticisms. Two major strands of critique emerged: one that revolves around "medicalization" and one that revolves around "lack of validity." At first, these critiques seem diametrically opposed to each other, as if they were replaying C. P. Snow's ([1959] 2012) struggle between the "two cultures" of the humanities and the natural sciences. Looked at more closely, however, both critiques turn out to be variants of cultural critique.

The first type of "cultural" critique is that the DSM-5 devalues cultural patterns of feeling and behaving in favor of excessive medical interventionism. The media response to the DSM-5 highlighted the fear that, if the new manual was correct, "we are all mad" and "abnormal is the new normal" (Rosenberg 2013). According to this line of critique, the new DSM exacerbates an ongoing process of psychiatric medicalization of everyday life. The "medicalization" critique had been around at least since the antipsychiatry days of the 1950s. The DSM-III had already received a great deal of criticism for medicalizing normal responses to adversity (e.g., Kutchins and Kirk 1997). Each subsequent edition of the DSM pushed medicalization to new heights.

The medicalization critique comes from both social scientists and other psy- sciences. In 2011, for example, the British Psychological Society (BPS) published a response to the DSM-5 that opens with a rejection of medicalization: "The Society is concerned that clients and the general public are negatively affected by the continued and continuous medicalisation of their natural and normal responses to their experiences" (BPS 2011). According to the BPS, mental distress is caused by *social* relations. The DSM-5 locates the roots of mental illness within the individual, but this "misses the relational context of problems and the undeniable social causation of many such problems" (BPS 2011). The BPS statement continues by reiterating that DSM categories themselves are "clearly based largely on social norms" (BPS 2011).

A much-cited example of how the DSM-5 had gone awry is the relation between bereavement and depression. Previous editions of the DSM recommended that clinicians use a bereavement exclusion: someone might present all the symptoms of depression, but if this happened in response to bereavement, then it should not be labeled depression. Experiencing other people's death was a normal life-cycle event. The DSM-5 removed the bereavement exclusion so that anyone who "actually" develops depression is "not denied" diagnosis and treatment only because its onset coincides with a traumatic life event (Wakefield 2013). For the critics, the DSM-5 further expands the realm of the pathological into what should properly be seen as normal (Greenberg 2010). This critique assumes that there is a culturally "normal" way to experience suffering and to respond to adverse life events that is increasingly pathologized and medicated. The rationale for this kind of medicalization was, ultimately, to profit a "mental health medical-industrial complex" (Sadler 2013).

Allan Horwitz and Jerome Wakefield (2008) also argue that psychiatric medicalization undermines feelings of "normal" sadness. They say that the life experiences that lead to depression are the loss of social status, the loss of valued personal attachments, and the failure to reach valued life goals. All these experiences are "normal," and to respond with sadness to them is also "normal." Feeling depressed about these losses and frustrations is not pathological. These feelings become pathological only if they persist for too long. Within their evolutionary model of depression, sadness is biologically normal. It turns into a harmful dysfunction only through *cultural* ways of evaluating these feelings: "A mental disorder exists when the failure of a person's internal mechanisms to perform their functions *as designed by nature* impinges harmfully on the person's well-being as defined by social values and meanings" (Horwitz and Wakefield 2008: 17, emphasis added). This version of the medicalization critique also turns against the social sciences. Horwitz and Wakefield think the social sciences fail to distinguish inner sadness from culturally defined depressive disorder. But Horwitz and Wakefield's critique of cultural consensus falters because it is based on a separation between fact and value, which makes historical changes to both diagnostics *and* experiences impossible (Ehrenberg 2010: xxviii). All emotions are "unnatural" (Lutz 2011) in the sense of being always already coconstituted by the inner in relation to an outer.

Another attack against medicalization came from Allen Frances, chairman of the DSM-IV Task Force. Frances (2009) predicted "a bonanza for the pharmaceutical industry but at a huge cost to the new false positive 'patients' caught in the excessively wide DSM-V net." He chided the epidemic increases in autism, bipolar disorder, and attention deficit hyperactivity disorder (ADHD) as unfortunate consequences of the DSM—including the DSM-IV he chaired. Frances went on to publish many versions of this critique both in psychiatric journals and leading news media such as the *New York Times*.

For bereavement, Frances argues, humans have cultures of mourning that developed over the course of history. Cultures found many ways of dealing with loss and sadness. Cultures thrived without any need to administer drugs: "Turning bereavement into major depression would substitute a shallow, Johnny-come-lately medical ritual for the sacred mourning rites that have survived for millenniums. To slap on a diagnosis and prescribe a pill would be to reduce the dignity of the life lost and the broken heart left behind" (Frances 2010).

It is ironic that Frances adopted such a heavily cultural view in his critique of the DSM-5. As chairman of the DSM-IV, he did not take up most of the recommendations given by the Group on Culture and Diagnosis, funded by the National Institute of Mental Health (NIMH), and he felt that existing evidence on "culture" was not "hard" enough to include them in the DSM-IV (Mezzich et al. 1999).

Another line of critique is that the DSM-5 is "too cultural" because all that are looked at are superficial behavioral symptoms that cannot be commensurated with genetics, neurological findings, or biological markers. A few weeks before the DSM-5 was published, Thomas Insel, then the director of the NIMH, ridiculed the DSM's approach to disease classification as an intuitive art rather than a hard science: "The weakness [of the DSM] is its lack of validity. Unlike our definitions of ischemic heart disease, lymphoma, or AIDS, the DSM diagnoses are based on a *consensus* about clusters of clinical symptoms, not any objective laboratory measure. In the rest of medicine, this would be equivalent to creating diagnostic systems based on the nature of chest pain or the quality of fever" (Insel 2013, emphasis added) (see chapter 11). Because it could never get beyond mere "opinions" arrived at through "consensus" decisions, he said, the NIMH "will be re-orienting its research away from DSM categories." Instead of outward symptoms, the new classifications should be based on measurable biomarkers. This project is called the Research Domain Criteria Project (RDoC).

Insel's attack on the DSM caused a stir beyond the research field. In response to the outcry caused by his critique, Insel cowrote a press release with J. A. Lieberman, president-elect of the APA, that supported the DSM as "the key resource for delivering the best available care" (Insel and Lieberman 2013; Psychiatric News Alert 2013). Patients and insurance companies, they said, could be "confident that effective treatments are available" (Insel and Lieberman 2013). Superficially, it appeared as if the NIMH had retreated, but this is not what happened. Insel just said that the "best available care" might be based on the DSM today, but that did not mean that it would be based on the DSM tomorrow. Some NIMH statements about the relation between the DSM and RDoC published since 2013 tend to portray the two frameworks as complementary, not competing (Lupien et al. 2017: 8), but it is difficult to see how these approaches could ever be commensurated.

Insel's critique stands in a tradition of privileging biology (as hard science) over symptoms (as "mere consensus"). Hopes for a neurobiological reorientation of DSM-5 were prominent in the Revision Agenda the NIMH and APA had published eleven years earlier: refining, reshuffling, and expanding disease definitions "may never be successful in uncovering their underlying etiologies" (Kupfer et al. 2002: xix). Biopsychiatrists have questioned the validity of DSM categories since the 1980s. The search for biological substrates is "build on quicksand" if it is based on invalid categories (see chapter 11).

These two critiques attack different kinds of commensuration processes. The medicalization critique rejects that normal symptoms are "the same" as pathological symptoms. The form of commensuration is one of similarity to and difference from prototypical symptom constellations. In turn, the validity critique rejects that outward symptoms signify the true causes, which are underlying biomarkers. The commensuration is one of proxy to cause.

Yet both lines of critique are based on the *same* principle of cultural relativism (see chapter 2). The medicalization critics say that the DSM is a cultural document cooked up by arbitrary committees of psychiatrists who are collaborating with pharmaceutical manufacturers. This can be remedied only by revealing the DSM as a cultural artifact with pathogenic consequences. The validity critics say that the DSM is a cultural document cooked up by clinicians who go by superficial symptoms only. This can be remedied only by replacing cultural constructs with hard scientific data.

What the DSM-5 Says about "Culture" (I): Interpretative Frameworks

Another irony is that neither the medicalization critics nor the validity critics stop to ask how the DSM *itself* deals with culture. None of them recognizes that the new edition entails a substantial new definition of culture. The new sections on culture in the DSM-5 have received almost no attention or commentary.

At first, what the DSM-5 says of "culture" seems uncontroversial. For some, though, the new DSM is a revolutionary chapter in the history of psychiatry. For Laurence Kirmayer, a prominent transcultural psychiatrist and contributor in the revision process, what ended up in the final version of the DSM-5 challenges "the fundamental logic of psychiatric nosology" and undermines the biopsychiatric position that all mental illnesses are "located inside peoples' heads" only. The new DSM supports the assumption that there cannot be any diagnosis of mental illness beyond dealing in the cultural languages of suffering: "We are embedded in social networks and interpersonal relations and local worlds" (quoted in Cummings 2013).

The discussion of culture in the DSM-5 is based on copious research. Preparations for the cultural aspects go back to Juan Mezzich and his colleagues' reviews of how the DSM-IV deals with culture and context (Mezzich et al. 1999). The Revision Agenda for the DSM-5 included "the importance of culture in psychopathology" as one of six key agenda items (Kupfer et al. 2002).

The treatment of culture in the DSM-5 comprises three sections. "Cultural Issues" are discussed in the introduction (APA 2013: 14–15). A whole chapter (749–59) is devoted to "Cultural Formulation," which extends the discussion of culture and outlines the Cultural Formulation Interview (CFI), a semi-structured interview schedule containing sixteen questions that try to capture a patient's cultural definition of a problem; cultural etiology; cultural factors affecting coping and help seeking; and cultural factors affecting current help seeking. The most intriguing pronouncements on culture are at the end of this chapter, hidden behind the outline of the CFI. The third "culture" section is the "Glossary of Cultural Concepts of Distress" (833–37), which lists syndromes such as *ataque de nervios*, *dhat*, and *susto*. These syndromes were called "culture-bound syndromes" in the DSM-IV.

Most of what the DSM-5 discusses as "culture" echoes classic definitions taken from anthropology. In the new DSM, "culture" is the totality of norms and values held by individuals, families, social systems, and institutions. Culture comprises both ideas and practices; "systems of knowledge, concepts, rules, and practices" (APA 2013: 749). Meanings, habits, and traditions are all encompassed in the culture concept. Language, religion, spirituality, family structures, life-cycle stages, rituals, and moral and legal systems are features of culture. One becomes a member of a culture by internalizing shared "norms" and "values" (749). Part of this internalization process is that norms are applied by significant others to the individual, and these others can include clinicians. Culture remains relatively stable over time but also remains open to change. It is not internalized by individuals uniformly but is revised and re-created in the process of internalization.

The DSM-5 argues that most people live in "multiple cultures" (APA 2013: 749). Some primarily belong to a "majority" culture; others belong more to a "minority" culture (750). Self-identities are fashioned from various cultural influences and rarely from a single culture only. Cultural diversity also derives from a diversity of social groups that are based in ethnic, religious, or occupational differences (750). An "ethnic" group is made up through a "culturally constructed group identity" (749). These group identities are "rooted" in different historical, geographical, linguistic, and religious experiences. Like culture, ethnicity is mixed, multiple, and hybrid, especially where mobility, intermarriage, and social intermixing are increasing (749).

According to the DSM-5, culture matters for psychiatric practice on many levels. First, culture provides patients with an "interpretive framework" that shapes both the "experience" of mental distress and its "expression." In this view, every psychiatric consultation is influenced by cultural differences. Psychiatric diagnosing has to rely on the symptoms, signs, and behaviors of patients, and since these are steeped in culture, clinical treatment decisions, prognostics, and outcomes are potentially affected.

Cultures vary by their "thresholds of tolerance" for symptoms and behaviors. What counts as normal and what is already pathological will differ according to cultural norms and expectations. Cultural awareness can help clinicians avoid misdiagnoses and "correct mistaken interpretations of psychopathology" (APA 2013: 758). It enhances the efficacy of treatments, helps transcultural research projects, and improves rapport by "speaking the language of the patient" (759).

The DSM-5 values the role of culture as good and bad. Culture has a good effect when it provides sources of support, which can be emotional, instrumental, and informational. Culture provides coping strategies and may enhance resilience. Traditional, alternative, and complementary forms of healing can be cultural resources of such resilience as well (APA 2013: 750).

Culture can also have negative effects. First, psychic suffering can be caused by "culture" in the widest sense. For example, vulnerabilities can emerge from interpersonal and intergenerational conflicts that are motivated by cultural differences (APA 2013: 749). "Panic disorder" and "health anxieties" can be triggered by cultural influences. People can get stressed by the "environment" (750) in which they live. This environment encompasses the family, religious groups, and social networks of friends, neighbors, or coworkers. "Psychosocial stressors" can be both in the immediate environment and in temporarily and spatially distant events. Problems can arise whenever the "adaptation" of an individual to the cultural norms around it is disturbed (749). The DSM-5 also mentions "racism" and "discrimination" as culture-based stressors.

"Economic inequity" as a source of suffering is mentioned once in passing (APA 2013: 749). The impact of economic inequities in the emergence of mental suffering has been more prominent in other publications (see chapter 10). For example, Robert Desjarlais and his colleagues (1995) claimed that economic poverty should be seen as the principal reason for mental suffering around the world. Most of the transcultural psychiatrists involved in the DSM-5 position themselves as hermeneutic (Mezzich et al. 1999), hence it is not surprising that socioeconomic determinants receive only scant attention. Socioeconomic factors are subsumed under culture.

The DSM-5 further points out that culture can have a negative impact on health seeking. Culturally based stigmatization can prevent people from seeking psychiatric treatment. When they decide to accept psychiatric help, cultural norms can impede diagnoses, treatment decisions, and outcomes. The relationship between the individual patient and the clinician is marked by differences of social status, cultural backgrounds, and language. These can lead to difficulties in communication (APA 2013: 750), and these can, in turn, adversely affect both the accuracy of the clinical diagnosis and the acceptance of the diagnosis by the patient. The same applies to the acceptance or rejection of the prescribed treatment, which then hampers adherence.

An important notion in the DSM-5 is the "adaptation" of the individual to both the cultural environment and to the clinical encounter. Cultural sensitivity is meant to increase adaptation, and without adaptation, good outcomes are unlikely. The Cultural Formulation Interview (CFI) is explicitly designed to enhance patient "adaptation" especially when there are deep cultural differences between the patient and the clinician, when there are disagreements between them, and when a patient shows "limited engagement" (APA 2013: 751).

The culture sections of the DSM-5 are trying to give a systematic list of reasons for how culture introduces *differences* into universal experiences of symptoms. The DSM-5 does not argue for cultural incommensurability, but it argues for cultural differences. The forms that culture make are commensurated with each other, so that it becomes possible to say that a certain kind of distress is correlated with certain kinds of cultural features.

What DSM-5 Says about "Culture" (II): Beyond Culture-bound Syndromes

A similar process of commensuration becomes visible in how the DSM-5 deals with the problem of culture-bound syndromes. These syndromes pose the possibility of incommensurability more than any other aspect ascribed to culture. Previously, the DSM dealt with culture only in the form of culture-bound syndromes. The concept had been introduced in the DSM-IV in 1994 and was taken up again in the DSM-IV-TR. Culture-bound syndromes were defined as "recurrent, locality-specific patterns of aberrant behavior and troubling experience that may or may not be linked to a particular DSM-IV diagnostic category. Many of these patterns are indigenously considered to be 'illnesses,' or at least afflictions, and most have local names. . . . [C]ulture-bound syndromes are generally limited to specific societies or culture areas and are localized, folk, diagnostic categories that frame coherent meanings for certain repetitive, patterned, and troubling sets of experiences and observations" (APA 2000: 898).

In the 1990s, the inclusion of "culture" in the DSM was seen as a productive step toward a better understanding of how factors outside the individual brain could make a difference to the prevalence and therapeutic outcome of psychiatric disorders. Yet the notion of culture-bound syndromes was soon regarded as outdated. The way culture-bound syndromes were listed made them look more like a museum of exotic curiosities than a clinically relevant guide to syndromes (Mezzich et al. 1999).

The DSM-5 considers the culture-bound syndromes concept a historical "construct" (APA 2013: 14) and replaces it with three other concepts: "cultural syndromes," "cultural idioms of distress," and "cultural explanation/perceived causes." A cultural construct can belong to any one of these analytic levels or to several of them. "Depression," for example, is simultaneously a cultural syndrome, a cultural idiom of distress, and a cultural explanation (758). All three influence symptoms, health seeking, clinical presentation, expectations of treatment, illness adaptation, and responses to treatments.

What is now called a *cultural syndrome* is nearly the same as what used to be called a *culture-bound syndrome*. The new term tries to avoid an emphasis on boundedness (APA 2013: 758). Most conditions previously dubbed culture-bound syndromes, such as dhat or susto, are now cultural syndromes: cultural patterns of distress that can be located within a cultural group or community. Cultural syndromes are co-occurring constellations of symptoms. The DSM-5 adds a new take on the old emic-or-etic debate by stating that cultural syndromes can be detected by an outsider even when they are not detected by local people. Hence, local groups can have distinct ways of experiencing and expressing suffering without a locally agreed label. It is also possible that the same cultural syndrome receives different labels within the same cultural setting (14).

"Cultural idioms of distress" emphasize that distress is expressed differently in different localities. Kirmayer and Sartorius (2007: 835) have recommended that *culture-bound syndromes* be replaced with *cultural idioms of distress*. Drawing on cognitive linguistics, they point out that bodily experience, language, and culturally shared illness narratives co-constitute one another. What had, so far, been described as "syndromes" were not discrete disorders. Instead, they were "culturally prescribed modes of understanding and narrating health problems and broader personal and social concerns" (835). To speak of *idioms* of distress emphasized the communicative dimension of suffering: what seemed like an exotic complaint might be "a way to express dissatisfaction with living conditions, legitimate difficulties in performing social roles, and allow the individual to seek outside help" (835). The new edition of the DSM endorses this notion of cultural idioms of distress as "a linguistic term, phrase, or ways of talking about suffering" (APA 2013: 14).

The DSM-5 further points out that there is no direct match between a word or label, on the one hand, and the underlying problems that are being talked about, on the other. For example, when a patient talks about "feeling depressed," this "may refer to widely varying forms of suffering without mapping out the discrete set of symptoms syndrome, or disorder" (APA 2013: 758). Even when a patient talks about "depression" and shows depressive symptoms, that does not mean that the diagnosis should be "depression" in all cases.

In turn, if a patient experiences symptoms that do not match any in the DSM-5 catalog, treatment should still be given: "Individuals whose symptoms do not meet DSM criteria for a specific mental disorder may still expect and require treatment" (APA 2013: 759). This statement is ambiguous because the term *require treatment* could either mean that both the clinician and the patient feel that treatment is necessary or that treatment is demanded by a patient but the clinician does not necessarily want to comply with the demand.

Despite all of its emphasis on language, the DSM-5 does not say that cultural idioms *coconstitute* the experience of suffering. In the DSM-5, words "express," "communicate," and "name" problems, but they do not shape them. A separation between "mere words" and "real problems" is intact. The only hint at such an argument is the statement that cultural constructs "influence how the individual experiences . . . his or her symptoms" (APA 2013: 750). The DSM-5 allows for the language of "professional diagnostic systems" to influence "cultural concepts" (758), but not for psychiatric diagnostics to influence the experience of distress.

The third concept replacing culture-bound syndromes, "cultural explanation or perceived cause," is a "culturally conceived etiology" within an "explanatory model." The concept of "explanatory models" has been a mainstay of medical anthropology since the 1980s (Kleinman 1980: 104–18). Anthropologists have approached the encounter between a healer and a patient as an encounter between different sets of causal presuppositions (Helman 2007: 122–55). These presuppositions entail, more or less explicitly, what caused the illness's symptoms, what would happen without medical intervention, and why improvements could be expected. In the DSM-5, a specific example for such a cultural explanation is *maladi moun*, a "human-sent illness" among Haitians (APA 2013: 835). Maladi moun can be sent because of the evil eye, envy, or malice. The label highlights the cause of the disorder rather than the symptoms, which can range from depression to psychosis or failure in daily life.

The word *bound*, in *culture-bound syndromes*, attracted the most discussion. The critics said that, instead of thinking of cultures as static and demarcated, one should think of cultures as dynamic and overlapping. Several alternatives to the "boundedness" were suggested in transcultural psychiatry. For example, *culture* really meant *context*; hence, culture-bound syndromes should be renamed context-bound disorders (Helman 2007: 266). Others emphasized that most, if not all, so-called culture-bound conditions could be detected in other cultures (Sumathipala et al. 2004). A case in point is semen loss anxiety, known as dhat in South Asia. Far from being "culture-bound," semen anxieties can be diagnosed in other world regions—for example, Sushrut Jadhav (2007) tried to show that dhat can be diagnosed among white British men, even though they have no cultural concept of dhat. But applying dhat in the United Kingdom presented a "category error" that could lead to "cultural iatrogenesis" if applied badly. Instead of culture-bound syndromes, psychiatry needs better conceptualizations of distress (Jadhav 2007). The DSM-5 also held that the culture-bound syndromes notion "overemphasizes the local particularity and limited distribution" of conditions (APA 2013: 758).

It was also said that many—if not all—disease labels used in the DSM are "bound" to North American and European cultures. All of the disease labels came from there, and translating them into other languages was cultural imperialism. Long before the term *culture-bound syndromes* entered the DSM-IV, some psychiatrists had argued for the cultural biases of psychiatric classification. For example, Marvin Opler (1959: 141, emphasis added) suggested that "*psychiatrists* remain fairly culture bound in their theorizing about psychopathology" and that the influence of culture is not confined to lay people. Roland Littlewood and Maurice Lipsedge (1987: 290) developed the related argument that conditions such as anorexia, obesity, overdosing, menopause, and even kleptomania are "historically and geographically . . . specific to industrialized cultures." Hence, culture-bound syndromes could be found not only among the exotic "Other" but right in the middle of Western *medical* discourse. Just because a condition has an officious Latin name does not mean that it has left the shackles of "culture" behind.

The authors of the DSM-5 have taken this on board, stating that, like culture, psychiatric categories change through history: "Like culture *and* DSM *itself*, cultural concepts may change over time in response to both local and global influences" (APA 2013: 758, emphasis added). All the diagnostic labels used in the DSM had specific cultural origins: "The current formulation acknowledges that *all* forms of distress are locally shaped, including the DSM disorders" (758).

Such a recognition of cultural relativism seemed impossible until recently. Critics long held that psychiatry is not as hard a science as it pretends to be; that DSM classifications will always be provisional; and that disease labels are "the product of negotiations around a conference table" (Greenberg 2010). As late as 2013, critics assumed that the authors of the DSM-5 would never depart from universal truth claims: "Each DSM aspires to carry out this classification mission in a scientific manner. . . . The authors of the successive manuals would thus be reluctant to see their creations as historical, cultural, ideological products rather than as scientific documents" (Phillips 2013: 159).

The DSM-5 countered the criticisms with a twist on its own cultural specificity: culture-specific *origins* were not the same as culture-specific *futures*. Being "shaped locally" (in Europe and America) did not mean that a concept could never travel to other parts of the world and be applied there. What was included in the DSM-5 were, basically, culture-bound syndromes of the West that became enculturated elsewhere. Even when a label's origin was local, it could *become* universal: "From this perspective, many DSM diagnoses can be understood as operationalized prototypes that started out as cultural syndromes and became widely accepted as a result of their clinical and research utility" (APA 2013: 758). This is an interesting riff on culture-bound syndromes: rather than arguing that culture makes concepts "bound" to a particular locality, it says that culture shapes concepts but does not keep them particular. The DSM suggests that its categories can pragmatically be called "universal" because they can leave their cultural origins behind. In this way, the DSM-5 manages to include cultural difference without forgoing biological sameness. Culture-based differences are acknowledged, but they never come to undermine the full commensurability of disorders across all cultures. The DSM-5 argues for a kind of consensus-based commensurability of mental illnesses. It effectively proposes the opposite of Michael Walzer's (1983) consensus-based *in*commensurability (see chapter 2): other people can agree culturally that their brains suffer from the same biologized mental disorders from which anyone else in the world is suffering.

What the DSM-5 Does Not Say about Culture

Despite the DSM-5's surprising cultural and historical self-reflexivity, there are some glaring holes in how it thinks about culture. The fifth edition reads as if its authors had stopped engaging with social theory in the 1980s. The group of psychiatrists behind the DSM-5 culture chapters come, by their own self-labeling, from a "meaning-centered" tradition (Mezzich et al. 1999). A purely symbolic approach was perhaps most popular in the 1970s and the 1980s, and this is the era from which the DSM-5's ideas about culture are derived.

Even the most ardent symbolic anthropologists, including Clifford Geertz (1973), were fully aware that *things* needed to be part of any viable definition of culture. Take the classic definition by A. L. Kroeber and Clyde Kluckhohn (1952: 35): "Culture consists of patterns of and for behavior acquired and transmitted by symbols, constituting the distinctive achievements of human groups, including their embodiments in artifacts; the essential core of culture consists of traditional (historically derived and selected) ideas and especially their attached values." Kroeber and

Kluckhohn were pioneers of cross-cultural comparisons of values. They are usually put within the lineage of symbolic anthropology that goes back to Franz Boas. But it is notable how even they emphasized the place of material stuff in the constitution of culture.

There is a thing-shaped hole in the DSM-5. Its authors ignore all definitions of culture that include things. Even a rudimentary inclusion of things as coconstituting agents would have improved the DSM. Here I want to highlight two types of "things" that all critics of the DSM mention, in one way or another. The first is the DSM manual as a material artifact itself; the second is the pharmaceutical.

There is a difference between how things are intended to be used and how they are actually used. This difference matters in the uses of the DSM. Psychiatrists who have to use the DSM in their daily practice, especially in the United States, like to say that the manual is not used to diagnose mental health problems. Instead, they say they see patients and come up with diagnoses based on clinical experience. They pick up the DSM only when there is either a serious doubt about how to label the condition or the insurance paperwork needs to be done (Carlat 2010).

Anywhere the DSM dominates, it does so not because of its diagnostic finesse but because its use is bureaucratically entrenched. In the United States, insurance payments and disability benefits are based on the DSM. The Social Security Administration demands diagnoses according to DSM criteria to evaluate benefit claims. Evidence in legal cases needs to refer to DSM categories. Classifying illness for bureaucratic and legal requirements is the main reason to use the DSM in practice: "Most psychiatrists and other clinicians do not bother with a DSM coding until they have to fill in the paperwork. They do their thinking in terms of prototypes, not definitions" (Hacking 2013). Gary Greenberg (2010) relates an anecdote about a former APA president who diagnosed and treated a patient for several months, then eventually picked up the DSM to look up how to label the condition. Asked whether the DSM changed his diagnosis or treatment, the eminent psychiatrist said "no." Asked whether the DSM had increased the "value of the diagnosis," the psychiatrist answered, "Yes. I got paid." The value added of the DSM is not diagnostic; it is financial. The biocommensuration that the DSM allows psychiatrists to perform is a value conversion of diagnostics into reimbursements.

Even pro-DSM advocates employ the "how the DSM is actually used" argument. For example, Sally Satel, a psychiatrist at Yale University and resident at the American Enterprise Institute, a neoliberal think tank cofounded by pharmaceutical giants, says that the "fuss" about the DSM-5 is unnecessary. The media may "trumpet" that the DSM-5 was a disaster, "but practicing psychiatrists will largely regard it as a nonevent" (Satel 2013). Changes to the DSM would not change psychiatric diagnostics; all that would change were the practices of institutions such as "insurance companies, state and government agencies, and even the courts" (Satel 2013). Once mental illness entered these bureaucratic contexts, DSM categories were taken to be entirely scientific and entirely precise. The psychiatrists themselves were sophisticated enough to know the difference between their own well-rounded care and the pseudo-exactness of the DSM. Since the key manual for psychiatric diagnostics was not used for actual psychiatric diagnostics, practicing clinicians would not be swayed by revised classifications.

By distinguishing the DSM's uses in bureaucracy from the DSM's uses in psychiatry, Satel tries to save the image of the uncompromised caring psychiatrist. According to her—and here lies the neoliberal twist of the argument—it is not the DSM that overdiagnoses and overmedicates patients; it is the anonymous bureaucratic machinery run by the federal government. Satel's argument is not clever enough, though, to get past a theory of culture that does not lose sight of the coconstitution of things and people. That psychiatric practice would not be shaped by the DSM, in some way or another, is implausible.

The second kind of thing that every critic mentions, in one way or another, is the pharmaceutical. Biopsychiatry and psychopharmacology have been developing hand in hand since the 1950s. There cannot be any understanding of psychiatry in practice without understanding the development, distribution, and prescription of pharmaceuticals. But drugs are excluded from the DSM-5. Any "cultural" account of psychiatric diagnostics that does not even mention pharmaceuticals misses the point.

Since the DSM-III, psychopharmacology has been based on symptoms-based diagnostics. Without specificity of symptoms, clinical trials could not be conducted, and without these clinical trial results, US Food and Drug Administration approval would not be given (see chapter 1). The proliferation of diagnostic categories also allowed companies to market "new" drugs for hitherto untreated problems. The logic of care has been replaced by the logic of profits: "Clinical trials are being designed in order to answer the question, What is the largest, safest, and most profitable market that can be produced?" (Dumit 2012: 103).

Ian Hacking coined the term *looping effects* to describe what happens when people, experts, institutions, and knowledge come back to change classifications (see chapter 11). Disease classifications are interacting with the "people" who are labeled and "made up" through them, with the "experts" who devise them, with the body of "knowledge" on which they are based, and with the "institutions" that assemble experts and legitimate knowledge. The DSM classifications are interacting with all these levels.

In the United States, direct-to-consumer marketing for prescription drugs is allowed. This establishes a direct link between patients and pharmaceutical producers and puts added pressure on doctors ("Ask your doctor if drug X is right for you"). The DSM gets criticized for "inventing" new diseases, but the industry is just as invested in making people consume drugs for the same, established conditions. The boom in prescriptions for selective serotonin reuptake inhibitors (SSRIs), kicked off by Prozac in the late 1980s, was as much about getting existing patients off "older" drugs as it was about getting new patients on new drugs.

Psychopharmaceutical looping effects have been extensively described. For example, Carl Elliott (2011) argues that the availability of psychotropic drugs changes practices in schools, hospitals, the armed forces, and many other areas. If it becomes normal that a drug such as Provigil (modafinil) is used by shift workers (including hospital doctors) to get through two night shifts without sleep, this will loop back into classifications of normal and pathological: "We introduce a new technology to satisfy a need, but it changes society in such a way to increase the demand of the technology, which then forces more and more people to use it, even if they would prefer not to" (Elliott 2011: 368).

The powerful affordance presented by psychotropics is very obvious in psychiatric practice outside North America and Europe. Indian psychiatrists are not worried about whether their patients' symptoms fit into DSM categories. They worry only about finding the best combination and dosage of drugs for each patient. In India, insurance companies do not reimburse for mental health treatments; no social benefits are available for sufferers; and the legal system does not use the DSM. Hence, Indian psychiatrists are unfettered by bureaucratic demands to use the manual.

Indian doctors' diagnostics are focused on the effects of psychotropic drugs. For Indian clinicians, the problem is not whether a patient's depression is of subtype XYZ but whether a patient's symptoms profile responds better to drug A than to drug B, at what dosage, for how long, and in what combinations. The diagnostic differences that actually matter are about prescribing for mental or physical comorbidities. Amitriptyline, for example, is the drug of choice for "rural somatizers"—that is, patients who complain about physical problems such as sleeplessness and all-body pain. And SSRIs are distinguished not by mental symptoms but by physical comorbidities, such as that some seem to have fewer cardiovascular side effects than others, which matters for patients who also have heart problems.

The doctors' lack of interest in finessing their diagnoses according to DSM classifications may look like bad practice. However, I think this is good practice. Psychiatry is still grappling with adopting the same specific etiology paradigm that was established in the rest of medicine during the nineteenth century (Ecks 2013). Specific etiology assumes that there are distinct diseases, such as "depression." The drugs that are developed to deal with specific diseases, in turn, are *magic bullets*, a term coined by Paul Ehrlich (1854–1915) to describe drugs that target only the pathogenic source of a disease and leave everything else in the body unchanged. In the 1950s, this magic bullet model was adopted by psychiatry to emulate the successes of antibiotics. If there is a distinct disease called "depression," then the drugs used to target it become "antidepressants." The emphasis on specificity carried over into further drug classifications. The idea of "selective" serotonin reuptake inhibitors is that the active ingredient targets a single neurotransmitter mechanism, as if the whole problem lies specifically in this one neurochemical process.

Joanna Moncrieff (2008), a psychologist and prominent critic of psychopharmacology, argues that psychiatry should move from a "disease-centered" to a "drug-centered" model. If psychiatry started with the multiple effects of drugs rather than with disease classifications, it could stop misleading patients about the specificity of the drug effects. There would no longer be a need to call psychotropic substances antidepressants, as if these drugs specifically targeted a disease entity called depression. Drugs clearly have all sorts of effects—some of them good, some of them bad—but they never target pathologies in the way that antibiotics target pathogenic bacteria: "A drug-centered model of drug action would lead to a new classification of psychotropic drugs according to their characteristic global effects and their chemical class, rather than their effects on a hypothetical disease" (Moncrieff 2008: 212). A drug-centered model does not require a specific nosology of symptoms in the style of the DSM. The ethnography of psychiatric practice shows that a "drug-centered" paradigm is already in place in India. Psychiatrists prescribe in a drug-centered way, not in a disease-centered way. They improvise with all kinds of substances and tailor doses and combinations to the individual patients' symptoms. That is also why they hardly ever consult DSM or *International Classification of Diseases* classifications when coming up with their treatments.

A Thing-Shaped Fix for the DSM-6

The APA's motto for its lucrative diagnostic manual is "After the Game Is before the Game"; planning for the next version is already underway. The ferocity of the critiques of the DSM-5 might make it seem that there will be no DSM-6 in the future. But the need for the DSM by both pharmaceutical industries and bureaucratic regimes makes it unlikely that there will not be a sixth edition. Here the "actual uses of the the DSM manual" argument returns. The DSM is too deeply linked to complex people, experts, institutions, and knowledge to be taken out of the equation. Even Hacking (2013), who argues that any attempt to create discrete disease classifications is flawed, expects the DSM juggernaut to carry on: "Some suggest that there will never be a 'DSM-6,'" he says. "Don't count on it. It is on the contrary likely that the manual will become more attuned to neurological causes." He is probably right that the "lack of validity" critics will gain further momentum and that the DSM has to come to terms with the RDoC project sponsored by the NIMH (see chapter 11).

While the APA is straining to commensurate symptom classifications with biomarkers, is there any chance for future editions of the DSM to respond to the medicalization critique? Supporters of the DSM-5 might say that the manual has reached its peak level of cultural sensitivity. After all, it now says that disease classifications change just like the rest of culture changes. If the DSM-5 says that "*all* forms of distress are locally shaped, including the DSM disorders" (APA 2013: 758), what more can a culturalist critic ask for?

A future revision of the DSM should focus on bringing things into the concept of culture. Leaving out things and their looping effects is in line with the DSM's "atheoretical" stance, but it makes for a weak grasp of psychiatry of cultural practice.

Bringing things back into cultural practice is also important because the many effects of drugs—on the mind, the body, and social relations—emerge only after they have long been in circulation. Adverse side effects and off-label uses of psychotropics take a while to loop back into psychiatric understandings of diagnosis and treatment. That is why the omission of pharmaceuticals in the cultural section is a mistake. Ignoring actual patterns of diagnosing and prescribing makes for bad medicine. The DSM-6 needs a habitography of pharmaceuticals more than another round of relabeling culture-bound syndromes.

NINE

Generic

Distinguishing Good Similarity from Bad Similarity

The Chimeric Generic

In this chapter, I think through things called "generic drugs." These things are even more context-dependent than other entities. Biocommensuration helps to grasp how some similarities are "good" and some are "bad." Most of the drugs prescribed in India are generics in the sense that they are copied drugs without product patent protection. However, in India, most generics are called "brands," a term that Europeans and North Americans would reserve for drugs with a product patent. That looks like a small difference, but if analyzed carefully the small difference emerges as a big difference. These differences reveal new layers of valuing life through establishing similarity. The smallest differences reveal the highest stakes: distinctions between chemical compounds become distinctions between life and death.

Generics mobilize different kinds of biocommensurations. Medicinal stuff is valued by how it enhances and prolongs life. A generic is a copy that is valued as "good" if it improves life and as "bad" if diminishes life. But valuations of whether these things are good or bad depend on how life is valued. Generics are good when they allow affordable access to health. This was the reason behind Indira Gandhi's changes to the Indian patent laws in the 1970s: the good generic was meant to prevent private companies from profiteering from life and death. As I argue in this chapter, generics are "good" when they are as therapeutically efficacious as the brand—when they are like "old friends" who can be entrusted with a patient's life more than some newfangled stuff that costs more but is less effective. In turn, generics are "bad" when they hinder investment into new, better, more life-enhancing drugs (as Big Pharma argues). Generics are bad when they imperil life due to substandard doses or spurious ingredients. Generics are bad when they foster irrational prescribing habits by giving *too much choice.*

"Generics" are different things depending on place and time. Distinctions between generics and their various opposites are elusive (Hayden 2007, 2013; Greene 2014). As a first approximation, a generic drug can be defined as a medicinal product that is identified by its chemical, nonproprietary name rather than a brand name. Fluoxetine is the generic name of a chemical composition, or "molecule," whereas Prozac is the name of the original brand. Generic drugs are medicinal products that are similar or identical in therapeutic efficacy, dosage, strength, and route of administration in relation to a "reference" drug. In Europe, a "generic medicinal product" must have "the same qualitative and quantitative composition in active substances and the same pharmaceutical form as the reference medicinal product" (European Parliament 2019). Generics are often defined both by what they share with a reference drug (such as bioavailability of the active substance) and what must be different. The brand name must be different; the physical appearance must be different; the packaging must be different; and the name of the manufacturer must be different (Greene 2014).

The reference drug is usually a substance that used to be patent-protected and proprietary to a company but has gone off patent after a period of time. That entangles chemical substance with intellectual property rights and turns generics into "copied drugs that circulate at the end of the patent" (Hayden 2011: 286). In this sense, generics are "legal" copies, as opposed to "counterfeit" products.

If generics can be defined only in relation to reference drugs, then for the definition of generic drugs to be stable, the definition of reference drugs needs to be stable as well. However, these reference drugs are moving referents. Jeremy Greene (2014) shows that the concept of a generic name emerged only *after* two other types of names were already established. In the nineteenth century, chemical companies started to discover therapeutic uses of various compounds. To make it easier to commercialize and market these compounds, the emerging industry gave them easy-to-remember names. For example, the company Bayer developed (5α,6α)-7,8-didehydro-4,5-epoxy-17-methylmorphinan-3,6-diol diacetate for the treatment of bronchitis and tuberculosis. A name like this hardly rolls off the tongue. From 1898 on, however, Bayer promoted the compound under a memorable brand name: Heroin. Having a brand name helped sort out some of the similarities and differences between compounds. However, brand names were not enough to name compounds independently of a producer. What was needed was a *third* name for the compound, easy to remember and beyond intellectual property rights. A regulatory need for such a third name became evident when, during World War I, the US government encouraged domestic companies to produce medicines marketed by German companies. The US pharmaceutical industry started to make the substance "diacetylmorphine" and marketed it under names different from heroin. The Food, Drug, and Cosmetic Act of 1938 required all US firms to give their products a brand name, as well as a "common or usual name" (Greene 2014: 22–23). Hence the "reference" for generics can be either the chemical compound or the brand name.

Another reason reference drugs are unstable referents is that *all* drugs are copies. There are no "originals." Drugs are manufactured objects that do not have a single original of which other drugs are "duplicates." There is no museum showcasing original drugs, like museums that showcase original Picassos. Generics are so confusing because they can be classified neither by primary oneness nor by original separateness (Sovran 1992; see chapter 2). Generics are complex assemblages of different materials (chemical substances) and different forms (manufacturing processes, naming, packaging, and so on).

Patents protect reference drugs against bad copies. Yet patents are given not just for active ingredients but also for a host of other properties, such as delivery method or therapeutic indication. Changes to these other aspects of drugs allow companies to "evergreen" patents. For example, Eli Lilly repackaged fluoxetine in pink-and-purple capsules, gave it the brand name Sarafem, and marketed it for premenstrual dysphoric disorder (see chapter 1). Pfizer's Viagra turned into Revatio, which treats pulmonary hypertension. The antidepressant drug imipramine (Tofranil) returned in a patented form in 1973 as a medicine that reduces bedwetting in children. Even one of the most infamous drugs, Grünenthal's Contergan (thalidomide), made a comeback in 1998 as Thalomid, an anti-leprosy drug. There is no good name for drugs that were first valued as good, then bad, and then good again. They could be called *Wiedergänger*, after the German word for a corpse that "walks again" after death. They were first biocommensurated as life-enhancing, then as life-diminishing, and then as life-enhancing again.

Understanding generics gets even more difficult when clinical practice comes into play. Let me illustrate this with an episode from fieldwork in India. In the middle of our conversation about how he treats depression, the Kolkata psychiatrist Dr. Bose's mobile phone rings. He picks up the call and switches to loudspeaker. A patient, a woman in her early twenties, is calling from Delhi. She says that the medicine Dr. Bose gave to her last time worked very well, but she has run out and needs a refill. She wants to buy the medicine from a shop in Delhi but finds it too expensive. Can Dr. Bose "substitute" a cheaper drug in the prescription? she asks. While her husband's family had enough money to buy the prescribed brand, she has only had a limited amount of "pocket money" and cannot spend it all on medications. Dr. Bose suggests that she see a psychiatrist in Delhi to get a different prescription, but the woman is anxious to keep her antidepressant treatment hidden from her in-laws.

In this moment, generics and people come together in peculiar ways. A patient asks a pharmacist for a drug, finds out that the drug is expensive, and asks the prescribing doctor for a more affordable substitute. Sometimes the doctor agrees; sometimes she does not. It is a common situation in a market where patients have to buy drugs out of pocket, where these drugs are relatively cheap, where patients know that all drugs can be substituted, but where patients do not always know whether one drug is a good substitute for another. Doctors, like everyone else in the Indian industry, do not say they are using "generics"; they use the term *brand*. A branded drug is any generic that is marketed under a brand name rather than the name of the active ingredient. These generic brands compete with many other generic brands of the "same" molecule. The intense attention to branding is necessary because of the intense competition among generics. Hundreds of different brands of common psychotropics are available (figure 9.1).

No company markets its products under the name of the active ingredient; all market under brand names. This applies to best-selling brands such as Fludac (Cadila) and Flunil (Intas) and to less well known brands, such as Persona (Yash Vision) and Prodac (RPG Life Sciences). The Indian

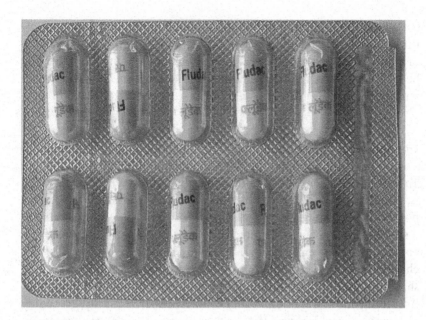

Figure 9.1 | Generic Prozac

subsidiaries of the original brand-owning companies market previously patent-protected products under different brand names. For example, Pfizer's selective serotonin reuptake inhibitor Zoloft (sertraline) is sold in India under the name Daxid (see chapter 4). Dr. Bose is a keen prescriber of fluoxetine—"Three out of ten get fluoxetine," he said—which is not just an antidepressant but has many other uses, including as an "antiobsessive." For major depression, he said, it is best combined with olanzapine (Zyprexa), which can be used "for all age groups, with minimal side effects." Dr. Bose would not use just any brand of fluoxetine; he used only the products from a few reputed companies that "we trust." And among them, the brand Flunil was his favorite. For Dr. Bose, market novelty does not trump clinical experience: "Newer drugs are coming up with a bang, but in a country like India, you cannot experiment. I cannot experiment with my patients from whom I take 300 rupees [as a consultation fee]. I have to be sure that it clicks. So my old drugs are my better friends than my new drugs." Innovation resulted not from the substances contained in the drugs but from the clinician's virtuosity in finding combinations and modulating dosages. "We do it in our own style," said Dr. Bose, "not the copycat style."

When a patient asks a doctor for a "substitute," what is being substituted for what? For both the patient and the doctor, the question is one of brand substitution. The efficacy of the drug is meant to stay the same, but what is changing? The brand name and the price are two obvious answers, but the problem does not end there.

Good Generic Practice

To show how difficult any definition of copied/generic/substitute drugs is, it helps to go back to a distinction between "possession" and "exemplification" introduced by Nelson Goodman (1976, 1992). For Goodman, it should not be taken for granted that one thing seems "different" from another. The problem is that all things are *similar* in *infinite* ways (see chapter 2). Things can be in the same place; they can have the same shape, price, colors, or weight; or they can be produced on the same day. According to Goodman, similarity is "insidious": "Similarity, ever ready to solve philosophical problems and overcome obstacles, is a pretender, an impostor, a quack" (Goodman 1992: 13).

To say that any two things are different, one needs to know what properties of the things are being compared. If a sample from a batch of generic drugs is compared with the whole that it is meant to represent, the sample is only a good sample if it exemplifies *relevant* properties. When a batch of drugs is tested for quality, the sample is only a good sample when it does not just possess the same properties as the batch but also exemplifies specific properties. The possession of properties is context-independent, whereas exemplification depends on context. What is being exemplified must be relevant, and what is relevant is a pragmatic question. One cannot compare two things outside a context.

Applied to Dr. Bose and his patient's request for a "substitute," it would have been possible for him to recommend a brand whose tablet or capsule was the same color as that of the brand used before. Or he could recommend a brand with the same expiration date or that was manufactured in the same factory. The list of possibly relevant criteria could also include potency, purity, disintegration time, choice of base, and viscosity (Greene 2014: 46). But none of these properties "possessed" would have made the difference between a "good" and a "bad" substitute. In the context of this patient's need for the same, but less expensive, drug, what mattered were efficacy and price.

Health-policy makers want clear names for medicinal things. But when it comes to generics, they find themselves bewildered by an array of local meanings. Núria Homedes and Antonio Ugalde (2005: 65) complain that "the term generic is used differently across countries and it may even have different meanings within a country depending on the context in which the term is used." Regulation by general standards is impossible when the entities to be regulated are so strangely context-dependent. Every country's regulatory context varies the meaning of *generic* (Babar 2017). Drugs can be similar or different in myriad ways: color, shape, smell, size, weight of active ingredient, weight of nonactive ingredients, packaging, and so forth. They are also similar or different in terms of availability in pharmacies or affordability according to income levels. They can be compared by country of origin and by producer. They are under different patent regimes and quality control protocols. Add to this the endless ways in which the forms of difference between good and bad copies can be labeled for the purpose of regulation. Julia Hornberger (2018: 380) compiles a devilishly long list of possibilities that drug regulators have to address: "Medication can be imperfectly tested, faultily produced, wrongly labeled, deficiently stored, deceivingly named, misleadingly marketed, incorrectly prescribed, illegitimately traded, inadequately consumed, and stolen, smuggled, faked, and re-produced under conflicting legal regimes." Reason demands that fakes get exposed (Copeman 2018), but to do so, one must be able to distinguish fakes from the real, the bad copy from the authentic good. If the properties to be compared are unclear or unknown, the bad copy cannot be exposed.

Generic Glut

Mr. Mittal is busy at work at one of his medicine shops at a traffic-choked intersection in the center of Kolkata. The shop sits on a corner lot and has two sales counters looking out onto different streets. The space is impossibly crammed, with medicine stacked up high in glass cabinets and along all the available walls. The shop's storage also includes the building's upstairs floor. After receiving a prescription note from a customer, a shop floor assistant downstairs shouts out the name and dosage of a medicine. Another assistant, sitting upstairs, throws the requested packet through a hatch in the ceiling. The shop is part of a family business founded by Mr. Mittal's father in the early 1970s. It employs thirty-two staff across two shops and a diagnostic laboratory. The Mittals have built up a "good" reputation over the decades; their shops command more trust than the hole-in-the-wall shops mushrooming across the city and the large corporate chains where managers may change frequently.

According to a rumor that circulated among owners of other medicine shops in the vicinity, Mr. Mittal's business had a history of smuggling brand-name drugs into India that were otherwise unavailable in the country. Mr. Mittal did not deny the rumor when I asked him about it but said there was no need to source medicine made abroad. For example, one could buy Prozac in India, but the US-manufactured product was fifty times more expensive than what was available from domestic manufacturers. Eli Lilly never bothered to sell Prozac in India because of the competition from generics. India joined the "antidepressant era" decades ago, but the country has never been on Prozac.

At a later point in the conversation, Mr. Mittal said emphatically, "We hardly sell generics," which were "only for government hospitals and institutions." Private medicine shops such as his sold only brands. The endless proliferation of brands was why he struggled to keep his stock in order. Decisions about what to stock depend on what the doctors are prescribing. Doctors in India do not prescribe by active ingredients because this would allow pharmacists to decide which products to give to the customer (and a doctor can make a profit only by prescribing a specific brand). Thus, for example, rather than writing "fluoxetine" on a prescription, doctors write "Fludac," "Prodep," or the brand name of some other medication produced by an Indian company.

As a shop owner, Mr. Mittal had to make difficult decisions about what to order from distributors. If he ordered too few pills of a particular brand, he might be unable to fill prescriptions brought to the shop and lose that business to his competitors. If he ordered too many pills of a brand, he might not be able to sell them all before the expiration date. It was possible to get limited refunds from distributors for products that were about to expire, but this involved a lot of work. Going by the reputation of the manufacturer helped to get a better sense of what might sell well: drugs from "good companies" sold more than from less trusted or less well known companies.

An obvious solution to the problem of an excessive number of brands was to recommend to customers a substitute drug. For example, if Fludac was out of stock, it could be replaced with Prodep, because they contain the same molecule. Although there were slight differences in price between brands, the "quality is all the same," Mr. Mittal said. Yet only a few customers—in his estimation, no more than 5 percent—would accept brand substitutions and would insist instead on getting the product named by the doctor or go to another shop. For owners of medicine shops such as Mr. Mittal, this problem was exacerbated by manufacturers' trying to make him order up to five new brands each day. "Five new brands daily come in," he said, "but they are all the same." Simultaneously, doctors continued to write prescriptions for "old" brands, and, indeed, no brand ever seemed to disappear entirely.

For Mr. Mittal, this brand culture is a headache. There was no profit for his shop in this abundance of copies (*copy* literally means *abundance*). On the contrary, it resulting in a loss because he had to invest in large storage spaces and managing overabundant stock. Instead of an ever-increasing range of brands, Mr. Mittal felt, the government should allow a maximum of thirty brands of the same molecule at any given time: "They can distribute all over India. You manufacture the same thing; I manufacture the same thing; she manufactures the same thing. The rest is all marketing—how much you sell and what profits you get out of it." He was not optimistic, however, that the current situation would change. Changes to India's patent laws in 2005 did not make any difference to brand abundance, and high-price patented drugs hardly made a dent in the overall medication market. The Indian market was already so crowded with low-price brands that a handful of expensive drugs licensed after 2005 were insignificant for daily business.

The situation described by Mr. Mittal supports Cori Hayden's (2011) proposal that the dynamics of pharmaceutical copies cannot be contained by opposing them to "originals." Instead, differences are drawn between different kinds of copies. Mr. Mittal's labeling of "generics" and "brands"—describing as a "brand" what would, outside of India, be considered a "generic"—does not present a matter of concern. The Indian pharmaceuticals market is driven not by competition among research-intensive companies trying to bring out "original" patented drugs earlier than their rivals but by competition among manufacturers of the "same" formulations who can differentiate themselves only by quality, price, and reputation. A "brand" medication is distinguished from the "generics" not by the patent status of the active ingredient but by the brand-name recognition of both the manufacturer and the product—hence, Mr. Mittal's insistence that his shop sells not generics but brands. "Generics," according to Mr. Mittal, are used in India's public sector only, where drug procurement is based not on brand recognition but on price and quality alone. In India, "generics" are not "copied drugs that circulate at the end of the patent" (Hayden 2011) but copied drugs that circulate *at the low end of the brand-recognition spectrum*. This also means that there is no firm distinction between *generic* and *brand*, or between copy and original. There are only different kinds of copies.

The differences and similarities between one "generic" and another are what Mr. Mittal describes as his key problem as a pharmacist. He does not care whether brands and generics are different or, as long as any generic brand is available, whether "original" brands are available in India or not. Instead, he cares that the drugs are efficacious (and he generally found that "all" of them were equally efficacious). He cares how much they cost. Above all, he cares when there are too many of the "same" drugs that he is forced to treat as completely different from one another. He had to squeeze thousands of items into his shop and worry about not being able to sell them quickly enough in the context of free-market proliferation of manufacturers, an absence of product monopolies, and a plethora of doctors prescribing an endless variety of brands.

Mr. Mittal's shop is just one *context* for comparison, in Goodman's sense of the term. There are many more contexts, each having its own criteria for "good practice." What Goodman calls "good practice" is a successful biocommensuration. Practice is "good" when it is life-enhancing. Goodman's "good practice" is a form of good life. In what follows, I detail other contexts. Each refractures what a "copy" is, and each presents a different valuation of what makes copies good or bad. They all seem to proliferate copiously, like the tens of thousands of tablets in Mr. Mittal's shop.

The Generic Pharmacy of the World

India is often called "the pharmacy of the world." In the first half of the twentieth century, the epithet was coined not for the Indian but for the German pharmaceutical industry (Kaiser and Prange 2004: 396). With the shift from Germany to India, the meaning of "world" has changed. Before, it meant that one country led global production. By contrast, the "world" for which India produces drugs are countries of the global South and the low-price segments of rich countries that consume them.

The first to call India the world's pharmacy were pro-access activists. Organizations such as Médecins sans Frontières (MSF) applauded the Indian drug industry for producing low-price copies of drugs that were protected by patents elsewhere. The standard example cited by MSF and similar organizations are antiretroviral (ARV) drugs. In 2000, an ARV triple combination of stavudine, lamivudine, and nevirapine was marketed at $10,439. Within two years, the price had fallen to just $209 for the "same" combination of drugs produced by Indian and Brazilian generic manufacturers, and it continued to fall further in the following years. For health activists, sharp price drops were possible only because of the fierce price competition that generics introduced. Since that time, India has been seen as a supplier of lifesaving drugs that otherwise would be unaffordable to most poor people.

Off-patent medicines are used in all countries of the world—indeed, they are the most widely used type of pharmaceutical even in markets with strong patent protections, such as the United States and Western Europe. Up to 80 percent of all prescriptions written in the United States are for off-patent drugs. Generics are also manufactured around the world, with many of the leading generics specialists located in Europe (e.g., Ratiopharm, Gedeon Richter) and North America (e.g., Mylan, Actavis, Mallinckrodt). Multinational pharmaceutical corporations such as Novartis, Abbott, Pfizer, and Sanofi all have large generics businesses, as well. India's generics industry is based in private, profit-driven corporations, including Ranbaxy, Cipla, Dr. Reddy's Laboratories (DRL), Lupin, and Sun Pharmaceuticals. Most of the large Indian corporations have become multinationals either by buying up production plants in established markets (e.g., DRL producing drugs in the United Kingdom) or by being bought up by other multinationals (e.g., Ranbaxy was acquired by the Japanese firm Daiichi Sankyo in 2008).

Still, the Indian industry is different. India is one of the world's top-three generics producers. Whereas European and North American countries have only a few dozen producers, there are an estimated 4,800 different companies in India employing 450,000 people. In the past decades, the Indian pharmaceuticals sector continued to grow 10–17 percent annually. The sheer number of companies, workers, products, and customers make India different from other major generics-producing countries.

India's position in the global generics market was made possible by the Indian Patents Act of 1970, which allowed manufacturers to bypass international product patent protections and reverse-engineer any molecule. This act, effective between 1972 and 2005, with some amendments and a ten-year transition period since 1995, lowered the threshold of entry into the pharmaceutical production business, and a plethora of Indian companies sprang up, all of them competing primarily on price. The market share of multinationals plummeted as the Indian companies rose. By the early 1990s, the industry had expanded and consolidated to such an extent that India became a net exporter of pharmaceuticals, a development unmatched by other developing countries.

Before the Patents Act of 1970, drug prices in India were high, even by the standards of other postcolonial countries. In the immediate post-Independence years, the domestic drug market was dominated by multinational companies that imported medicines and sold them at a premium price. During Indira Gandhi's first term as prime minister of India (1966–77), this situation was seen as unsustainable and politically unacceptable, and a new patent regime was introduced. In a speech at the World Health Assembly in 1982, Prime Minister Gandhi emphasized the political exigency of making drugs affordable: "The idea of a better-ordered world is one in which medical discoveries will be free of patents and there will be no profiteering from life and death." Ironically, Gandhi's patent regime was neither "free of patents" nor free of private industry "profiteering." Process patents were forms of patenting as well, even if they resulted in a different industry. Long before India accepted global terms on intellectual property rights as set by the World Trade Organization (WTO), the question was no longer whether pharmacological knowledge *should* be in private ownership. Even Gandhi's government asked only *who* should own intellectual property and under what conditions (Halliburton 2017). The Patents Act of 1970 compares entities not by whether they should have intellectual property protection but by what specific aspects of intellectual property should be protected. Capitalist profiteering is what drove so many companies to enter the generics manufacturing business. Nevertheless, the Patents Act of 1970 is driven by a logic of biocommensuration that values the health of the population over the profitability of pharmaceutical corporations.

In 2005, a new Patents Act came into force that again requires Indian companies to respect product patents. The 2005 act was negotiated under the WTO's Trade-Related Intellectual Property Rights (TRIPs) agreements. The TRIPs-compliant act of 2005 is seen as a victory of multinational companies over Indian generics producers. Yet even the 2005 act maintained provisions that were meant to protect affordable medicines and to stall excessive and unfounded applications for product patent by multinationals. The best-known provision is section 3(d) (see chapter 1). The 1970 act already stipulated that "the mere discovery of a new form of a known substance which does not result in the enhancement of the known efficacy" should be "considered to be the same substance." This provision was retained, with some minor modifications, in the 2005 act. Section 3(d) prevents companies from "evergreening" patents by launching modified versions of known substances, combinations, delivery methods, or simply disease indications. The key issues to be considered by patent officers are whether a substance is "not known" already and the difference in efficacy is "significant."

Multinational companies have filed thousands of lawsuits against patent decisions and against the patent law itself, arguing that parts of the 2005 act violate international trade agreements and prevent research-intensive companies from earning patents they have rightfully earned in other countries. The best-known case of this kind is *Novartis v. Union of India* (Supreme Court of India 2013), which revolved around a patent application for the beta crystalline version of imatinib mesylate (brand name Glivec/Gleevec), a flagship drug to fight blood cancer. Worldwide interest in the outcome of the Glivec case was not stirred by the affordability and availability of imatinib for cancer treatments in India or elsewhere. Instead, it focused on the status of section 3(d). Pro-access advocacy groups, including MSF, worried that multinational drug companies would start evergreening patents for other lifesaving drugs, including ARVs, and that this would lead to great price increases in the global market. Section 3(d) is seen as safeguarding the continuing supply of affordable generics from India to countries of the global South. The lives of millions of people depend on whether two chemical entities are "considered to be the same substance" or not. Drawing distinctions between molecules becomes drawing distinctions between who can live and who must die.

The litigation began in 2006 in the Madras (Chennai) High Court and caused an international outcry. After coming before different Indian courts and appellate bodies, the case was concluded in 2013, when the Supreme Court of India rejected Novartis's patent application for a beta version of imatinib (Gabble and Kohler 2014). The court found that the beta version was not a new "invention" but only a tweaked update of the alpha crystalline version. It also found that the beta crystalline version of imatinib mesylate showed no significant improvement in "therapeutic efficacy."

One of Novartis's crucial concerns, to protect its European and American markets from any "spillage" of Indian-produced generic imatinib, was largely successful (Ecks 2008). Branded Glivec (in the beta version) continues to be one of Novartis's most profitable products. In

2012, total net sales of the drug were a staggering $4.7 billion (Novartis 2012: 155). In 2018, net sales were lower, at a mere $1.6 billion, but even now Glivec is one of the company's best-selling drugs. In India, one can currently buy the alpha version of imatinib from ten companies—one of them is Novartis. The price of these drugs is vastly lower than that of the beta version, which remains exclusive to Novartis. In all of the countries where the beta version has a patent, the alpha version cannot be sold.

The language of the Indian Supreme Court ruling makes no mention of the concept of "copy." Not even the term *generic* features in the proceedings. In the Supreme Court judgment, the word *generic* appears only in statements made by pro-access advocates and Indian parliamentarians. For example, an Indian politician is cited in the Supreme Court verdict for his statements in support of section 3(d) and "immunity for generic drugs which are already available in the market" (Supreme Court of India 2013: para. 80).

The case hinged, instead, on *degrees of similarity* in terms of therapeutic efficacy. The court admitted that the beta version of imatinib was different from, and an enhancement of, the alpha version based on several significant criteria, including better "flow properties," "thermodynamic stability," and "lower hygroscopicity." But the none of these improvements, the court held, "have anything to do with therapeutic efficacy" (Supreme Court of India 2013: para. 187). Crucially, the court ruled that increased bioavailability was "not in itself a determination of effectiveness"; instead, it showed only "the rate and extent of absorption" in a living organism (para. 188). Novartis failed to prove that improved bioavailability of the beta version of the molecule also meant superior therapeutic efficacy (para. 189). The biocommensurating work of the High Court consisted of paring down an array of possible comparisons between the alpha and beta versions of Glivec to only one difference, "therapeutic effectiveness." Increasing bioavailability *could* enhance effectiveness and, hence, merit patent protection, but in the specific case of Glivec, its enhanced bioavailability did *not* enhance its effectiveness.

Pro-access organizations and Novartis reacted to the 2013 verdict with the same arguments they had used in previous years (Ecks 2008; Halliburton 2017). Médecines sans Frontières greeted the Supreme Court's "landmark decision" to "uphold Indian's Patents Act" despite Novartis's seven-year legal siege. The decision was a "huge relief" for everyone who depended on "affordable medicines from India" (MSF 2013). According to Novartis, however, India denied the patent because the country was hostile to the protection of intellectual property rights. The beta version of Glivec, the company argued, was recognized as an "innovation [in] nearly 40 countries including China, Russia, and Taiwan," and the verdict was a "setback for patients" because research-intensive drug innovation was not properly protected. Novartis has been threatening to withdraw research-and-development investments from India ever since it lost the first legal challenge in 2007 and has vowed to find other avenues to fight off generic competition from India. One of them is support for the global policing of "bad" copies.

Generic Crimes

In 2013, the battle between Big Pharma and Indian generics producers reached a new level. Indian newspapers reported that multinational companies had given 4.5 million euros to the International Criminal Police Organization (INTERPOL) to support is fight against "fake/counterfeit medicines" (Nagarajan 2013). Because India's Central Bureau of Investigation (CBI) is a member of INTERPOL, some feared that this would lead to prosecutions of generics producers. The reputation of the Indian manufacturers is built on claims that their drugs are "good" copies: generic versions that have the same efficacy as the original brands, but at a much lower price. Allegations of bad-quality copies strike at the heart of the industry.

Also in 2013, Ranbaxy USA Inc., a subsidiary of its Indian parent company, agreed to pay $500 million to settle allegations filed against it for inadequate testing of some of its drugs produced in India. This was the largest financial penalty ever paid by a producer of generics in the United States. The settlement consisted of a criminal fine of $150 million and a $350 million civil fine under the False Claims Act. The Ranbaxy case exemplifies the policing of Indian drugs that are marketed under US Food and Drug Administration (FDA) regulations and that fell under the jurisdiction of the US Department of Justice (DOJ). The second case, of the so-called Declaration of Rome and the strange fate of the International Medicinal Products Anti-counterfeiting Taskforce (IMPACT), speaks to alliances among brand pharmaceutical producers, the World Health Organization (WHO), and transnational police action.

At stake in the Ranbaxy case was whether some of the company's generics manufactured in India and exported to the United States were "adulterated." The definition of *adulteration*, as applied here, was whether current Good Manufacturing Practice (cGMP) regulations had been maintained. According to the DOJ, only strict adherence to cGMP protocols can ensure that "a drug meets the requirements as to safety and has the identity and strength, and meets the quality and purity characteristics, which the drug purports or is represented to possess" (DOJ 2013).

The US press coverage sensationalized the case and called into doubt the quality of *all* generics produced in India. For example, a feature story on *CBS News* (2013) pointed out that, of the 80 percent of all drugs prescribed in the United States that are generics, 40 percent were made overseas, "where oversight is weaker." Ranbaxy had exploited the weak surveillance of the Indian drug industry to consistently falsify drug safety records. Business investors' publications were equally alarmist: NASDAQ *News* quotes a former vice-president of Ranbaxy's US operations, Vince Fabiano, as saying that the company "used the fraud as a competitive advantage to build and grow the business" in the United States and conjured the image of a cancer patient who is getting worse despite taking drugs: "Is it because of the drug? Is it because of the disease process? No one would know" (quoted in Bullock 2013).

Bruno Latour once compared two ways of interpreting laboratory test results. If all goes well for the scientists, their research reveals the universal features of, say, mammal kidney structures. But "if all goes badly, it shrinks to three hamsters in one laboratory in 1984" (Latour 1987: 51). A similar scaling and exemplification problem is at work in the Ranbaxy case. The company was clearly falsifying test data, but that did not mean that all of its drugs were dangerous to take.

One irony of this case is that the whistleblower who brought the fraud to the FDA's attention, and walked away with nearly $50 million from the settlement money, first noticed that something was wrong when the test data on bioavailability were not just *similar* to those that the original companies had published but *identical*. Ranbaxy's fraud would never have been noticed if the company had plagiarized the test data more cleverly rather than copying them so faithfully. The fraud consisted in Ranbaxy making *perfect* copies of existing test data instead of introducing a little bit of variation.

The slippage between legitimate off-patent drugs and "fake" or "counterfeit" drugs has been part of the brand-versus-generic distinction since at least the 1940s (Greene 2014). The current approach to criminal fakes by the WHO goes back to the early 1990s. The first international meeting on counterfeit medicines was organized in 1992 by the WHO together with the International Federation of Pharmaceutical Manufacturers and

Associations (IFPMA), an industry lobby group. At that meeting, the following definition was endorsed: "A counterfeit medicine is one which is deliberately and fraudulently mislabeled with respect to identity and/or source. Counterfeiting can apply to both branded and generic products and counterfeit products may include products with the correct ingredients or with the wrong ingredients, without active ingredients, with insufficient active ingredient or with fake packaging" (WHO 2019a). Not least, the odd inclusion of "correct ingredients" in this definition reinstates the slippage between brands and generics that informs the debates to date.

In 2006, the International Conference on Combating Counterfeit Medicines published a manifesto against bad copies known as the Declaration of Rome. It states that making and selling counterfeit drugs is a "vile and serious criminal offence" (World Health Organization 2006: para. 1). Since counterfeiting has become a global health problem, it needs "effective coordination and cooperation at the international level" (para. 4). The WHO was to lead the establishment of IMPACT (para. 6). The Declaration of Rome was endorsed by a group of national drug-regulating authorities; international organizations; and associations representing patients, prescribers, pharmaceutical companies, and wholesalers. However, the actual composition of the conference group was never made public. It appears that "patients" were represented only by the International Alliance of Patients' Organisations, which receives funding from big pharmaceutical corporations (People's Health Movement et al. 2011: 237).

In its first report, which was also its last report, IMPACT emphasized the limitations of the objects it was policing (AIFA 2009). "Generic" in the sense of off-patent was meant to be off-limits. Judgments "related to intellectual protection are not within the scope of the task force" (22). The goal of IMPACT was only to protect public health against bad medicines, and "both counterfeit-branded products, as well as counterfeit generic medical products" were included. Introducing the report, IMPACT's Vice-Chair P. B. Orhii rebutted critics who saw the task force as an attack on legitimate generics: "I cannot see how fighting counterfeits can negatively affect generics" (5). The counterfeit agenda had become the "victim" of intellectual property debates to such an extent that it was "hindering" the fight against fakes. Where the lines between good and bad copies should be drawn was obvious, as Orhii stated sulkily: "We know what we mean when we say counterfeit medicine. . . . [W]e make no confusion between counterfeit medicines, substandard medicines and legitimate generic medicines. We know that counterfeit medicines are a global public health menace" (5).

Many pro-access groups within and outside the WHO, as well as representatives from the Indian government (Shukla and Sangal 2009), have argued for a complete separation between the WHO and IMPACT. For the nongovernmental organization Medico International, for example, claims that IMPACT was not about patent protection are "half-hearted, insincere, and deceptive" (People's Health Movement et al. 2011: 241). Secretive influence of companies in rich countries, exerted through the International Federation of Pharmaceutical Manufacturers (IFPAM), corrupted the task force's credibility. The very legitimacy of IMPACT was questionable, not least since the WHO is not allowed to be influenced by industry lobbyists. Thus, IMPACT *itself* was a "counterfeit" (People's Health Movement et al. 2011: 243).

Tacitly acknowledging concerns about IMPACT's problematic stance toward generics, the WHO withdrew its support. As a first step, the IMPACT headquarters were removed from Geneva and housed instead at the Italian drug regulator Agenzia Italiana del Farmaco (AIFA). In 2013, the WHO launched the "Global Surveillance and Monitoring System for Substandard and Falsified Medicinal Products" as an alternative to IMPACT (WHO 2019b). Orhii, in turn, was appointed director-general of the NAFDAC, Nigeria's FDA, which is fighting "substandard, spurious, falsely labeled, falsified, and counterfeit" (SSFFC) drugs. That office was established with approval of the WHO under its Member State (MS) mechanism. The MS was established in 2011 in the wake of controversy around IMPACT and suspicions that it served the interests of multinational companies in their battle against generic-manufacturing competitors.

The problem with the label "counterfeit" was that it was tied up with legal and economic dimensions, expressing that the makers of the copy were posturing as the makers of the rightful brand. The challenge was to define generics *without* reference to brands and intellectual property rights. Labels for bad copies proliferate further, such as "compromised" drugs. After years of classificatory work, the MS mechanism presented its solution in 2017 (WHO 2017), replacing the SSFFC label with three categories: "substandard medicinal products," "unregistered/unlicensed medicinal products," and "falsified medicinal products." The new labeling avoids all mention of "counterfeit" and presents a classification "with no account taken of intellectual property concerns" (3). Now, the copied drug is "good" as long as it is of the same standard, registered, licensed, and not falsified. This is a better definition of *generic* than previous ones, but with the extreme instability of this chimeric object, the definition is likely to change again.

Even if there is a new global definition for generics, it still needs to be implemented in individual countries' regulations. This is not a straightforward task and has been done very unevenly. Also, in 2020 the Indian government drastically expanded the definition of *drug*. It now includes anything that can be used to treat, mitigate, or prevent any health problem in any living being. In the wake of COVID-19, the government now treats disinfectants, soap, and face masks as "drugs." Anything that potentially improves health in any way can now be treated under "drug" regulations. Good luck prosecuting the manufacturers of substandard, spurious, falsely labeled, falsified, or counterfeit hand sanitizer.

TEN

Same Ills, Same Pills

Genealogies of Global Mental Health

Globalizing Mental Illness

In May 2018, a report announced that diagnoses of depression are rising dramatically in the United States (BlueCross BlueShield 2018). Between 2013 and 2016, rates increased 63 percent among adolescents and 47 percent among millennials. The highest rates were found in the richest states of the Pacific Northwest and New England. The rise of mental disorders is said to be a global phenomenon, striking rich and poor countries alike. In October 2018, the Lancet Commission on Global Mental Health and Sustainable Development (Patel et al. 2018) advised that low- and middle-income countries needed to take "urgent action" to "fully implement" psychiatric diagnostics and therapies developed in the United States and Europe—as if these interventions had lowered rates of suffering in the countries from which they came. It is as if the global scaling up of interventions scales up the suffering, as well. This is the key paradox of mental health in the world today.

Global mental health (GMH) is an interdisciplinary field of research, policy, and advocacy that seeks equal access to basic mental health care for everyone in the world. The most globalized version of psychiatry to date, GMH fully biocommensurates all minds in all places as suffering from the same ills; takes therapies to be universally valid; presumes that the same policy interventions will work anywhere; and believes that links between economics and mental health are the same across the globe. The "communicative" phase of psychopharmaceutical globalization was completed when Indian companies started to export antidepressants to European and North American markets (see chapter 6). Global mental health completes psychiatry's metaphysical and terrestrial globalization. In its best moments, GMH says it wants to complete a form of communicative globalization in which the Other is allowed to speak back. Yet the universalist assumptions of GMH make this impossible.

In theory, the "global" in GMH means that people from all parts of the world are included: "All countries can be thought of as developing countries in the context of mental health" (Patel et al. 2018: 1). In practice, GMH is focused on low- and middle-income countries, where the gap is deepest between what GMH advocates think should be done and what is actually done. Although GMH is described as a global collaboration, all of its leading proponents are based in elite European and American institutions. The same elite bias applies to the Movement for Global Mental Health (MGMH), GMH's civil society arm. The MGMH's advisory board consists of the same researchers who run GMH. Global mental health has a growing influence on national mental health policies, especially in countries with weak national health sectors and a strong international donor presence.

As a field, GMH is about two decades old. The current meaning of *global mental health* emerged in the 2000s. Until that time, a more common term was *world mental health*. The World Development Report (World Bank 1993), the influential book *World Mental Health* (Desjarlais et al. 1995), and the *World Health Report 2001* (WHO 2001) do not contain the phrase *global mental health*. Until the 2000s, *global mental health* was used to describe a population's overall stress levels (Cohen et al. 2014). The replacement of *world* and *international* came with a wider shift in health policy to *global* concerns. Changing the name from *world* to *global* inserts GMH into the global health assemblage.

Global mental health became the dominant discourse upon publication of a series of articles in *The Lancet* in 2007. "No Health without Mental Health," the first article in the series (Prince et al. 2007), says that all "health" should be refocused on "mental" health. Better mental health would reduce all other health problems (including infectious diseases) and all other social problems (including gender inequalities and poverty). Mental health should become central in "all aspects of health and social policy, health-system planning, and delivery of primary and secondary general health care" (Prince et al. 2007). A year later, the World Health Organization (WHO) published the *World Mental Health Gap Action Programme*. Other key reports were the *Grand Challenges in Global Mental Health* program by the US National Institute of Mental Health (NIMH) (Collins et al. 2011) and the WHO's *Mental Health Action Plan* (2013). The latest phase integrates mental health into the sustainable development goals (SDGs), so that good mental health is defined as an integral aspect of social and economic development (Patel et al. 2018).

Global mental health is the latest moment in the global history of Euro-American psychiatry, which began in the nineteenth century. It emerged when psychiatry teamed up with public health and health economics to scale up its impact beyond richer countries. Global mental health is an assemblage of disparate concerns, methods, institutions, actors, and infrastructures, each with its own genealogy. It contains an epidemiology of who is suffering and at what rates. The relation to health economics has been fundamental to its rise: what are the impacts of poor mental health on economic growth, and how does economic growth impact on mental health? Therapies proposed by GMH are derived from "best practices" in the psy- sciences: psychiatry (mostly psychotropics), clinical psychology, and counseling. An area in which GMH contributes to what has already been established is the trialing of psychosocial interventions for larger groups. Education is another field of GMH, in terms of both spreading awareness and reducing stigma and inserting mental health into educational settings. It employs methods from health systems analysis to assess what kinds of service provisions are in place in the community, primary, secondary, and tertiary levels. Finally, GMH defines itself as human rights advocacy. This includes lobbying governments for legal safeguards for people with mental health problems. In what follows, I focus on three pillars of GMH: epidemiology, economics, and service provision. In each section, I attempt to trace where this concern emerged and chart where it might be heading.

Epidemiology

The first pillar of GMH is epidemiology. To make mental health a global project, it was necessary to show that these disorders could be found in all countries of the world. Preferably, prevalence rates should be similar because this would validate both universal neurobiological disease etiologies and the cross-cultural reliability of the symptom classifications.

Even after decades of epidemiological work, the worldwide data remain disputed. For example, rates of depression vary dramatically among countries. Evelyn Bromet and her colleagues (2011) found that the highest-scoring countries could have rates of depression thirty-three times higher than those of the lowest-scoring countries. Even for studies that aimed at a high standardization of methods used, twelve-month prevalence of depression in high-income countries ranged from just 2.2 percent in Japan to 10.4 percent in Brazil. Too much variance is troubling: it means that the data are wrong, the methods are wrong, or assumptions of universal biological etiology are wrong. A fourth possibility—that mental disorders are coconstituted by economic, social, and environmental contexts so that they become "local biologies" (Lock 2001)—is not considered in GMH.

Advocates of GMH—influenced by Lancet Commission members such as Arthur Kleinman—say that the field emerged from a confluence of a medical "etic" approach that treated mental disorders as scientifically as other medical conditions and an "emic" approach taken by anthropologists "who analysed mental disorders as shaped by social and cultural forces" (Patel et al. 2018: 4). It is debatable how important the emic perspective ever was, but it is clear that GMH, in its current formulation, is an etic project that considers local definitions of mental health irrelevant to the GMH project. The only importance accorded to local meanings is that they produce "stigma" and erect "barriers to care." The question of whether diagnostics and treatments allow symptoms in non-Western cultures to be commensurated is not raised. The global spread of interventions becomes a matter of "scaling up" the standardized interventions. The perspective of "activists championing a cultural perspective" who fear that GMH is "a western psychiatric framework dominated by pharmaceutical interventions" (8) is strategically mentioned but not taken seriously. Worse, a "cultural perspective" has been blacklisted as one of six "threats to global mental health" (7).

As in most other fields in biomedicine, mental disorders began to be quantified in the nineteenth century. Yet unlike in other fields in biomedicine, the epidemiology of mental disorders took much longer to settle in (Lovell 2014). The leading framework for epidemiological quantification is the Global Burden of Disease (GBD) project (see chapter 11), which introduced a new metric to measure the global impact of mental illnesses: the disability-adjusted life year (DALY). They measure disease burdens as the number of years lost due to ill health, disability, and early death. First developed by Harvard University for the World Bank in 1990, DALYs were adopted as a method by the WHO in 2000. Previously, health liabilities were expressed using only years of life lost, without taking disability into account. The introduction of DALYs produced surprising insights into population health. It came as shock that five of the ten leading causes of disability were psychiatric conditions. Like no methodological innovation before or since, DALYs made mental health a global concern (Wahlberg and Rose 2015).

Nevertheless, doubts remain about the quality of the GBD data and about the validity of the disease categories. Critical evaluations of how global burdens of mental disorders are calculated find that the amalgamation of disparate studies suffers from many problems. The individual studies compiled are of uneven quality and representativeness. When global statistics are put together from separate small studies, the specificities and limitations of the individual studies are brushed aside. Petra Brhlikova, Allyson Pollock, and Rachel Manners (2011: 25) argue that many studies included in global burden calculations "exhibit significant shortcomings and limitations with respect to study design and analysis and compliance with GBDep (Global Burden of Depression) inclusion criteria" and that the "poor quality" of the data make many conclusions questionable. Nevertheless, the numbers are performative: "To say the numbers are constructed is to miss the point that all such estimates in social epidemiology are the product of specific, and questionable, practices of calculation. The key point here is not about accuracy . . . but about what the numbers are intended to do: in this form of politico-moral argument, it is hoped that the sheer weight of numbers will do important rhetorical work in demonstrating that here is scandalous neglect of suffering and 'something must be done'" (Rose 2018: 140).

An additional problem with the epidemiology informing GMH comes from a long-standing suspicion that psychiatric epidemiology cannot extrapolate the results of clinical studies to the population at large (Shorter 2013). The number of people found to suffer from major depressive disorder within the definition of the *Diagnostic and Statistical Manual of Mental Disorders* (DSM) in clinical settings could not be used to make claims about urgent needs in the population. Vikram Patel (2014: 18), the most prominent proponent of GMH, has even called for the abandoning of global burden statistics because they produce a "credibility gap" for psychiatric research. Large numbers of people in any country can be said to be "distressed," as in sad or fearful, yet they are not "disordered."

Epidemiological claims about the burden of depression being both immense and incredibly specific undermines trust in psychiatry: "Only a small fraction of the global population truly believes any of the astonishingly large figures that these surveys throw up. Those figures simply lack face validity because they conflate emotional distress with mental disorders" (18). If the epidemiology of global mental disorders is in doubt, the whole GMH project is in doubt. Patel argues that "more or less distress" estimations would be more believable than pseudo-exactness along strictly defined criteria.

Even worse for the epidemiology is the crumbling faith in symptoms-based diagnosis, which is used in the DSM-5 and the eleventh edition of the *International Classification of Diseases* (ICD). Psychiatric epidemiology only took off in the 1980s, when DSM-III classifications were structured enough to be applied in community surveys. The DSM has been the key source for psychiatric epidemiology since that time. Prior research was hampered by a lack of consensus about how to classify the disorders to be counted (Eisenberg 2010: 94).

A revolt within psychiatry against the DSM and symptoms-based diagnosis has been brewing since the 1990s. Biopsychiatric doubts about the validity of symptoms as true phenotypes of organic problems have been voiced since the 1980s. These doubts deepened even more when the symptoms could not be commensurated with biomarkers. The disillusionment with the DSM became a paradigm shift when the NIMH declared that it was turning its research strategy away from the DSM and toward the Research Domain Criteria Project (RDoC [see chapter 11]).

These dramatic changes in research-based psychiatry are hardly ever discussed in relation to GMH, although they make a fundamental difference to the ground on which GMH is standing. One of the direct engagements with the diagnostic crisis within GMH has been the question of whether DSM-style categories "really do overlap with the main issues that global mental health must address" (Stein et al. 2013). Some authors point to other indicators of mental health issues in the population, such as social inequality. In any case, no diagnostic alternative to symptoms-based diagnosis in the style of the DSM and the ICD exists. Recent moves toward a "dimensional" approach that is more sensitive to shades of severity (Patel et al. 2018) does not solve any of the problems of validity and reliability of symptom classifications.

The GMH publications make only a few mentions of the crisis of symptoms-based diagnostics. In the new GMH manifesto (Patel et al. 2018: 11), the DSM/RDoC problem is cited in relation to a "staging" approach to be developed in GMH. In the future, RDoC-style research might allow "deep phenotyping," meaning that individual patients' risks could be assessed on multiple biological levels. Eventually, this could make inventions more targeted—for example, by looking for markers of inflammation in cases of depression. But deep phenotyping is only a future possibility, and even if it existed, it would have little clinical relevance.

The Lancet Commission recognizes that symptom-based diagnostics have "limitations" because they can be "simplistic," "not always helpful," and "reductionist" (Patel et al. 2018: 11). While the commission "does not advocate for the abolition of classification systems" (11), it recommends paying greater attention to the fact that mental disorders develop gradually. During the prodromal stages, signs of coming disorder are not distinct enough to be caught by symptoms-based classifications. In most cases, "non-specific psychological distress"—said to be the most common manifestation of mental problems in large populations—does not need a diagnostic label, but it still needs a full intervention: "The staging model . . . recognizes opportunities for intervention at all stages" (12). It is ironic that GMH went from a critique of the tendency of the DSM and the ICD to overly medicalize populations to an even *more* medicalizing vision of everyone being prodromally disordered. The proposed staging model solves nothing; GMH epidemiology is still built on the same quicksand as in the 1980s.

Economics

Disability-adjusted life years allowed a new way to measure economic impacts of mental illnesses. Global mental health would not have emerged without the economic burden argument. Mental health became a priority because worsening mental health indicators are dragging down whole economies. The first studies on the mental-economic nexus are from the early 1990s. Dorothy Rice, Sander Kelman, and Leonard Miller (1992) brought US national survey data together with a "newly developed methodology for calculating costs" and arrived at a staggering figure of an annual loss to the US economy of $104 billion. Of that, $43 billion was spent on treatments; $47 billion was lost because morbidity reduced productivity; and $9 billion was lost because of premature death. One key finding was that there are direct and indirect costs of rising mental illnesses. The direct costs (including medications and clinical treatments) are already huge, but the indirect costs due to reduced productivity, higher rates of social benefit payments, higher rates of incarceration, and higher rates of homelessness were just as draining. Economic burdens continue to be calculated in this way (Insel 2008). Economic cost calculations are now included in public health research and policy development in most places. For example, in the United Kingdom the National Health Service recognizes mental health problems as the largest single cause of disability in the country, making it not only a quarter of the national burden of ill health but also the leading cause of illness-related work absence. It is estimated that mental health problems cost the country £100 billion each year—including the costs to individuals and society of treating preventable illness, the impact on quality of life, lost working days, and lost income.

All of the initial research focused on rich countries, while a scarcity of data hampered extending this perspective to poor countries. From early on, however, causal relations between mental ill health and loss of economic wealth were seen in poor countries. Patel and Kleinman (2003: 612) have argued that mental ill health and lower economic wealth are typical of people with low levels of education. There is a "vicious circle of poverty and mental disorder," with one dragging the other down. Mental health interventions should therefore also include financial aid interventions, such as microcredit schemes.

The mental health-and-economics nexus took a while to get onto the political agenda. It was only in 2014 that "mental health became a hot topic" (Insel 2014) among the world's political leaders. Echoing the GMH motto that there can be no health without mental health, Thomas Insel said that governments had finally realized that there could be "no wealth without mental health." Links between good mental health and good productivity were intensifying because of economic shifts toward the tertiary service sector. Mood disorders were rampant in the service sector. Insel's point tallies perfectly with Alain Ehrenberg's (2010) thesis about the rise of the fatigued self (see chapter 3). To date, however, psychiatry has not explored this correlation between rising rates of service sector work and rising rates of mood disorders. If true, it would mean that mental disorders are going to increase along with the growing dominance of service work; it would also mean that any further deepening of economic globalization is not the solution to the world's mental health problems. Instead, economic globalization is driving the problem.

Scholars in the GMH field are optimistic that global economic growth reduces mental illnesses. Poverty makes you depressed, and wealth lifts up your mood. Economic growth becomes the engine of growth in population mental health. The "vicious cycle" model was a major component of the WHO's *World Health Report 2001*: poverty led to a higher prevalence of mental disorders. Higher prevalence, lack of care, and more severe course of disease had negative economic consequences. To turn the vicious cycle into a virtuous one, the WHO report advocated investments in psychiatric drugs as investments in economic growth. Investments in drugs as first-line treatments became investments in global economic growth, and growth became a cure for mental illnesses. But maybe the true return on the economic investment is a worsening of mental health.

In the 2010s, the WHO and the World Bank continued to propagate the vicious cycle model (figure 10.1). Much of the research continues to be focused on depression and anxiety because they are the most common and most draining. The WHO and the World Bank now put the cost of depression and anxiety at $1 trillion per year worldwide (Chisholm et al. 2016). The association between socioeconomic poverty and poor mental health is taken as an unquestionable fact: poverty is one of the "key risk factors for the onset and persistence of mental disorders that, in turn, were associated with loss of income due to poor educational attainment and reduced employment opportunities and productivity. These complex, multidirectional pathways led to a vicious cycle of disadvantage and mental disorders" (Patel et al. 2018: 5). The vicious cycle model subscribes to a pro-capitalist approach holding that material wealth leads to mental health.

The next question is whether interventions should focus on mental health or on material wealth. Either investment in economic growth is prioritized to enhance mental health or money is spent on targeted mental health interventions that improve economic growth. Crick Lund and his colleagues (2011: 1502) compared these two possibilities and concluded that targeted interventions are more powerful than broader economic growth: "We found that the mental health effect of poverty alleviation interventions was inconclusive. . . . By contrast, mental health interventions were associated with improved economic outcomes in all studies, although the difference was not statistically significant in every study." The study "supports the call to scale up mental health care, not only as a public health and human rights priority, but also as a development priority" (1513).

Yet the causal links between mental health and material wealth remain fraught with unproven assumptions. Lund and his colleagues (2011: 1502) observe that the "vicious cycle" hypothesis was "fairly robust" in

Investing in treatment for depression and anxiety makes sense.

$1

US$1 of investment in treatment for depression and anxiety leads to a return of US$4 in better health and ability to work.

This is good for people, and good for economies.

WORLD BANK GROUP

World Health Organization

Figure 10.1 | The vicious/virtuous cycle
(World Bank/World Health Organization infographic)

rich countries, but not in poor countries. They describe two kinds of causation models: the "social causation hypothesis" and the "social drift hypothesis." The social causation model assumes that poverty lessens social capital and increases stress, bad diets, and trauma. The social drift model assumes that people who are already distressed are at a higher risk of falling into poverty because of higher health expenditures, reduced productivity, and unemployment. The main problem is that there are hardly any "robust" studies on the topic. Despite screening thirteen thousand articles, Lund and his colleagues found only fourteen that met their inclusion criteria. Out of more than 1,500 randomized trials identified in the 2007 *Lancet* series on mental health, "only four measured economic status outcomes." The entire discipline was, therefore, "in its infancy" (1508, 1513). There is a complete disconnect between the high confidence levels of GMH policy statements about economic growth and better mental health, on the one hand, and reliable evidence on what these connections might be, on the other. Global mental health has failed to produce any solid evidence that clear links between more and less wealth and more and less mental well-being exist.

A study on mental health featured on the World Bank's web page estimates productivity losses due to all mental, neurologic, and substance use disorders at $8.5 trillion in 2010. This is expected to double by 2030 "if a concerted response is not mounted" (Chisholm et al. 2016: 416). These calculations work with two kinds of value: the "intrinsic" value of having good mental health and the "instrumental" value of working productively, as well as being able to "form and maintain relationships, . . . pursue leisure interests, and to make decisions in everyday life" (416). The treatments considered are six months of continuous antidepressant treatment with fluoxetine; regular visits to outpatient and primary care services for medications and psychosocial treatments; and, for a few severe cases, hospital admissions of up to fourteen days. Overhead costs— for administration, for example—are also factored in. The global treatment gap stood at 72 percent in high-income countries and at 93 percent in low-income countries. Only 7 percent of people in poor countries received treatment for depression (Chisholm et al. 2016: 418). These figures on treatment gaps leave out entirely what is provided *beyond* the formal public sector (a fatal weakness of the methodology that I return to in the next section). When treatments were scaled up, the returns on investment were 5.7:1, meaning that an overall economic return of $5.70 could be realized for every $1 spent on treatments (Chisholm et al. 2016: 422). This sounds impressive, until the return-on-investment ratios are compared with those of most other health interventions. For malaria, the benefit to cost ratio is 40:1 (Chisholm et al. 2016: 422). The evidence on economic returns is extremely weak. Citing Lund and his colleagues (2011), Dan Chisholm and his colleagues (2016: 422) repeat that "the evidence base for the mental health effect of interventions targeted at the poor remains insubstantial." The argument that "economic wealth means mental health" is not well evidenced.

Another hypothesis is that greater material wealth puts mental health at risk. Mental disorders, especially mood disorders, are correlated with increasing social isolation, competitiveness, secularization, materialism, unhealthy diets, and sedentary lifestyles. Reviewing the evidence on the links between modernization and depression, Brandon Hidaka (2012: 211) concludes that "more money does not lead to more happiness." Instead, "Economic and marketing forces of modern society have engineered an environment promoting decisions that maximize consumption at the long-term cost of well-being." Modernity's "overfed, malnourished, sedentary, sunlight-deficient, sleep-deprived, competitive, inequitable and socially isolating environment" is toxic for the mind. This hypothesis of the toxic influences of economic growth is never seriously considered by GMH.

A related hypothesis focuses on relative wealth changes rather than absolute wealth levels. In this view, socioeconomic change in and of itself tends to be detrimental to mental health. This is especially so when people are torn from long-standing social networks and faced with more competition and higher aspirations (Heaton 2013). In this vein, Dinesh Bhugra and Anastasia Mastrogianni (2004: 10) argue against money producing better mental health: "We have entered the brave new world of globalization. . . . Societies alter rapidly through urbanization, acculturation, modernization, and social and cultural change. The quality of life in many countries is affected by economic disintegration, unequal distribution of collective wealth, social disruption, political repression, migration and even war. . . . Global economic forces have weakened poor countries and communities on the one hand, and reinforced the economic status of wealthy countries on the other."

This line of argument was prominent in WHO publications prior to the era of DALYs but can still be heard. For example, in the *Mental Health Action Plan 2013–2020*, the WHO acknowledges a link between the downsides of capitalism and the mental health of populations. The financial crisis of 2007 has had a particularly detrimental effect: "The current global financial crisis provides a powerful example of a macroeconomic factor leading to . . . higher rates of mental disorders and suicide as well as the emergence of new vulnerable groups. . . . In many societies, mental disorders related to marginalization and impoverishment . . . and overwork and stress are of growing concern" (World Health Organization 2013: 7).

Versions of this theory have been disappearing and reappearing over the past decades. For example, it is plausible, and supported by WHO studies since the 1960s, that schizophrenia patients have a better prognosis in poor countries than in rich countries (Halliburton 2021). The WHO's own research on better recovery in poor countries is never mentioned in GMH publications because it contradicts the "material wealth is mental health" model.

Where the older argument converges with GMH is that economic decline, especially if it is rapid and sudden, is bad for mental health. When people move quickly from relative wealth to relative poverty, mental health suffers (Lorant et al. 2007). But in contexts in which people move slowly from relative poverty to relative wealth, it is not clear that the opposite effect—of improving mental health—happens.

Missing from the GMH discourse on the economics of mental health is an engagement with *relative* gains or losses. The importance of change *relative* to the past and *relative* to social others has been highlighted by critical health economists such as Richard Wilkinson (2002; see also Wilkinson and Pickett 2010) and Michael Marmot (2005). Similarly, GMH does not consider the "mental ills of marginality" (Ecks and Sax 2005). Socioeconomic marginalization has negative health effects. People at the margins suffer more from stigmatization, poverty, low education, and limited access to health services. Marginalization can make existing illness worse, and it can push people into illness. Marginalization is always relational: who is on the margins and who is in the center depends on the relations between them. For economic wealth, marginalization is not about absolute levels (of income, wealth, and so on) but about relative levels: where others stand and how things are valued in local contexts. Being economically marginalized is not an absolute state; it is relative to the whole economy. Links between economic change and mental health can be grasped only by focusing on relative status. When the WHO argues that the global financial crisis has increased the incidence of mental illnesses, the explanation for this must lie in relative changes to multiple people and groups. Any model that treats economic wealth in a static and absolute way is going to fail.

A relational way to study the mental-economic nexus can be found between the lines of a few WHO publications. For example, in 2009, the WHO report *Mental Health, Resilience and Inequalities* (Friedli 2009) took the idea of relational status to mental health. The report argued that mental ill health cannot be reduced to absolute wealth levels; it has to be seen as relative. The report not only argued that "higher national levels of income inequality are linked to a higher prevalence of mental illness," but, even more worryingly, "as countries get richer, rates of mental illness increase" (Friedli 2009: 35). Similarly, Wilkinson and Kate Pickett (2010: 67) highlight inequality as source of mental illness, writing, "Differences in inequality tally with more than threefold differences in the percentage of people with mental illness in different countries."

A relational approach to socioeconomic status is missing in GMH. In the Lancet Commission's report, socioeconomic relations are mentioned only in a static, absolute sense: "Structural inequities . . . can have a negative effect on mental health and wellbeing" (Patel et al. 2018: 11). Inequality "erodes social capital" and "amplifies social comparisons and status anxiety" (15). A deeper analysis is missing. The field of GMH completely fails to reckon with economic status as relative, self-worth as relative, and ascriptions of value as relative. It has no theory of value or values because it banned all considerations of culture.

In every way, mental health is an outlier among different medical conditions. With all other illnesses, the more money that is spent on them, the more they are reduced. But with mental illnesses, more money does not seem to bring reductions. Without a relational approach to studying wealth and mental health, this paradox will not be resolved.

Scaling Up Services

The treatment gap motivates all GMH work. The epidemiology shows that people are in need. The economic modeling shows that people in need are unproductive. The health systems analysis shows that those in need are not being helped. The treatment gap notion could emerge only from the epidemiology, and the epidemiology could emerge only from standardized diagnostic criteria. In turn, interventions are justified as cost-effective. Economic losses from mental disorders are made calculable, like other economic liabilities, and the expected returns on investment into therapies can be assessed by measures of return on investment. Global mental health presents a perfectly closed loop. A leading GMH representative summarizes this drive toward drugs and prescribers: "In order to reduce mental health problems in people that have depression . . . you need to deliver care. In order to deliver care you need care to be available. In order for care to be available you need to make drugs available, people need to be trained. I mean, that basic part is the same, in all of the countries" (quoted in Bemme 2019: 10).

One of the first moments of discovering treatment gaps occurred in the United States in the 1980s when the NIMH used DSM-III criteria to study the prevalence of mental disorders. Its study found that mental disorders were highly prevalent (20 percent annually) and that only a minority of people with problems received care: "The message was unambiguous: the magnitude of the need for treatment is such that the only possible public health solution is to enhance the capacity of the primary health-care system to provide mental health treatment" (Eisenberg 2010: 94). The rise of depression to the most common mental disorder is part of the changes in diagnostic criteria introduced in the DSM-III. It expanded the definition of depressive disorder by merging severe melancholia with milder symptoms of nervous disorders. The DSM-III laid the foundations of the global depression epidemic (Horwitz and Wakefield 2007; Shorter 2013).

The discovery of high prevalence rates in the general population and the treatment gap was proffered by psychiatric deinstitutionalization (see chapter 6). Global mental health also says that deinstitutionalization and care in the community offer better value than asylums (Patel et al. 2018: 5); GMH criticizes brick-and-mortar mental institutions as places of poor treatments and human rights abuses. The notion of community care gathered pace along with deinstitutionalization and eventually became the dominant discourse in the 1980s. In India, the first Mental Health Programme (NMHP), launched in 1983, called for the deinstitutionalization of psychiatry and a move toward community care (Jain and Jadhav 2009). The "community care" and "human rights" pillars of GMH both stem from this turn against asylum-based care. If there had been as many asylums in the global South as in the global North, GMH would have taken a different turn. But the mental asylums in European colonies during the nineteenth century were thin on the ground and catered almost exclusively to Europeans, not to the "natives." There were few institutions in the South that could be deinstitutionalized.

The landmark *World Health Report 2001* (whose principal author was the Indian psychiatrist R. S. Murthy) embraced all the assumptions of the DALY era: mental illnesses are widespread and highly burdensome; effective drugs exist but are neither widely available nor affordable; and closing the treatment gaps should be a top priority of global health interventions. The report warned about an "increasing" burden of mental disorders and a "widening" treatment gap: "Today, some 450 million people suffer from a mental or behavioural disorder, yet only a small minority of them receive even the most basic treatment" (WHO 2001: 3). It went further by pointing out that "the poor and the deprived have a higher prevalence of disorders, including substance abuse" (xiv). The treatment gap is deeper not just because services are not offered to the poor but because the poor are suffering more. The report predicted that depression would become the world's second-leading health problem by 2020.

In the report, psychotropics held the promise of better treatment for all, and "new" hope came particularly with "new" drugs. Drugs "provide the first-line treatment" (World Health Organization 2001: xi). Psychotherapy, counseling, and other nonpharmaceutical interventions were favorably discussed, but the report questioned whether they could be cost-effective and whether the lack of skilled personnel did not rule them out as a viable option for poor countries (62). The problem that needed a policy solution was to make psychotropics accessible to everyone, especially to poor people. "Make psychotropic drugs available" is the second out of ten points for future policies (xi). "Essential" drugs should be on every country's essential drugs list, and "the best drugs" should be available "whenever possible" (xi). In the antidepressant segment, drugs are said to be effective "across the full range of severity" (65), including mild depressive symptoms. The "new" drugs—meaning selective serotonin reuptake inhibitors (SSRIS)—were highly effective for all forms of depression, including severe depression. There were no doubts about the efficacy of antidepressant drugs and no doubts about using them across the world as a first-line treatment. The new antidepressants were costlier than the older ones, but their better side-effect profile meant a "reduced need for other care and treatment," so that even expensive drugs were ultimately more cost-effective (61). No one in the world should be "deprived, on economic grounds only, of the benefits of advances in psychopharmacology" (61).

The confidence in "new" drugs as the best first-line treatment peaked in the 2000s. Later publications by the WHO maintained the severity and depth of the global treatment gap but became more reluctant to tout drugs as the best first-line treatment. For example, the WHO-sponsored Mental Health Gap Action Programme (mhGAP) of 2008 calculated that there were vast gaps between what national governments were investing in mental health and what was needed. The report held that the treatment gap was "more than 75%" worldwide—that is, only 25 percent of people who need treatment receive it. When examined by type of mental disorder, the treatment gap ranged from 32 percent for schizophrenia to 78 percent for alcohol use disorders. Depression had a gap of 56 percent. The same report also listed "treatment with antidepressant medicines" as the first of two "evidence-based interventions"; the second was "psychosocial interventions" (World Health Organization 2008: 11).

In the 2010s, WHO started to shy away from an all-out embrace of psychotropics to treat all major mental disorders. Depression treatments became less pharmaceuticalized. The mhGAP Intervention Guide, first published in 2010 (with a second edition in 2016), split "mild" depression from moderate and severe depression and moved it into a separate section for "other significant emotional or medically unexplained complaints" (WHO 2010: 80). (Why "mild depression" should not count as "depression" is not explained.) Moderate and severe depression, meanwhile, are said to be best treated by nonpharmacological interventions, such as addressing psychosocial stressors or reactivating social networks (10). The demotion of antidepressants from first-line treatment to an intervention to be merely "considered" can only be read between the lines.

The WHO *Mental Health Action Plan 2013–2020*, published in 2013, mentions the treatment gap only once, in an appendix (WHO 2013: 35). Whenever the treatment gap gets less attention, psychotropic treatments also get less attention. The *Mental Health Action Plan* does not make any statements about psychotropics. In the document, the word *drug* refers only to illegal and addictive substances, not to psychotropics. At one point, the availability of "basic medicines for mental disorders in primary healthcare" is said to be low, but so was the availability of "nonpharmacological approaches" (9). The *Mental Health Action Plan* insists that "mental health strategies and interventions for treatment, prevention and promotion need to be based on scientific evidence or best practice, taking cultural considerations into account" (10). It does not spell out what the best evidence is for psychotropics, but statements such as these can be taken as a nod to the growing doubts about the efficacy of medications.

When GMH calculates treatment gaps for countries of the global South, private-sector services are entirely excluded. The exclusive focus on what happens in the public sector produces a skewed picture of treatment gaps in countries of the South. Not only are private-sector pharmaceutical prescriptions ignored by GMH, but private practitioners providing mental health care are also ignored. When GMH says that there are, for example, only "0.31 mental health professional per 100,000 population in India" (World Health Organization 2008: 34), this captures only specialized personnel in public-sector facilities. The fact that at least 90 percent of all mental health treatments are given by nonspecialists and in the private sector is never even considered as a possibility. Nor is the possibility ever entertained that psychotropics are used by unlicensed people. In India, unlicensed "quack" doctors and people who work in medicine shops are often the first point of call (Ecks and Basu 2009). The calculation of mental health treatment gaps by GMH is faulty because it ignores everything happening outside the public biomedical sector.

Global mental health's key idea for closing the treatment gap is "task sharing" (formerly known as "task shifting"). To train enough specialized psychiatrists in poor countries, training requirements had to be reduced and low-skilled health workers employed. This is not a shift in tasks but a shift in who is performing tasks: "Specific tasks are moved, where appropriate, from highly qualified health workers to health workers with shorter training and fewer qualifications" (Patel et al. 2011: 11). With basic supervision by a psychiatrist or similar specialist, these low-skilled health workers were just as good at diagnosing problems, dispensing drugs, and offering behavioral therapy. The "mobilization and recognition of nonformal resources in the community—including community members without formal professional training," is the essential element in delivering services for all (Patel et al. 2011: 11).

One of the many problems of task sharing is that it embraces a strategic ignorance about healers that are deemed unqualified or irrelevant (Ecks and Basu 2014). It is also well established that many forms of distress are helped by religious and ritual practices (e.g., Heim and Schaal 2014; Sax 2014). The wide variety of treatment options for mental health problems gets pushed aside (Fernando 2014; Mills 2014). The way that GMH operationalizes the treatment gap is based on a biomedicalized concept of healing (Ingleby 2014). Scaling up biomedical services through task sharing either treats forms of healing that do not fit into the GMH agenda as quackery or ignores them altogether. In many countries, informal biomedical providers easily outnumber trained formal providers. The presence of these informal providers gets entirely ignored. In other fields, such as tuberculosis control, the presence of informal practitioners is not only recognized but also used for the extension of treatment protocols in areas where no formal provider would be present. This move has not yet happened in GMH (Ecks and Basu 2014).

Global Mental Illness, Local Mental Health

During fieldwork on the uses of psychotropics in India I explored how rural medical practitioners (RMPs) in West Bengal make sense of depression (e.g., Ecks and Basu 2009, 2014). The RMPs have no formal training in biomedicine and are viewed as illegal quacks by the government. But in rural areas, they outnumber trained biomedical practitioners by a large margin. Because they are a first point of call for people with health problems, the police tolerate their presence. The RMPs are not meant to know anything about how depression is diagnosed, how it is treated, and what its causes are. Yet all of them spoke about how many patients nowadays come with depression symptoms and how they treat them routinely with drugs. The drugs are supposed to be dispensed by prescription from licensed practitioners only, but RMPs have no trouble sourcing antidepressants from drug wholesalers.

The RMPs said that depression was increasing by leaps and bounds among the rural poor. "A recent addition to the list of diseases has been depression," RMP Malla told me. "It has reached frightening proportions." The present era was clearly more stressful and unhappy than previous times. The cause of rising rates of depression was rampant socioeconomic change, which, in turn was, caused by globalization and market capitalism. People used to be more content with their situation; now, however, television shows them affluent lifestyles of big-city folks, while their own economic status seems to become ever more precarious. If the root cause of depression was socioeconomic, the psychotropic drugs could only tinker with symptoms. Echoing popular ideas about how to deal with low moods and the mind "feeling bad" (Ecks 2013), the RMPs also used nonpharmacological treatments: counseling ("Don't think too much"), practical advice on life problems, and spiritual encouragement ("Try praying").

Even small insights into local practices trouble key assumptions of GMH. Global mental health says that there is a huge gap between rich and poor countries both in the awareness of mental disorders and in the effective treatments that are provided. Global mental health holds that rising levels of material wealth around the world lowers the risks of suffering from mental illnesses. The treatment gap in poor countries is so severe that only the drafting of lay people into psychiatric task-sharing schemes can begin to close it. However, the example of RMPs in West Bengal shows, on the contrary, that there are many more mental care providers in the real world than is acknowledged in GMH policies; treatment deemed to be effective by GMH circulates much deeper and further than is apparent; mental illnesses are not nearly as unknown or stigmatized as GMH assumes; and rising levels of wealth are not necessarily good for mental health.

One point that GMH representatives and RMPs agree on is that mental suffering continues to rise. Both GMH advocates and RMPs hold that the available treatments can have a limited positive effect on some individual patients, but none of the treatments seems to get a grip on the actual underlying problems. Even the Lancet Commission admits that "pharmacological and other clinical interventions for mental disorders . . . could have limited effects on the population-level burden of mental disorders" (Patel et al. 2018: 8). In rich countries, the prevalence of mental health problems "has not decreased, despite substantial increases in the provision of treatment (particularly antidepressants) and no increase in risk factors" (8). That mental ill health is increasing during the same era when more money is put into improving mental health is one of the fundamental paradoxes that GMH must face. Only an approach to mental health within complex relational contexts can provide an answer. There can be no global mental health without understanding social mental health and the local contexts of valuing one's own life in comparison with other lives.

ELEVEN

Failed Biocommensurations

Psychiatric Crises after the DSM-5

The Double Crises of Diagnostics and Psychopharmacology

Psychiatry is in crises—not just one, but several. These crises come from its failure to commensurate diagnostics and treatments. Psychiatry tried to find commensurations between reported symptoms, on the one hand, and findings on brain circuitry, genetics, and life events, on the other. Finding these relations should have led to new mechanisms for drug action and the development of new psychotropics. As I argue in this chapter, psychiatry was unable to integrate bioneurological research with symptoms-based diagnosis. What appears as phenotype does not correlate with the genotype. At the same time, pharmaceutical companies failed to create an economic return from their research and development (R&D) investments into new molecules. My focus is the disease category of major depressive disorder. I argue that the crises of psychiatric diagnostics and therapy reflect deeper uncertainties about where the discipline is heading. There have been attempts at reinvention, but there is no clear path forward. Even a decade ago, most of the resistance against psychiatry came from outside the discipline. Now, psychiatry has become its own fiercest critic. Different strands of psychiatry have become practically incommensurable with one another.

Two events exemplify this crisis. The first is the departure by the National Institute of Mental Health (NIMH) from the new edition of the *Diagnostic and Statistical Manual of Mental Disorders*, the DSM-5, published by the American Psychiatric Association (APA), and its move toward the Research Domain Criteria Project (RDoC). This new framework was in preparation for some years before the DSM-5 was published, yet it was right before the APA unveiled the DSM-5 in 2013 that the NIMH declared that DSM categories lacked validity and research on mental disorders should not use the manual any longer. The DSM-5 was greeted with unprecedented criticism from many different directions, but its jettisoning by the leading funding body in US neurosciences marked a low point.

The second event is the retreat of major pharmaceutical companies from funding research into new psychopharmaceuticals. While generic versions of existing drugs continue to be best sellers, pharmaceutical companies found investing in new medicines too risky to be continued. Major companies, including AstraZeneca, GlaxoSmithKline, Merck, Novartis, Pfizer, and Sanofi, abandoned or drastically reduced research into neuropsychiatric disorders in the 2010s (Abbott 2011; Harrington 2019; Wegener and Rujescu 2013). H. C. Fibiger, a former vice-president of neuroscience at Eli Lilly, even asked why it "took so long for the industry to abandon psychiatry" when it was clear that "not a single mechanistically novel drug has reached the psychiatric market in more than 30 years" (Fibiger 2012: 649). When no new products were on the horizon, the industry could not sustain spending any more money on it.

Each of these events could mark a crisis of its own, but in combination they give psychiatry an air of despair: the established approach got ditched by the NIMH, and hopes for future drugs got dashed by pharmaceutical companies. These two critical events are deeply connected to each other. The DSM sets the standards for how pharmaceutical companies get approval for the treatments they want to market. Since the DSM-III, there has been an inseparable nexus of the manual and psychopharmacology: "DSM-III locked psychiatry in a symbiotic relationship with the pharmaceutical companies. For drug companies, DSM provides a compendium of possible markets and new drug targets, a universe that has grown with each subsequent revision" (Whooley 2019: 178). Clinical trials need to enroll patients with specific problems rather than a wide spectrum of complaints. The more specific the diagnosis, the easier it is to conduct trials and provide the evidence needed to get approval from the US Food and Drug Administration (FDA).

Previously, diagnostic innovation seemed to foster pharmacological innovation, and pharmacological developments influenced diagnostic revisions. With the double crisis of DSM and the withdrawal of pharmaceutical R&D, this nexus looks broken. The double crisis of psychopharmacology and psychiatric diagnostics has been brewing for a long time, but it is only now that a new horizon for innovation is explicitly defined by a rupture with the past. If psychopharmacology *had* made continuous progress over the past decades, and if it *had* come up with many novel drugs, the DSM would still be deemed a success. But the lack of innovation in psychopharmaceuticals drags the DSM down with it (Lilienfeld and Treadway 2016: 443–44).

Psychiatrists do not need critics outside the field to tell them about these combined crises: they diagnosed them first. Painting a dark picture of the future of psychiatry, Philip Mitchell and Dusan Hadzi-Pavlovic (2014: 350) present a list of reasons that the field is so troubled: growing evidence that psychotropics are no better than placebos; a "failure to clarify the pathophysiology of the major psychiatric disorders"; a failure to "identify targets for tailored and improved drug therapies"; "the pharmaceutical industry has retreated from the psychiatry/central nervous system arena"; and doubts about the "integrity of the relationship between the psychiatric profession and the pharmaceutical industry, with very public exposés of opaque and questionable professional and industry behaviour."

To disentangle psychiatry's inability to make its different domains commensurable with one another, I draw on Ian Hacking's "engines of discovery" model, which he developed from work on autism and multiple personality disorder. Hacking (2007) finds ten processes that trigger and accelerate innovation: counting, quantification, creation of norms, correlation, medicalization, biologization, geneticization, normalization, bureaucratization, and resistance. He is interested in how disease classifications emerge, how they get disseminated, and how long-term experiences by both patients and clinicians loop back into the classificatory work. For Hacking, disorders come into circulation when they are defined by "experts" who are based in established "institutions" where they devise authoritative "knowledge" about the "people" who are labeled in specific ways. Hacking's work has been influential in debates on how and why psychiatric disease classifications are changing historically.

Here I want to put his model to work on the question of how psychiatry tries to make its different goals commensurable with one another.

I focus my analysis on the diagnosis and treatment of unipolar depression. Psychiatry has too many disparate subfields to allow a single assessment of whether progress is being made or not. Some areas of psychiatry experience a higher level of change in diagnostic labeling than others. For example, "depression" has remained relatively stable, whereas "autism" has changed substantially. Some areas have a strong consensus on the urgency of psychiatric treatments; some do not. Severe forms of psychosis, for example, are usually seen as in urgent need of treatment, whereas sadness after bereavement is not. Innovation in psychopharmacology has also been highly uneven across various psychiatric conditions. While many drugs have come to market for depression, no drug for autism has ever been developed.

Hacking's engines of discovery provide a powerful frame for analysis, but they are also a bit of a ragbag. It is not clear why there should be exactly ten engines, or why they should be ordered in the way they are. Some of the engines are so similar that they might be combined, and some engines are better subdivided. But going through these engines helps to find different kinds of biocommensurations in attempts at innovative work. In what follows, I look at all the ten engines while also tweaking the model as I go along.

Engines of Discovery

Hacking's first engine of discovery is "counting," which asks how many people suffer from a condition. Numerical value comparisons are a key mode of biocommensuration. As a diagnostic and statistical manual, the DSM is explicitly meant to allow quantification. Counting is done on regional, national, and international levels, by demographic groups, and so on. One of the first times depression was counted was in 1844, when the Association of Superintendents of American Asylums—the precursor of the APA—was founded, and an attempt was made to develop statistics for what the asylum inmates were suffering from (Hacking 2013; Horwitz and Grob 2011; Solomon 1958). The first sustained studies in psychiatric epidemiology did not come from psychiatrists but from social scientists—for example, Émile Durkheim's ([1897] 1951) study on suicide or Robert Faris and Warren Dunham's (1939) environmental study on mental disorders in a Chicago neighborhood. Psychiatric epidemiology got a boost after World War II, when concerns about "unserved populations" of mentally ill people intensified (Rose 2018: 30). Hampered by changing diagnostic criteria, psychiatric epidemiology took off only in the 1980s, when the DSM-III classifications were applied in community surveys (Bromet and Susser 2006: 9). Since the 1980s, prevalence numbers have skyrocketed (Rose 2018: 31).

Currently, the most influential framework for epidemiological counting is the Global Burden of Disease (GBD) project, which began in the 1990s (see chapter 10). Based on GBD calculations, the *World Health Report 2001* claimed that depression would be the world's second-leading health problem after heart disease by 2020. The same report also promoted the idea that the "new" antidepressants, selective serotonin reuptake inhibitors (SSRIs), should be made available for all people in need (WHO 2001: 65).

Counting people suffering from depression, as well as counting the economic costs of depression, became a key engine of discovery in the 1990s. Nearly every research article on depression now begins with dire figures on the burden of disease that depression presents. The need for more research, the need for new drugs, and the need for better services are justified by counting depression and other disorders. Introducing an article on new directions in psychopharmacology, for example, Thomas Insel and his colleagues (2013: 2438) go from "burden" to "cost" to "unmet need": "Psychiatric conditions account for five of the top ten causes of disability and premature death . . . The global cost for disorders of mental health in 2010 was $2.5 trillion and projected to markedly increase to $6.5 trillion in 2030 . . . a considerable proportion of people with mental health problems remain untreated." In this way, psychiatrists say that there is an urgent crisis in the form of a treatment gap: people need treatments, but the treatments are not available to them.

Yet counting depression is in crisis for at least two reasons: the quality of the epidemiological data is questionable, and the transcultural validity of disease categories is questionable. Critical evaluations of GBD analyses conclude that its syntheses of disparate and often unreliable studies suffer from severe commensuration problems (Brhlikova et al. 2011). Most studies used in GBD calculations are of questionable value. The grand conclusions drawn from bringing these data together do not stand up to scrutiny (see chapter 10).

The second engine of discovery is "quantification." Hacking points out that psychiatric conditions usually come not in the form of either "present" or "not present" but in shades of severity and duration. What

Hacking calls "quantification" is counting and comparing units along a scale. The use of scales or standards is another basic mode of biocommensuration. For depression, various scales have been designed to assess its severity, among others the Hamilton Depression Rating Scale, the Beck Depression Inventory, and the Zung Self-Rating Depression Scale. None of these scales has ever been adopted exclusively. The DSM-5 continues a tradition of quantifying depression by the number, duration, and severity of different symptoms. It is typical for this approach to say that "x number or more" of a list of symptoms must be present for a diagnosis to be made. There were hopes of getting better diagnoses and prognoses through more fine-grained dimensional assessments that measure the frequency, duration, and severity of symptoms. The DSM-5 task force could not come up with a consensus on how many dimensions there should be or how to distinguish severity from functionality (Whooley 2016). The dimensional approach was ultimately dropped in the final version of the DSM-5 (Cuthbert 2014; Lupien et al. 2017). "Quantification" remains an active engine of discovery in psychiatry.

The third engine is "creation of norms." For Hacking, quantification of mental conditions may entail cutoff points between "normal" and "pathological" states. Devising cutoff points is another basic mode of biocommensuration. It establishes a comparison between two overall states ("healthy" and "sick") and commensurates different cases as belonging to "the same" state. The DSM-5 lists nine key symptoms of major depressive disorder, then creates the norm that "5 (or more) of the following symptoms have been present during the same 2-week period." If only four symptoms are present, "depression" is not to be diagnosed.

There is an unending debate over whether these boundaries between normal and pathological states exist and, if they do, whether they exist merely by convention. Why "5 (or more)" less significant symptoms rather than four highly significant symptoms? Norm creation can be said to have been in deep crisis for some time. Fears that the "normal" is getting lost by the encroachment of the "pathological" have long been voiced, especially in relation to depression (Horwitz and Wakefield 2007). Disorders according to the DSM have often been said to contain "scientifically arbitrary diagnostic cut-offs" (Lilienfeld and Treadway 2016: 439). Treatments have been shown to loop back into perceptions of what is normal. Carl Elliott (2011), for example, shows that the availability of psychotropic drugs makes the normal look pathological, and treatments for a few can become routinely expected enhancements for everyone.

This criticism was leveled at the DSM-5 even more than at earlier editions. The removal of the bereavement exclusion for depression diagnoses in the DSM-5 exemplifies the problematic relation between the normal and the pathological (Blumenthal-Barby 2013; Zachar et al. 2017). In previous editions of the manual, it was recommended that clinicians should not diagnose depression when a patient was newly bereaved. The fifth edition removed the bereavement exclusion (see chapter 8). The chorus of outrage, from both inside and outside psychiatry, was deafening. If not even bereavement after losing a loved one was normal, then what else would remain untouched by psychiatric overreach? "Creation of norms" is clearly an area of crisis in psychiatry.

Hacking's fourth engine, "correlation," proposes that the discovery of correlations among different disease conditions is a source of innovation in diagnostics and treatments. "Correlation" is a mode of biocommensuration that compares classes of entities by their influence on one another. Research designed to find correlations between depression and other conditions constitutes a large segment of all research in psychiatry. For example, studies are devoted to showing connections between depression and diabetes (De Groot et al. 2001), cancer (Massie 2004), and irritable bowel syndrome (Fond et al. 2014). This work of correlating also includes socioeconomic factors, such as asking whether poor people suffer more from depression than rich people. This work of correlating usually focuses on the linkages between two conditions, but it can also include three or more conditions—for instance, depression, gender, and poverty (Patel et al. 2002).

A problem that has long haunted psychiatry is comorbidity, a kind of correlation in which two or more psychiatric problems occur together (Feinstein 1970; Lilienfeld and Treadway 2016: 440; Lupien et al. 2017: 3). Comorbidity is a biocommensuration that is less valued than correlations between discrete disorders, because it is uncertain what the units of comparison are. There is, for example, a long discussion about whether, and how, depression and anxiety are related to each other—whether they are truly separate entities or, rather, always co-occurring, with anxiety as a prodrome or a residue of depression (e.g., Kessler et al. 2001; Lenze et al. 2000). Research on comorbidity can also arrive at the conclusion that several conditions are sufficiently closely correlated to suggest that a new, overarching label should be introduced into the diagnostic catalog. An example is the suggestion that a new label called "complicated grief" should be introduced in a future edition of the DSM that reckons with commonly found constellations of prolonged sadness, anxiety, and a range of other symptoms (Shear et al. 2011). Many critics of DSM-style diagnostics hold that "comorbidity" is just a clumsy way to diagnose when, ideally, only a single condition should be diagnosed. The comorbidity problem comes from the DSM's use of a Linnaean style of classification that treats mental disorders as if they were separate species of beings, like plants or animals (see chapter 2). However, the assumption that mental disorders behave like plants and animals is probably spurious. The widespread occurrence of comorbidity—and, related to it, the widespread occurrence of "Not Otherwise Specified (NOS)" diagnoses—point to a "fatal flaw" in the DSM classifications (Hacking 2013). In one form or another, "correlation" will continue to be a major engine of discovery in psychiatry. What is not yet clear is whether this work on correlations will use a categorical approach or a multidimensional approach. A noncategorical approach to correlation is the goal of the RDoC.

Hacking orders the next six engines as medicalization, biologization, geneticization, normalization, bureaucracy, and resistance. For my analysis of failed biocommensuration in psychiatry, it makes more sense to reorder these engines. Normalization goes with medicalization. Biologization and geneticization are best discussed together, and I do so toward the end of the chapter. Bureaucracy and resistance are more straightforward than the other engines, so I discuss them before the others.

"Bureaucratization" comprises all processes in which disease categories become inserted into, and acted on, by a variety of bureaucratic institutions, including insurance companies, state health authorities, mental health policies, social benefits administrations, border controls, asylum courts, criminal courts, schools, and so forth. "Bureaucratization" is a form of biocommensuration that makes health impairments comparable with financial compensation. Depression is now a major concern for health bureaucracies in most countries, especially in relation to long-term sick leave and disability benefits; it is a leading reason for long-term sick leave. The need to administer depression bureaucratically is one of the reasons that the DSM has become so entrenched, and that the manual is unlikely ever to disappear (Hacking 2013; Rose 2013; see chapter 8). Bureaucratic demands for psychiatry to provide a reliable list of diagnoses was a major reason for the redesign of the DSM-III in the 1970s (Fein 2016). Once psychiatric labels and treatments are bureaucratically entrenched, their bureaucratization unfolds its own consequences (McGoey 2012; Pickersgill 2013). "Bureaucratization" was an engine of discovery for the DSM-III, but it has become a force of resistance against future paradigm shifts.

"Resistance" consists of all processes in which "kinds of people who are medicalised, normalised, and administered, increasingly try to take back control from the experts and the institutions, sometimes by creating new experts, new institutions" (Hacking 2007: 311). "Resistance" is about setting up and legitimating alternative biocommensurations. One example of how people's resistance can loop back into diagnostics is the removal of homosexuality as a form of mental disorder from the DSM in 1973. Nothing quite as dramatic has happened to the diagnosis of depression. People resist being labeled "depressed" or "as living with depression," but not nearly as vocally as people with other conditions. While the definition of *depression* has not encountered much resistance among patients, therapeutics for depression have. This kind of resistance starts with a patient questioning the need to take pills against the symptoms of depression and silent nonadherence to prescribed drugs (Ecks 2011). Resistance gets stronger whenever people protest openly against antidepressants or even sue pharmaceutical producers over the effects of their drugs. In the United States, thousands of court cases have been brought against pharmaceutical corporations over SSRIs such as Prozac, Lexapro, and Zoloft. Patients have sued companies successfully for not revealing evidence on violent behavior and birth defects. Increased risk of suicide due to SSRIs has been prominent (Healy et al. 2007; Liebert and Gavey 2009). There is a substantial group of anti-pharma activists who describe the ordeals they suffered from taking drugs (e.g., Newman 2016). In all of its forms, "resistance" adds serious doubts about psychiatric innovation.

"Resistance" can happen against any of the other nine engines of discovery. In the case of depression, it is especially strong in relation to "medicalization," a process of turning seemingly natural problems of human existence, such as emotional suffering, into medical problems in need of treatment (Conrad 2007). In this definition, "medicalization" is a form of "creation of norms" and of "normalization." For Hacking, "medicalization" is about treating people defined as depressed in a medical setting. Psychiatry as a knowledge form that aims at the "normalization" of thinking and behaving has been discussed at great length. Michel Foucault's work on disciplinary power (Foucault 1975, 2008) is all about "normalization" and possibilities of resistance.

The crisis of psychiatric biocommensuration is not confined to psychopharmacology. As Stefan Priebe, Tom Burns, and Tom Craig (2013) argue, "The past 30 years have produced no discoveries leading to major changes in psychiatric practice." All of the current schools of psychotherapeutic thought have been around for decades. All of the kinds of service provision, including outpatient clinics, have been used for decades. Even the methods to assess the efficacy of treatments, such as the randomized controlled trial, have been used for more than half a century. The proliferation of rival therapeutic streams that see themselves as incommensurable with one another has been dubbed a "narcissism of minor differences" (Denig 2017).

Hacking's ten engines of discovery do not separate nonpharmacological and pharmacological forms of "medicalization," but I think this is a crucial distinction. Pharmaceuticalization has a different dynamic from medicalization (Abraham 2010; Bell and Figert 2012; Cloatre and Pickersgill 2014), especially in psychiatry (Ecks 2011; Healy 1997; see chapter 5). Depression was medicalized long before it was pharmaceuticalized, and pharmaceuticalization can proceed without medicalization. The profitability of antidepressants "established an economic incentive for broadening the criteria and bringing many conditions under the umbrella of depression. Thus, recent years have seen an enormous expansion of the range of mood disturbances and other common problems treated with antidepressants, even as evidence for the efficacy of these medications has been challenged" (Kirmayer et al. 2017).

Given that changes to DSM criteria have been so deeply connected to the development of the psychopharmaceutical market, it is all the more startling that the nexus between economic incentives and therapeutic incentives could break down. A crisis of innovation in psychiatry is visible in all of the treatments for depression, but particularly in the pharmaceuticalization of depression. The withdrawal of pharmaceutical companies from psychiatric drug development requires a new kind social science critique (Pollock 2011). Let me focus on this crisis of psychopharmacology in detail.

The Crisis of Psychopharmacology

Whereas the second half of the twentieth century has been characterized as the "antidepressant era" (Healy 1997), the last decade has seen "the end of the psychopharmaceutical revolution" (Tyrer 2012). Even a decade ago, any suggestion of a crisis of psychiatry in the field of pharmacology would have seemed outlandish. Psychopharmacology used to be celebrated as going from strength to strength, and antidepressants were among those drugs showcased as great success stories. The pinnacle of this era was reached in the 1990s and early 2000s. The *Beyond Therapy* report by the President's Council on Bioethics never even asked whether psychopharmaceuticals were safe and effective; it only asked whether the drugs were also safe and effective for people who wanted to be "better" than well (see chapter 5). It seemed beyond doubt that psychopharmacology was making rapid progress in all areas of mental health. The bioethical question was not whether drugs should be used at all but whether stimulants, antidepressants, and antipsychotics could and should be used to enhance cognitive functioning beyond normal levels—for example, in children: "Opportunities to modify behaviour in children using psychotropic drugs are growing rapidly, and the young but expanding field of neuroscience promises vast increases in understanding the genetic and neurochemical contributions to behaviour and comparable increases in our ability to alter it, safely and effectively" (President's Council on Bioethics 2003: 70). No one would write this today.

If only prescription rates were considered, no crisis could be detected. Sales of antidepressants, and psychopharmaceuticals more generally, remain extremely strong across the world. Global statistics all point to steadily increased uses of antidepressants over the past decades. Across Organization for Economic Cooperation and Development (OECD) countries, rates of antidepressant use have roughly doubled between 2000 and 2013 (OECD 2015). While prescription rates have increased, the money spent on antidepressants has remained roughly the same. In England, prescriptions for antidepressants increased 165 percent between 1998 and 2012, with accelerated growth between 2008 and 2012—the years of the global financial crisis (Spence et al. 2014: 4). In the United States, 11.2 million people used these drugs in 1998; by 2010, that figure was 23.3 million ("Antidepressants" 2013). While US prescription rates have more than doubled, the costs of the treatments have stayed the same ($621 in 1998, compared with $651 in 2010). The expiration of patents and competition from generics' pushing down drug prices explains the simultaneous increase in prescriptions and stagnant sales values.

These globally increasing rates of antidepressant prescriptions occurred despite mounting evidence against the drugs' efficacy. In the mid-2000s, meta-analyses of clinical trial data, including findings that had been withheld by pharmaceutical companies, concluded that antidepressants are no better than placebos for mild and moderate depression (Kirsch 2010). Even more alarming are suspicions that rising prescription rates of psychotropics are the *cause* of the current epidemic of mental illnesses and chronic disability (Whitaker 2010). Psychiatric drugs do have effects on brain chemistry, but it is still unclear what these effects are. The theory of a specific "neurochemical imbalance" of serotonin levels in the brain synapses has been disproved (Kirsch 2010; Moncrieff 2008; Whitaker 2010). Beneficial effects of the drugs seem to occur only—if they occur at all—in the early treatment phase. Over longer months and years, the drugs potentially prolong suffering. Assessments of efficacy systematically neglect the effects of long-term exposure (Whitaker 2010: 65).

Since the 1950s, the development of psychopharmaceuticals has been driven by private pharmaceutical companies. In times when the drugs were still protected by patents, the profits were staggering. Yet almost all the major patents for psychopharmaceuticals have now expired. Eli Lilly's patent for Prozac expired in 2001, and the company lost 80 percent of its market share in fluoxetine in the first year. Eli Lilly's patent for olanzapine (Zyprexa) expired in 2011, taking down the company's net income by 23 percent. AstraZeneca lost its patent on the blockbuster drug quetiapine (Seroquel) in 2012 and, with it, lost 25 percent of its pretax profits. Forest Laboratories' escitalopram (Lexapro) went off patent in 2013, and the company's first-quarter profits of that year sank by 79 percent (Drugdevelopment-Technology 2012).

Around the same time that their major drug patents expired, most multinational pharmaceutical companies, including AstraZeneca, GlaxoSmithKline, Merck, Novartis, Pfizer, and Sanofi, either closed or scaled back their R&D units for neuropsychiatric disorders (Abbott 2011; Greenberg 2013; Rose 2018: 129–31; Wegener and Rujescu 2013). For example, AstraZeneca shut down all research on depression and announced that, while "the patient need for better medicines in neuroscience is huge and the science is promising," the R&D investments had not paid off. The company had made "an active choice to stay in neuroscience" but not through in-house research. AstraZeneca moved neuroscience innovation to a "virtual" unit consisting of researchers employed by other organizations, some of them in public-sector institutions. The critical literature on Big Pharma's promotion of psychotropics started from the assumption of hugely powerful corporations investing cynically in a hugely profitable segment of the market.

New requirements to register and make public any ongoing drug trial has made it easier to get a sense of the pipeline of drugs under development. For example, the WHO International Clinical Trials Registry provides publicly accessible information on the status of ongoing trials. A recent survey of all drugs in development in phase I, II, or III of clinical trials between 2006 and 2011 (Fisher et al. 2015) confirms that the end of the psychopharmaceutical revolution is here, and likely here to stay. From among 2,477 drug entities in various stages of development, only 102 belonged to the neuropsychiatric spectrum. In other words, only 4 percent of all drugs that were recently in development were for mental illnesses. Broken down by diagnoses, drugs for anxiety and depression drugs up 31.5 percent; for addiction, 23.5 percent; for psychosis, 23.5 percent; for insomnia, 6.8 percent; for sexual dysfunction, 6.2 percent, and for attention deficit hyperactivity disorder (ADHD), 5.6 percent. Almost all the drugs that were tested in clinical trials were not new molecular entities but long-approved drugs merely being tested for new indications—for example, testing existing antipsychotics for the treatment of depression (Miller 2010: 502).

So is the pipeline for new psychopharmaceuticals drying up? Insel, former director of the NIMH, has lamented the dearth of new products: "The biggest problem isn't the announcements by GSK and AstraZeneca, it's when you look at the pipeline and see what companies are actually doing in psychiatric drug development. There are very few new molecular entities, very few novel ideas, and almost nothing that gives any hope for a transformation in the treatment of mental illness" (quoted in Miller 2010: 502; see also Insel et al. 2013). It can be argued that the pipeline is not even in a process of "drying up"—it has been nearly dry for decades. "Innovation" in the antidepressant era was confined to tweaking a handful of nearly identical molecules. Pharmaceutical companies focused their investments on finding "me-too" drugs rather than entirely different therapies. The profits to be made from drugs such as Prozac were so large that all that was needed, from an investment point of view, was to find a small variation of the same drug, or to find new indications for the same drug, and get a patent to protect the "innovation."

If there was a pipeline, it was awash with hype and not with innovation. One example is the drug Pristiq, which is one of the few psychopharmaceuticals that still has patent protection today. The brand is currently owned by Wyeth, which is part of Pfizer. Pristiq won a patent in the United States in 2008 despite a demonstrable lack of innovation. It is another version of the long-known venlafaxine (Effexor) and differs from it only in terms of its dosage. Pristiq does not have clinical advantages over other drugs. The Pristiq patent was challenged by a few generics producers, and in some jurisdictions, such as Australia, the patent was revoked. Pristiq has already become generic outside the

United States and Europe. Dozens of generic versions are produced in India. Pfizer India sells Pristiq as "Prestiq" for just 18 rupees (about 28 cents) per 100 mg tablet. In the United States, the same drug costs ten to thirty times more. Pristiq is not an innovative drug.

There were several attempts to go off the beaten path and find new drugs based on new pathways. For example, observations of circadian dysfunction led to the hypothesis that depression has something to do with melatonin metabolism (Kasper and Hajak 2013). A drug called agomelatine, a melatonin antagonist, was under development by Servier Laboratories up until phase III clinical trials. The drug received approval by the European Medicines Agency in 2009 and is marketed as Valdoxan. Servier sold the US rights to Novartis, which wanted to get marketing authorization in the United States, but Novartis stopped the development of the drug in 2011 because there was not enough evidence of efficacy, and there were indications of severe liver toxicity.

Similarly, an industry insider told me about a German pharmaceutical company trying to develop a drug for schizophrenia that targeted not the standard dopamine pathways but the body's melatonin metabolism (see Anderson and Maes 2012; Baandrup et al. 2011). After years of development, the company finally pulled the plug in 2015. The results from the clinical trials were too weak to take it any further.

A few substances from beyond the psychotropic spectrum are currently tested for their effects on depression. One of them is sirukumab, a human antibody that inhibits inflammation (Zhou et al. 2017). Sirukumab was developed to treat arthritis; it has not been licensed yet, but in 2016 Janssen Pharmaceuticals submitted a patent application to the FDA, and in Europe a similar patent application was submitted by GlaxoSmithKline and Johnson and Johnson. Trials looking at the antidepressant potentials of sirukumab assume that disturbances in the body's immune system can result in increased anxiety, psychomotor retardation, and circadian rhythm disturbances. If sirukumab helps alleviate these symptoms by targeting the immune system, then its "transdiagnostic" potentials include major depression. That a condition of the immune system ("inflammation") can now be connected to a mental illness ("depression")—something that the DSM-5 does not allow—is explicitly linked to the introduction of the NIMH's RDoC project (Zhou et al. 2017). It is too early to tell whether sirukumab will ever be marketed as an antidepressant drug, but it is important to note that the model underpinning these trials is based on RDoC, not on the DSM.

A rare recent success is the approval in the United States of Sage Therapeutics' drug Zulresso (brexanolone) as an injection for the treatment of postpartum depression (FDA 2019). Sage Therapeutics is a spin-off of the NIMH and was founded by a researcher with the NIMH, Steven Paul, who did much of the neuroscientific work on the drug. Zulresso's approval is based on a new therapeutic model that links changes in steroid hormones during and after pregnancy to depressive symptoms. The new treatment consists of a continuous sixty-hour intravenous injection of a steroid called allopregnanolone, which inhibits stress-inducing steroids in the brain. The original idea for this model goes back to Hans Selye, the discoverer of "stress" (Gordon 2019). The price tag of the treatment is $20,000 per patient (Shannon 2019).

Investing in new drugs has proved much riskier for psychopharmaceuticals than for other therapeutic segments. Psychiatric drugs take the longest to develop (after antineoplastic drugs), have the lowest approval rates, and take the longest to receive approval. They are also more expensive in clinical development because when they fail, they tend to fail in the final-stage trials with human subjects. Animal tests are not good at predicting effects in humans (Miller 2010: 504).

One problem of psychiatric drug discovery is that it has been run almost entirely by for-profit private companies. The profitability of the tried and tested molecules explains why pharmaceutical companies had little incentive to invest in basic research or in discovering substantially new treatments (Dumit 2018). The companies invested in highly similar yet ultimately non-innovative drugs aimed at keeping patients in chronic treatment. The industry will always prefer a chronic treatment to a short-term treatment to make steady and continuous sales (Whitmarsh 2013). Instead of making people well, Big Pharma "exchanged any interest in reducing treatments for the goal of increasing them" (Dumit 2012: 17).

A caveat to this argument is that R&D in other therapeutic segments is based on the same logic of profits, yet there the pipelines were not drying up as badly as in psychiatry. There is something peculiar about psychiatric innovation when compared with other fields of medicine. Cancerous cells and the cardiovascular system are complex, too, but no other part of the body is as complex as the brain and body-brain connections. Pharmaceutical companies could have invested more, but an aversion to financial risks alone cannot explain the lack of psychiatric innovation.

After DSM-5

The final two engines of discovery that appear in Hacking's heuristic model are "biologization" and "geneticization." As noted earlier, I think these two engines are better discussed together, as genetics are part of biology.

The search for the biology of depression has a long history. The notion that depression is *melancholia*, an excess of black bile in the body, is thousands of years old (Horwitz and Wakefield 2007: 54–55). An explicit attempt to make psychiatry a biological science dates to the middle of the nineteenth century and the work of Wilhelm Griesinger (1817–1868). The 1990s saw a renaissance in biopsychiatric approaches to depression, made possible by new methods in molecular neurosciences, as well as by neuroimaging technologies such as functional magnetic resonance imaging. During the same era, new research has focused on identifying genetic predispositions for depression. The search for genetic risk factors is conducted through family, twin, and adoption studies. To date, genetic relatedness seems to be correlated with higher risks of developing major depressive disorder (MDD), but no definitive genetic markers could be identified (Lohoff 2010). To date, genetic research has also failed to produce leads for therapy (Insel et al. 2013: 2439).

While the DSM may be psychiatry's bible, finding biological causes remains the holy grail (Geppert 2017). The inability of the DSM-5 to integrate symptom classifications with biological and genetic research findings (see Romelli et al. 2016) pushed RDoC up the NIMH's agenda. The NIMH publicly turned against the APA manual in 2013, with Insel disparaging symptoms-based diagnostics as an intuitive art (Insel 2013). Symptom classifications were not mirrors of nature but merely the mirror of consensus opinions (see chapter 8). To go beyond biocommensurations based on "mere consensus," the NIMH moved toward RDoC, a new research framework that puts objective and measurable biomarkers at the center (Fu and Costafreda 2013).

Although RDoC did not make any headlines prior to 2013, it has been part of the NIMH's strategic plan since 2008 (Cuthbert 2014). The hope for a neurobiological paradigm shift had already appeared in the DSM-5's Revision Agenda, published by both the NIMH and the APA eleven years earlier. In RDoC style, the agenda argued that refining, reshuffling, and expanding disease definitions would never find true biological causes (Kupfer et al. 2002: xix). Doubts about how valid DSM categories are has even deeper roots. In 1989, the British psychiatrist Robert E. Kendell

(1989: 313) proposed that the "discrete clusters of psychiatric symptoms we are trying to delineate do not actually exist." In the 1990s, many psychiatrists questioned the validity of DSM diagnostics in the same words. The Dutch psychopharmacologist Herman van Praag (1998: 179) wrote that a lack of validity of DSM categories would mean that "our biological studies are built on quicksand. The search for the biological determinants of invalid constructs will probably generate invalid and irreproducible results." The Research Domain Criteria Project transformed these doubts about the DSM into a research program.

The RDoC framework starts with the notion that mental disorders are dysfunctional patterns in brain activity that can be studied upward through behavior and self-reports and downward through cellular, molecular, and genetic traits. For psychiatrists invested in the DSM approach, RDoC threatens to push the field even deeper into a strictly biological approach. Even psychiatrists who were often critical of the DSM are wary of RDoC. Laurence Kirmayer and Daina Crafa (2014) warn that RDoC will push aside behavioral and experiential "phenotypes" in favor of biological endophenotypes and favor research driven to find specific anatomical locations rather than complex and distributed mechanisms that cannot be localized.

In terms of Hacking's engines, RDoC favors biology and genetics over other factors. The discovery of new correlations is key, but these correlations are to be established among "units of analysis." Hence, the discovery of correlations is emphatically not about finding comorbidities in the style of the DSM.

The creation of norms is also work of the future. For now, RDoC makes no distinctions between the normal and the pathological in the way that the DSM does. Two reasons are given for this. First, the DSM thresholds for pathology are branded as arbitrary and unable to detect "subclinical" symptoms. Second, RDoC wants to free up the recruitment criteria for the inclusion of research subjects.

In DSM-oriented work, one needs to identify subjects that fit into the classifications, such as "MDD." In RDoC-oriented work, however, other forms of sampling are encouraged. The rules for sampling can be entirely about life events. For example, RDoC allows comparisons of the brain scans of people who suffered childhood abuse with those who did not suffer abuse. There is no requirement to diagnose whether the people in the one sample show symptoms of depression, trauma, or any other recognized DSM category. Instead, it is sufficient to do the sampling by life events. For example, "parenting" could be turned into a unit of analysis

(Blair 2015). As Steven Hyman, a former NIMH director, points out, "The DSM system has itself impeded progress in the areas of neuroscience relevant to psychiatric disorders. If to obtain a grant or to publish a paper, one must select study populations according to a system that is a poor mirror of nature, it is very hard to advance our understanding of psychiatric disorders" (quoted in Casey et al. 2013).

Research under RDoC wants to find pharmaceutical cures in the long run, but this is not a short-term goal: researchers say that it can take ten to twenty years until this kind of work can be done (Rapp 2016: 6). The NIMH emphasizes that causal models must be discovered instead of mere outcomes. Hence, RDoC is also a turn against large randomized controlled trials that focus only on treatment outcomes without explaining *why* the treatment is supposed to work. The development of brexanolone is a good example of how neuroscientific modeling of why symptoms occur can indeed lead to the discovery of new therapies. The Research Domain Criteria Project also encourages research on nonpharmacological treatments. There are now published RDoC studies on, for example, the uses of mindfulness and yoga for training adolescents to better cope with stress (Henje Blom et al. 2014).

A few publications address what psychopharmacological research will look like after the DSM and after the withdrawal of the pharmaceutical industry. Insel and his colleagues (2013) issued a programmatic statement that lists opportunities for innovative solutions in drug development; it calls for a comprehensive "paradigm shift" in diagnostics and in how future research might be funded between nonprofit research and for-profit companies. A few paths to novel drugs exist, such as glutamate-based therapies (Zarate et al. 2010), which involves giving ketamine (an old anesthetic and party drug that is also known as "horse tranquilizer") to people with severe depression (Murrough et al. 2017). The time horizon for truly new treatments, the programmatic statement noted, is twenty years (Insel et al. 2013: 2439). The future horizons of RDoC thus are more about low expectations, deflation, and uncertainty than about future hope (Fitzgerald 2017).

From Symptoms to Behavioral Traces

The founders of RDoC thought the new framework would set the research agenda for decades to come. Yet there are signs that the RDoC era may be shorter than expected. The NIMH is not keen on pushing the

RDoC agenda as hard as it did under the directorships of Steven Hyman, Thomas Insel, and Bruce Cuthbert. When he became the new director of the NIMH in 2016, Joshua Gordon announced that the continuation of RDoC needed to be reviewed. In 2017, he wrote, "We have not yet reached a position to say whether RDoC has succeeded," but RDoC was going to continue until more evidence was available. Gordon then criticized RDoC for having fallen into the same "consensus" trap that its advocates had brought against the DSM: that the categories were merely based on a group of experts' opinions. "We constructed the RDoC domains using a similar method to what we used to construct DSM diagnoses," Gordon said. "We took a bunch of scientists and clinicians and locked them in a room together" (Gordon 2017). Whether RDoC could escape this trap was not clear, and that it would be branded as yet another "consensus" is supremely ironic, because RDoC was designed to do away with categories that were based merely on "consensus." Even more ironic is that the research community sees the mandated shift to RDoC, enforced through NIMH grant allocations, as coercive: RDoC came down from the top of the NIMH, and its abrupt introduction *lacked consensus* among researchers (Pickersgill 2019). In other words, the DSM was first introduced by consensus; then it was rejected because it was based on consensus; then the substitution of the DSM with RDoC was rejected because it lacked consensus. Psychiatry clearly struggles to figure out what it should do with "consensus." All successful biocommensurations have a high degree of consensus. Psychiatry has a consensus gap.

Beyond RDoC, another horizon opened up through big data: Gordon's NIMH proposed that a big data approach could be psychiatry's golden future. Researchers could enroll "1 million or more" volunteers willing to be tracked through "web-based behavioral measures" (Gordon 2017). These behavioral data would then be linked to volunteers' medical records. In a next step, algorithms would be developed to "parse behavior into its basic building blocks" (Gordon 2017), and these "basic building blocks" would eventually supplant DSM categories. The big data strategy collects habitual behavioral patterns from a massive sample of people and develops algorithms for detecting significant habit changes. Diagnosis of mental disorders will emerge, it is hoped, from biocommensurating habit changes with mental illnesses. Ideally, this new diagnosis will later become biocommensurable with new therapies.

The NIMH proposes the same big data strategy championed by private businesses. An example is the Silicon Valley startup Mindstrong, cofounded by former NIMH director Thomas Insel (Harrington 2019: 298). In 2015,

Insel raved about how mental disorders could be detected through data collected from mobile phones: "Technology can cover much of the diagnostic process because you can use sensors and collect information about behavior in an objective way" (quoted in Regalado 2015). Tracking habitual behavior supplants "biologization" and "geneticization." As Insel explains this shift: "I spent thirteen years at NIMH really pushing on the neuroscience and genetics of mental disorders, and when I look back on that I realize that while I think I succeeded at getting lots of really cool papers published by cool scientists at fairly large costs—I think $20 billion—I don't think we moved the needle in reducing suicide, reducing hospitalizations, improving recovery for the tens of millions of people who have mental illness" (quoted in Rogers 2017). The return on investment from extracting genetic and neurological data was so poor that it needed to be replaced by a new source for extraction: behavioral data (figure 11.1).

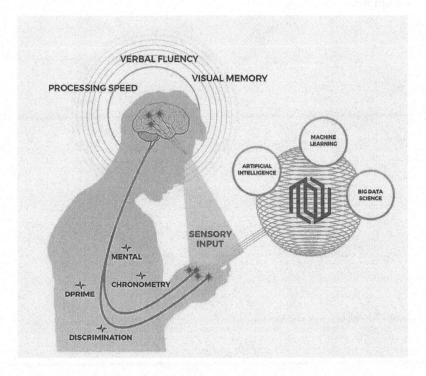

Figure 11.1 | Mental disorder goes big data (Mindstrong promotional material)

The big data strategy was initiated before the data privacy scandals at Facebook and other tech companies. It started before it came to light that DNA ancestry sites such as 23andMe are selling their customers' genetic data to pharmaceutical corporations (Brodwin 2018). Recording massive amounts of behavioral data through mobile devices to detect how people are at risk of going mad, then linking this up with confidential medical and genetic records, is the greatest privacy nightmare imaginable.

This inquiry into the failed biocommensurations in psychiatry has shown that there are fundamental crises in diagnostics and in drug treatments, as well as a range of smaller crises in all aspects of research and practice. Even the latest shift toward RDoC seems to be in crisis. A decade ago, it looked like mental disorders were authoritatively defined by experts in established institutions who collected solid knowledge on the mental conditions that afflicted people. If there was resistance, it came almost entirely from outside psychiatry. Now all of this is up in the air, and all of the most powerful critiques of psychiatry come from within itself.

References

Aakhus, Mark, and Michael Bzdak. 2012. "Revisiting the Role of 'Shared Value' in the Business-Society Relationship." *Business and Professional Ethics Journal* 31, no. 2: 231–46.

Abbott, Alison. 2011. "Novartis to Shut Brain Research Facility." *Nature* 480, no. 7376 (December 6): 161–62.

Abraham, John. 2010. "Pharmaceuticalization of Society in Context: Theoretical, Empirical and Health Dimensions." *Sociology* 44, no. 4: 603–22.

Abraham, John, and Graham Lewis. 2002. "Citizenship, Medical Expertise and the Capitalist Regulatory State in Europe." *Sociology* 36: 67–88.

Adams, Vincanne, ed. 2016. *Metrics: What Counts in Global Health*. Durham, NC: Duke University Press.

Agarwal, S. P., ed. 2004. *Mental Health: An Indian Perspective, 1946–2003*. New Delhi: Elsevier.

Agenzia Italiana del Farmaco (AIFA). 2009. *IMPACT International Medical Products Anti-Counterfeiting Taskforce: 2006–2010*. Milan: Agenzia Italiana del Farmaco.

Ahen, Frederick. 2017. "Responsibilization and MNC-Stakeholder Engagement: Who Engages Whom in the Pharmaceutical Industry?" In *Stakeholder Engagement: Clinical Research Cases*, ed. R. Edward Freeman, Johanna Kujala, and Sybille Sachs, 87–112. Cham, Switzerland: Springer.

American Psychiatric Association (APA). 2000. *Diagnostic and Statistical Manual of Mental Disorders*, 4th ed., text revision (DSM-IV-TR). Washington, DC: American Psychiatric Association.

American Psychiatric Association (APA). 2013. *Diagnostic and Statistical Manual of Mental Disorders*, 5th ed. Washington, DC: American Psychiatric Association.

Anderson, George, and Michael Maes. 2012. "Melatonin: An Overlooked Factor in Schizophrenia and in the Inhibition of Anti-psychotic Side Effects." *Metabolic Brain Disease* 27, no. 2: 113–19.

"Antidepressants: Global Trends." 2013. *Guardian*, November 20. Accessed November 18, 2020. https://www.theguardian.com/News/2013/Nov/20/Mental-Health-Antidepressants-Global-Trends.

Applbaum, Kalman. 2004. *The Marketing Era: From Professional Practice to Global Provisioning*. London: Routledge.

Ariely, Dan. 2009. *Predictably Irrational*. London: HarperCollins.

Aristotle. 1952. *Politics*. Chicago: Encyclopedia Britannica.

Astuti, Rita, and Maurice Bloch. 2015. "The Causal Cognition of Wrong Doing: Incest, Intentionality, and Morality." *Frontiers in Psychology* 6, no. 136 (February 18). Accessed November 18, 2020. https://doi.org/10.3389/fpsyg.2015.00136.

Baandrup, Lone, Birgitte Fagerlund, Poul Jennum, Henrik Lublin, et al. 2011. "Prolonged-Release Melatonin versus Placebo for Benzodiazepine Discontinuation in Patients with Schizophrenia: A Randomized Clinical Trial—The Smart Trial Protocol." BMC *Psychiatry* 11, no. 1: 160.

Babar, Zaheer-Ud-Din, ed. 2017. *Pharmaceutical Policy in Countries with Developing Healthcare Systems*. Cham, Switzerland: Springer.

Barandiaran, Xabier E., and Ezequiel A. Di Paolo. 2014. "A Genealogical Map of the Concept of Habit." *Frontiers in Human Neuroscience* (July 21). Accessed November 18, 2020. https://doi.org/10.3389/fnhum.2014.00522.

Barberis, Nicholas C. 2013. "Thirty Years of Prospect Theory in Economics: A Review and Assessment." *Journal of Economic Perspectives* 271: 173–96.

Barnes, Barry, David Bloor, and John Henry. 1996. *Scientific Knowledge: A Sociological Analysis*. Chicago: University of Chicago Press.

Baron, Jonathan. 2007. *Thinking and Deciding*, 4th ed. Cambridge: Cambridge University Press.

Barsam, Ara P. 2008. *Reverence for Life: Albert Schweitzer's Great Contribution to Ethical Thought*. Oxford: Oxford University Press.

Barua, Maan. 2016. "Lively Commodities and Encounter Value." *Environment and Planning D: Society and Space* 344 (January 20): 725–44.

Bayetti, Clement, Sushrut Jadhav, and Sumeet Jain. 2019. "Mapping Mental Well-being in India: Initial Reflections on the Role of Psychiatric Spaces." In *The Hospital in South Asia: Health Policies, Care Practices*, ed. Clémence Jullen, Bertrand Lefebvre, and Fabien Provost, 133–77. Paris: Éditions de l'École des Hautes Études Sciences Sociales.

Bear, Laura, Karen Ho, Anna Lowenhaupt Tsing, and Sylvia Yanagisako. 2015. "Gens: A Feminist Manifesto for the Study of Capitalism." *Fieldsights*, March 30. Accessed November 18, 2020. https://culanth.org/fieldsights/gens-a-feminist-manifesto-for-the-study-of-capitalism.

Bechara, Antoine, and Antonio R. Damasio. 2005. "The Somatic Marker Hypothesis: A Neural Theory of Economic Decision." *Games and Economic Behavior* 52, no. 2: 336–72.

Beck, Ulrich. 2009. *What Is Globalization?* Cambridge: Polity.

Bell, Susan E., and Anne E. Figert. 2012. "Medicalization and Pharmaceuticalization at the Intersections: Looking Backward, Sideways and Forward." *Social Science and Medicine* 75, no. 5: 775–83.

Bemme, Dörte. 2019. "Finding 'What Works': Theory of Change, Contingent Universals, and Virtuous Failure in Global Mental Health." *Culture, Medicine, and Psychiatry* 43, no. 4: 574–95.

Benedict, Ruth. 1934. *Patterns of Culture*. Boston: Houghton Mifflin.

Berlin, Isaiah. 1976. *Vico and Herder: Two Studies in the History of Ideas*. London: Hogarth.

Bernard, H. Russell. 2006. *Research Methods in Anthropology: Qualitative and Quantitative Approaches*. Lanham, MD: Altamira.

Bhaskar, Roy. 2010. *Reclaiming Reality: A Critical Introduction to Contemporary Philosophy*. London: Routledge.

Bhugra, Dinesh, and Anastasia Mastrogianni. 2004. "Globalisation and Mental Disorders: Overview with Relation to Depression." *British Journal of Psychiatry* 184 (January): 10–20.

Biehl, João. 2005. *Vita: Life in a Zone of Abandonment*. Berkeley: University of California Press.

Biehl, João. 2007. "Pharmaceuticalization: AIDS Treatment and Global Health Politics." *Anthropological Quarterly* 80, no. 4: 1083–126.

Birch, K., and D. Tyfield. 2013. "Theorizing the Bioeconomy: Biovalue, Biocapital, Bioeconomics or . . . What?" *Science, Technology, and Human Values* 38, no. 3: 299–327.

Blair, R. J. R. 2015. "Psychopathic Traits from an RDoc Perspective." *Current Opinion in Neurobiology* 30: 79–84.

BlueCross BlueShield. 2018. *Major Depression: The Impact on Overall Health*, May 10. Accessed November 18, 2020. https://www.bcbs.com/the-health-of -america/reports/major-depression-the-impact-overall-health#five.

Blumenthal-Barby, J. S. 2013. "Psychiatry's New Manual (DSM-5): Ethical and Conceptual Dimensions." *Journal of Medical Ethics* 40, no. 8. Accessed November 18, 2020. http://jme.bmj.com/content/40/8/531.

Bollnow, Otto Friedrich. 2009. *Das Wesen der Stimmungen—Schriften, Band 1*. Würzburg, Germany: Königshausen and Neumann.

Bourdieu, Pierre. 1990. *The Logic of Practice*. Stanford, CA: Stanford University Press.

Bourdieu, Pierre, and Loïc J. Wacquant. 1992. *An Invitation to Reflexive Sociology*. Chicago: University of Chicago Press.

Bradley, Bridget, and Stefan Ecks. 2018. "Disentangling Family Life and Hair Pulling: Trichotillomania and Relatedness." *Medical Anthropology* 37, no. 7: 568–81.

Braslow, Joel T. 1997. *Mental Ills and Bodily Cures: Psychiatric Treatment in the First Half of the Twentieth Century*. Berkeley: University of California Press.

Brhlikova, Petra, Allyson M. Pollock, and Rachel Manners. 2011. "Global Burden of Disease: Estimates of Depression—How Reliable Is the Epidemiological Evidence?" *Journal of the Royal Society of Medicine* 104, no. 1 (January 1): 25–34.

Brijnath, Bianca, and Josefine Antoniades. 2016. "'I'm Running My Depression': Self-Management of Depression in Neoliberal Australia." *Social Science and Medicine* 152 (March): 1–8.

British Psychological Society (BPS). 2011. "Response to the American Psychiatric Association: DSM-5 Development." Accessed November 18, 2020. http://apps .bps.org.uk/_publicationfiles/consultationresponses/DSM-5%202011%20 -%20BPS% 2oresponse.pdf.

Brodwin, Erin. 2018. "DNA-Testing Company 23andMe Has Signed a $300 Million Deal with a Drug Giant: Here's How to Delete Your Data if That Freaks You Out." *Business Insider*, July 25.

Bromet, Evelyn, Laura Helena Andrade, Irving Hwang, and Nancy A. Sampson et al. 2011. "Cross-National Epidemiology of DSM-IV Major Depressive Episode." *BMC Medicine* 9, no. 1: 90.

Bromet, Evelyn J., and Ezra Susser. 2006. "The Burden of Mental Illness." In *Psychiatric Epidemiology: Searching for the Causes of Mental Disorders*, ed. Ezra Susser, Sharon Schwartz, Alfredo Morabia, and Evelyn J. Bromet, 5–14. Oxford: Oxford University Press.

Bucher, Taina. 2018. *If . . . Then: Algorithmic Power and Politics*. Oxford: Oxford University Press.

Buckley, Chris, and Steven Lee Myers. 2020. "As New Coronavirus Spread, China's Old Habits Delayed Fight." *New York Times*, February 7, 2020.

Bullock, Diane. 2013. "What Ranbaxy's Fraud Says about the State of Big Pharma Research." *NASDAQ News*, November 8. Accessed November 18, 2020. http://www.nasdaq.com/article/what-ranbaxys-fraud-says-about-the-state-of-big-pharma-research-cm298353.

Bunzl, Matti. 1996. "Franz Boas and the Humboldtian Tradition: From Volksgeist and Nationalcharakter to an Anthropological Concept of Culture." In *Volksgeist as Method and Ethic: Essays on Boasian Ethnography and the German Anthropological Tradition*, vol. 8, ed. George W. Stocking Jr. Madison: University of Wisconsin Press.

Burton, Robert. [1621] 2001. *The Anatomy of Melancholy*. New York: New York Review of Books.

Caduff, Carlo. 2014. "On the Verge of Death: Visions of Biological Vulnerability." *Annual Review of Anthropology* 43 (October): 105–21.

Camic, Charles M. 1986. "The Matter of Habit." *American Journal of Sociology* 91, no. 5: 1039–87.

Camic, Charles M. 2015. "Habit: History of the Concept." In *International Encyclopedia of the Social and Behavioral Sciences*, 2d ed., 475–79. Amsterdam: Elsevier.

Candea, Matei. 2018. *Comparison in Anthropology*. Cambridge: Cambridge University Press.

Canguilhem, Georges. [1952] 2001. "The Living and Its Milieu." *Grey Room*, no. 3 (Spring): 6–31.

Carlat, Daniel. 2010. *Unhinged: The Trouble with Psychiatry—A Doctor's Revelations about a Profession in Crisis*. New York: Simon and Schuster.

Carlisle, Clare. 2014. *On Habit (Thinking in Action)*. London: Routledge.

Carrier, James. 2010. "Exchange." In *The Routledge Encyclopedia of Social and Cultural Anthropology*, ed. Alan Barnard and Jonathan Spencer, 271–75. London: Routledge.

Carsten, Janet. 2013. "What Kinship Does—And How." *HAU: Journal of Ethnographic Theory* 3, no. 2: 245–51.

Casey, B. J., Nick Craddock, Bruce N. Cuthbert, Steven E. Hyman, et al. 2013. "DSM-5 and RDoC: Progress in Psychiatry Research?" *Nature Reviews Neuroscience* 14, no. 11: 810–14.

Caspi, Avshalom, and Terrie E. Moffitt. 2018. "All for One and One for All: Mental Disorders in One Dimension." *American Journal of Psychiatry* 175, no. 9: 831–44.

Cassin, Barbara, Emily Apter, Jacques Lezra, and Michael Wood, eds. 2014. *Dictionary of Untranslatables: A Philosophical Lexicon*. Princeton, NJ: Princeton University Press.

Castells, Manuel. 1996. *The Rise of the Network Society*. Oxford: Blackwell.

Cavell, Stanley. 1989. *This New yet Unapproachable America: Lectures after Emerson after Wittgenstein*. Chicago: University of Chicago Press.

CBS News. 2013. "Ranbaxy Whistleblower Reveals How He Exposed Massive Pharmaceutical Fraud." Accessed November 18, 2020. http://www.cbsnews.com/8301-505263_162-57611023/ranbaxy-whistleblower-reveals-how-he-exposed-massive-pharmaceutical-fraud.

Center for Disease Dynamics, Economics and Policy. 2020. "IndiaSIM Model." Accessed November 18, 2020. https://cddep.org/covid-19/india.

Centers for Medicare and Medicaid Services. 2018. *National Health Expenditure Data: Historical*. Accessed June 29, 2021. https://www.cms.gov/Research-Statistics-Data-and-Systems/Statistics-Trends_and-Reports/NationalHealthExpendData/NationalHealthAccountsHistorical.htm.

Center for Systems Science and Engineering, Johns Hopkins University. 2020. "COVID-19 Dashboard." Accessed November 18, 2020. https://www.arcgis.com/apps/opsdashboard/index.html#/bda7594740fd40299423467b48e9ecf6.

Chakrabarty, Dipesh. 2000. *Provincializing Europe: Postcolonial Thought and Historical Difference*. Princeton, NJ: Princeton University Press.

Chang, Ruth. 2015. "Value Incomparability and Incommensurability." In *The Oxford Handbook of Value Theory*, ed. Iwao Hirose and Jonas Olson, 205–25. Oxford: Oxford University Press.

Chisholm, Dan, Kim Sweeny, Peter Sheehan, Bruce Rasmussen, et al. 2016. "Scaling-Up Treatment of Depression and Anxiety: A Global Return on Investment Analysis." *Lancet Psychiatry* 3, no. 5: 415–24.

Choy, Timothy K. 2011. *Ecologies of Comparison: An Ethnography of Endangerment in Hong Kong*. Durham, NC: Duke University Press.

Clark, Andy. 1998. *Being There: Putting Brain, Body, and World Together Again*. Cambridge, MA: MIT Press.

Clarke, Adele E., Janet K. Shim, Laura Mamo, Jennifer Ruth Fosket, and Jennifer R. Fishman. 2003. "Biomedicalization: Technoscientific Transformations of Health, Illness, and U.S. Biomedicine." *American Sociological Review* 68, no. 2: 161–94.

Cloatre, Emilie, and Martyn Pickersgill. 2014. "International Law, Public Health, and the Meanings of Pharmaceuticalization." *New Genetics and Society* 33, no. 4: 434–49.

Cohen, Alex, Vikram Patel, and Harry Minas. 2014. "A Brief History of Global Mental Health." In *Global Mental Health: Principles and Practice*, edited by Vikram Patel, Harry Minas, Alex Cohen, and Martin J. Prince, 3–26. New York: Oxford University Press.

Cohen, Bruce M. Z. 2016. *Psychiatric Hegemony: A Marxist Theory of Mental Illness*. London: Palgrave Macmillan.

Collier, Andrew. 1999. *Being and Worth*. London: Routledge.

Collins, Pamela Y., Vikram Patel, Sarah S. Joestl, Dana March, et al. 2011. "Grand Challenges in Global Mental Health." *Nature* 475, no. 7354: 27–30.

Conrad, Peter. 2005. "The Shifting Engines of Medicalization." *Journal of Health and Social Behavior* 46, no. 1: 3–14.

Conrad, Peter. 2007. *The Medicalization of Society: On the Transformation of Human Conditions into Treatable Disorders*. Baltimore: Johns Hopkins University Press.

Coombs, Nathan, and Ashley Frawley. 2019. "The Value in 'Value': An Exercise for Pluralising Economics Instruction." *International Review of Economics Education* 30 (January): 100–142.

Copeman, Jacob. 2008. "Violence, Non-violence, and Blood Donation in India." *Journal of the Royal Anthropological Institute* 14, no. 2: 278–96.

Copeman, Jacob. 2018. "Exposing Fakes." In *Fake: Anthropological Keywords*, ed. Jacob Copeman and Giovanni da Col, 63–90. Chicago: HAU.

Cordero, Ronald. 2018. "Sartre, Heidegger, and the Origin of Value." *Philosophy and Theology* 30, no. 2: 321–31.

Cosgrove, Lisa, Harold J. Bursztajn, Deborah R. Erlich, Emily E. Wheeler, and Allen F. Shaughnessy. 2013. "Conflicts of Interest and the Quality of Recommendations in Clinical Guidelines." *Journal of Evaluation in Clinical Practice* 19, no. 4: 674–81.

Cowling, Benjamin J., Sheikh Taslim Ali, Tiffany W. Y. Ng, Tim K. Tsang, et al. 2020. "Impact Assessment of Non-Pharmaceutical Interventions against Coronavirus Disease 2019 and Influenza in Hong Kong: An Observational Study." *Lancet Public Health*, no. 5: e279–88.

Cranford, Peter G. 1981. *But for the Grace of God: The Inside Story of the World's Largest Insane Asylum, Milledgeville*. Augusta, GA: Great Pyramid.

Crumley, Carole L. 2005. "Remember How to Organize: Heterarchy across Disciplines." In *Nonlinear Models for Archaeology and Anthropology*, ed. Christopher S. Beekman and William W. Baden, 35–50. London: Routledge.

Csordas, Thomas J. 2002. *Body, Meaning, Healing*. Houndsmills, UK: Palgrave Macmillan.

Cummings, Constance A. 2013. "DSM-5 on Culture: A Significant Advance." *Thefpr.org Blog*, June 27. Accessed November 18, 2020. https://thefprorg .wordpress.com/2013/06/27/dsm-5-on-culture-a-significant-advance.

Cuthbert, Bruce N. 2014. "The RDoC Framework: Facilitating Transition from ICD/DSM to Dimensional Approaches That Integrate Neuroscience and Psychopathology." *World Psychiatry* 13, no. 1: 28–35.

Cvetkovich, Ann. 2012. *Depression: A Public Feeling.* Durham, NC: Duke University Press.

Da Col, Giovanni, and David Graeber. 2011. "Foreword: The Return of Ethnographic Theory." *HAU: Journal of Ethnographic Theory* 1, no. 1: vi–xxxv.

Dalsgaard, Steffen. 2013. "The Commensurability of Carbon: Making Value and Money of Climate Change." *HAU: Journal of Ethnographic Theory* 3, no. 1: 80–98.

Darwin, Charles. [1859] 2008. *On the Origin of Species.* Oxford: Oxford University Press.

Deacon, Terrence W. 2011. *Incomplete Nature: How Mind Emerged from Matter.* New York: W. W. Norton.

Dean, Mitchell. 2014. "Michel Foucault's 'Apology' for Neoliberalism: Lecture Delivered at the British Library on the 30th Anniversary of the Death of Michel Foucault, June 25, 2014." *Journal of Political Power* 7, no. 3: 433–42.

Decker, Hannah S. 2007. "How Kraepelinian Was Kraepelin? How Kraepelinian Are the Neo-Kraepelinians?—From Emil Kraepelin to DSM-III." *History of Psychiatry* 18, no. 3: 337–60.

De Groot, Mary, Ryan Anderson, Kenneth E. Freedland, Ray E. Clouse, and Patrick J. Lustman. 2001. "Association of Depression and Diabetes Complications: A Meta-Analysis." *Psychosomatic Medicine* 63, no. 4: 619–30.

Denig, Carl F. 2017. "Minor Differences of Narcissism: Narcissistic Personality in Germanophone Europe and North America." PhD diss., University of Edinburgh.

Derrida, Jacques. 2016. *Of Grammatology.* Baltimore: Johns Hopkins University Press.

Desjarlais, Robert, Leon Eisenberg, Byron J. Good, and Arthur Kleinman, eds. 1995. *World Mental Health: Priorities, Problems and Responses in Low-Income Countries.* New York: Oxford University Press.

Di Schiena, Raffaella, Olivier Luminet, Betty Chang, and Pierre Philippot. 2013. "Why Are Depressive Individuals Indecisive? Different Modes of Rumination Account for Indecision in Non-clinical Depression." *Cognitive Therapy and Research* 37, no. 4: 713–24.

Dolan, Catherine, and Dinah Rajak, eds. 2016. *The Anthropology of Corporate Social Responsibility.* Oxford: Berghahn.

Downey, Gary Lee, Joseph Dumit, and Sarah Williams. 1995. "Cyborg Anthropology." *Cultural Anthropology* 10, no. 2: 264–69.

Dr. Reddy's Limited. 2006. *Annual Report 2005–2006: Creating Global Enterprise.* Accessed November 18, 2020. http://www.drreddys.com/investors /annualreports.html.

Drugdevelopment-Technology. 2012. "Top Five Expired Blockbuster Drugs." Accessed November 18, 2020. http://www.drugdevelopment-technology .com/features/featuretop-5-expired-blockbuster-drugs.

Dumit, Joseph. 2012. *Drugs for Life: How Pharmaceutical Companies Define Our Health.* Durham, NC: Duke University Press.

Dumit, Joseph. 2018. "The Infernal Alternatives of Corporate Pharmaceutical Research: Abandoning Psychiatry." *Medical Anthropology* 37, no. 1: 59–74.

Dumont, Louis. 1966. *Homo hierarchicus: Essai sur le système des castes*. Paris: Gallimard.

Dumont, Louis. 1975. *La civilisation indienne et nous*. Paris: Armand Colin.

Dumont, Louis. [1980] 2013. "On Value: The Radcliffe-Brown Lecture in Social Anthropology, 1980." *HAU: Journal of Ethnographic Theory* 3, no. 1: 287–315.

Duncker, Karl. 1945. "On Problem-Solving." *Psychological Monographs* 58, no. 5: 1–13.

Durkheim, Émile. [1897] 1951. *Suicide: A Study in Sociology*. Translated by John A. Spaulding and George Simpson. Glencoe, IL: Free Press.

Durkheim, Émile. [1905–1906] 1956. *Education and Sociology*. Translated by Sherwood D. Fox. Glencoe, IL: Free Press.

Ecks, Stefan. 2005. "Pharmaceutical Citizenship: Antidepressant Marketing and the Promise of Demarginalization in India." *Anthropology and Medicine* 12, no. 3: 239–54.

Ecks, Stefan. 2008. "Global Pharmaceutical Markets and Corporate Citizenship: The Case of Novartis' Anti-cancer Drug Glivec." *BioSocieties* 32: 165–81.

Ecks, Stefan. 2010. "Near-Liberalism: Global Corporate Citizenship and Pharmaceutical Marketing in India." In *Asian Biotech: Ethics and Communities of Fate*, ed. Aihwa Ong and Nancy Chen, 144–66. Durham, NC: Duke University Press.

Ecks, Stefan. 2011. "A Polyspherology of Psychopharmaceuticals: Globalization, Capitalism, and Psychiatry." In *Pharmaceutical Self: The Global Shaping of Experience in an Age of Psychopharmacology*, ed. Janis Jenkins, 97–116. Santa Fe, NM: School for Advanced Research Press.

Ecks, Stefan. 2013. *Eating Drugs: Psychopharmaceutical Pluralism in India*. New York: New York University Press.

Ecks, Stefan. 2015. "The Strange Absence of Things in the 'Culture' of DSM-5." *Canadian Medical Association Journal* 188, no. 2: 142–43.

Ecks, Stefan. 2017. "The Public and Private Lives of Psychopharmaceuticals in the Global South." In *The Sedated Society: The Causes and Harms of Our Psychiatric Drugs Epidemic*, ed. James Davies, 249–69. London: Palgrave Macmillan.

Ecks, Stefan. 2020. "A Medical Anthropology of the 'Global Psyche.'" *Medical Anthropology Quarterly* 34, no. 1: 143–47.

Ecks, Stefan. 2021. "Mental Ills for All: Genealogies of the Movement for Global Mental Health." In *The Movement for Global Mental Health: Critical Views from South and Southeast Asia*, ed. William S. Sax and Claudia Lang, 41–64. Amsterdam: Amsterdam University Press.

Ecks, Stefan, and Soumi Basu. 2009. "The Unlicensed Lives of Antidepressants in India: Generic Drugs, Unqualified Practitioners, and Floating Prescriptions." *Transcultural Psychiatry* 46, no. 1: 86–106.

Ecks, Stefan, and Soumi Basu. 2014. "'We Always Live in Fear': Antidepressant Prescriptions by Unlicensed Doctors in India." *Culture, Medicine, and Psychiatry* 38, no. 2: 197–216.

Ecks, Stefan, and Christine Kupfer. 2014. "'What Is Strange Is That We Don't Have More Children Coming to Us': A Habitography of Child Psychiatry and Scholastic Pressure in Calcutta." *Social Science and Medicine* 143: 336–42.

Ecks, Stefan, and William Sax, eds. 2005. "Introduction: Special Issue: The Ills of Marginality: New Perspectives on Subaltern Health in South Asia." *Anthropology and Medicine* 12, no. 3: 239–54.

Ehrenberg, Alain. 2010. *The Weariness of the Self: Diagnosing the History of Depression in the Contemporary Age.* Montreal: McGill-Queen's University Press.

Eilberg-Schwartz, Howard. 1986. *The Human Will in Judaism: The Mishnah's Philosophy of Intention.* Atlanta: Scholars.

Eisenberg, Leon. 2010. "Were We All Asleep at the Switch? A Personal Reminiscence of Psychiatry from 1940 to 2010." *Acta Psychiatrica Scandinavica* 122, no. 2: 89–102.

Eli Lilly. 2003. "Answers to Shareholders." Accessed November 18, 2020. https:// investor.lilly.com/financial-information/annual-reports.

Elliott, Carl. 2011. "Enhancement Technologies and the Modern Self." *Journal of Medicine and Philosophy* 36, no. 4: 364–74.

Elliott, Carl, and Tod Chambers, eds. 2004. *Prozac as a Way of Life.* Chapel Hill: University of North Carolina Press.

Epperson, C. Neill, Meir Steiner, S. Ann Hartlage, Elias Eriksson, et al. 2012. "Premenstrual Dysphoric Disorder: Evidence for A New Category for DSM-5." *American Journal of Psychiatry* 169, no. 5: 465–75.

Ernst, Waltraud. 1991. *Mad Tales from the Raj: The European Insane in British India, 1800–1858.* London: Routledge.

Ernst, Waltraud. 1997. "Idioms of Madness and Colonial Boundaries: The Case of the European and 'Native' Mentally Ill in Early Nineteenth-Century British India." *Comparative Studies in Society and History* 39: 153–81.

Espeland, Wendy Nelson, and Mitchell L. Stevens. 1998. "Commensuration as a Social Process." *Annual Review of Sociology* 24, no. 1: 313–43.

Espeland, Wendy Nelson, and Stacy E. Lom. 2015. "Noticing Numbers: How Quantification Changes What We See and What We Don't." In *Making Things Valuable,* ed. Martin Kornberger, Lise Justesen, Jan Mouritsen, and Anders Koed Madsen. Oxford: Oxford University Press. doi:10.1093/acprof :oso/9780198712282.003.0002.

European Parliament. 2019. "Regulation (EU) 2019/6 of the European Parliament and of the Council of 11 December 2018 on Veterinary Medicinal Products and Repealing Directive 2001/82/EC." Accessed June 27, 2021. https://eur-lex .europa.eu/eli/reg/2019/6/oj.

Everett, Caleb. 2017. *Numbers and the Making of Us: Counting and the Course of Human Cultures.* Cambridge, MA: Harvard University Press.

Faris, Robert E. Lee, and Warren H. Dunham. 1939. *Mental Disorders in Urban Areas: An Ecological Study of Schizophrenia and Other Psychoses.* New York: Hafner.

Fassin, Didier. 2018. *Life: A Critical User's Manual*. Cambridge: Polity.

Fein, Elizabeth. 2016. "Our Circuits, Ourselves: What the Autism Spectrum Can Tell Us about the Research Domain Criteria Project (RDoC) and the Neurogenetic Transformation of Diagnosis." *BioSocieties* 11, no. 2: 175–98.

Feinstein, Alvan R. 1970. "The Pre-therapeutic Classification of Co-morbidity in Chronic Disease." *Journal of Chronic Diseases* 23, no. 7: 455–68.

Ferguson, James, and Akhil Gupta. 2002. "Spatializing States: Toward an Ethnography of Neoliberal Governmentality." *American Ethnologist* 29, no. 4: 981–1002.

Fernando, Suman. 2014. *Mental Health Worldwide: Culture, Globalization and Development*. New York: Palgrave Macmillan.

Ferrari, Joseph R. 1991. "Compulsive Procrastination: Some Self-Reported Characteristics." *Psychological Reports* 68, no. 2: 455–58.

Fibiger, H. Christian. 2012. "Psychiatry, the Pharmaceutical Industry, and the Road to Better Therapeutics." *Schizophrenia Bulletin* 38, no. 4: 649–50.

Fischer, Bernd. 1995. *Das Eigene und das Eigentliche: Klopstock, Herder, Fichte, Kleist: Episoden aus der Konstruktionsgeschichte nationaler Intentionalitäten*. Berlin: Erich Schmidt.

Fisher, Jill A., Marci D. Cottingham, and Corey A. Kalbaugh. 2015. "Peering into the Pharmaceutical 'Pipeline': Investigational Drugs, Clinical Trials, and Industry Priorities." *Social Science and Medicine* 131: 322–30.

Fitzgerald, Des. 2017. *Tracing Autism: Uncertainty, Ambiguity, and the Affective Labor of Neuroscience*. Seattle: University of Washington Press.

Foley, Duncan K. 2000. "Recent Developments in the Labor Theory of Value." *Review of Radical Political Economics* 321: 1–39.

Fond, Guillaume, Anderson Loundou, Nora Hamdani, Wahid Boukouaci, et al. 2014. "Anxiety and Depression Comorbidities in Irritable Bowel Syndrome (IBS): A Systematic Review and Meta-Analysis." *European Archives of Psychiatry and Clinical Neuroscience* 264, no. 8: 651–60.

Fossati, Philippe, Anne-Marie Ergis, and J. F. Allilaire. 2002. "Executive Functioning in Unipolar Depression: A Review." *Encephale* 28, no. 2: 97–107.

Foucault, Michel. [1966] 2005. *The Order of Things*. London: Routledge.

Foucault, Michel. 1975. *Surveiller et punir: Naissance de la prison*. Paris: Gallimard.

Foucault, Michel. 1984. *Histoire de la sexualité: Le souci de soi*. Paris: Gallimard.

Foucault, Michel. 2008. *The Birth of Biopolitics: Lectures at the Collège de France, 1978–1979*, ed. Michael Senellart. Houndmills, UK: Palgrave Macmillan.

Fox, Richard G., and Andre Gingrich, eds. 2002. *Anthropology, by Comparison*. London: Routledge.

Frances, Allen. 2009. "A Warning Sign on the Road to DSM-V: Beware of Its Unintended Consequences." *Psychiatric Times* 26, no. 8: 1–4. Accessed November 18, 2020. https://www.psychiatrictimes.com/articles/warning-sign-road-dsm-v-beware-its-unintended-consequences.

Frances, Allen. 2010. "Good Grief." *New York Times*, August 14.

Frances, Allen, and A. M. Cooper. 1981. "Descriptive and Dynamic Psychiatry: A Perspective on DSM-III." *American Journal of Psychiatry* 138, no. 9: 1198–202.

Frank, Robert. 2004. *Globalisierung "alternativer" Medizin: Homöopathie und Ayurveda in Deutschland und Indien.* Bielefeld, Germany: Transcript.

Freeman, R. Edward. 2010. *Strategic Management: A Stakeholder Approach.* Cambridge: Cambridge University Press.

French, Peter A. 1979. "The Corporation as a Moral Person." *American Philosophical Quarterly* 16, no. 3: 207–15.

Friedli, Lynne. 2009. *Mental Health, Resilience and Inequalities.* Copenhagen: WHO Regional Office for Europe.

Friedman, Thomas L. 2005. *The World Is Flat: A Brief History of the Twenty-first Century.* London: Penguin.

Friston, Karl. 2013. "Life as We Know It." *Journal of the Royal Society Interface* 10, no. 86: 20130475.

Frost, Randy O., and Deanna L. Shows. 1993. "The Nature and Measurement of Compulsive Indecisiveness." *Behaviour Research and Therapy* 31, no. 7: 683–92.

Fu, Cynthia H., and Sergi G. Costafreda. 2013. "Neuroimaging-based Biomarkers in Psychiatry: Clinical Opportunities of a Paradigm Shift." *Canadian Journal of Psychiatry* 58, no. 9: 499–508.

Fuller, Christopher J. 1984. *Servants of the Goddess: The Priests of a South Indian Temple.* Cambridge: Cambridge University Press.

Fuller, Christopher. 1988. "The Hindu Pantheon and the Legitimization of Hierarchy." *Man* (n.s.) 23: 19–39.

Gabble, Ravinder, and Jillian Clare Kohler. 2014. "To Patent or Not to Patent? The Case of Novartis' Cancer Drug Glivec in India." *Globalization and Health* 10, no. 1. https://doi.org/10.1186/1744-8603-10-3.

Gandhi, Mohandas K. 1986. *The Moral and Political Writings of Mahatma Gandhi, Volume 2: Truth and Non-violence,* ed. Raghavan Iyer. Oxford: Clarendon.

Geertz, Clifford. 1973. *The Interpretation of Cultures.* New York: Basic.

Geppert, C. 2017. "Introduction: More Dives and Intellectual Jujitsu." *Psychiatric Times* 34, no. 5. Accessed November 18, 2020. http://www.psychiatrictimes.com/special-reports/introduction-more-dives-and-intellectual-jujitsu.

Gibson, James J. 1977. "The Theory of Affordances." In *Perceiving, Acting, and Knowing: Toward an Ecological Psychology,* ed. Robert Shaw and John Bransford. Hillsdale, NJ: Erlbaum.

Glenn, Evelyn Nakano. 2008. "Yearning for Lightness: Transnational Circuits in the Marketing and Consumption of Skin Lighteners." *Gender and Society* 22, no. 3: 281–302.

Glimcher, Paul W., Colin F. Camerer, Ernst Fehr, and Russell A. Poldrack. 2014. "Introduction: A Brief History of Neuroeconomics." In *Neuroeconomics,* ed. Paul W. Glimcher, Colin F. Camerer, Ernst Fehr, and Russell A. Poldrack. London: Academic.

Global Reporting Initiative and UN Global Compact. 2018. *Integrating the SDGs into Corporate Reporting: A Practical Guide.* Accessed November 18, 2020. http://sdghelpdesk.unescap.org/sites/default/files/2020-04/GRI_UNGC _Reporting-on-SDGs_Practical_Guide.pdf.

Goffman, Erving. 2009. *Stigma: Notes on the Management of Spoiled Identity.* New York: Simon and Schuster.

Goodale, Mark. 2006. "Ethical Theory as Social Practice." *American Anthropologist* 108, no. 1: 25–37.

Goodman, Nelson. 1973. *Fact, Fiction, and Forecast.* Indianapolis: Bobbs-Merrill.

Goodman, Nelson. 1976. *Languages of Art: An Approach to a Theory of Symbols.* Indianapolis: Hackett.

Goodman, Nelson. 1978. *Ways of Worldmaking.* Indianapolis: Hackett.

Goodman, Nelson. 1984. *On Mind and Other Matters.* Cambridge, MA: Harvard University Press.

Goodman, Nelson. 1992. "Seven Strictures of Similarity." In *How Classification Works*, ed. Mary Douglas and David Hull. Edinburgh: Edinburgh University Press.

Gordon, Joshua. 2017. "The Future of RDoC." June 5. Accessed November 18, 2020. https://www.nimh.nih.gov/About/Director/Messages/2017/The -Future-Of-RDoC.Shtml.

Gordon, Joshua. 2019. "A Bench-to-Bedside Story: The Development of a Treatment for Postpartum Depression." March 20. Accessed November 18, 2020. https://www.nimh.nih.gov/About/Director/Messages/2019/A-Bench -To-Bedside-Story-The-Development-Of-A-Treatment-For-Postpartum -Depression.shtml.

Graeber, David. 2001. *Toward an Anthropological Theory of Value: The False Coin of Our Own Dreams.* New York: Palgrave.

Graeber, David. 2005. "Value: Anthropological Theories of Value." In *A Handbook of Economic Anthropology*, ed. James G. Carrier. Cheltenham, UK: Edward Elgar.

Graeber, David. 2011. *Debt: The First 5000 Years.* London: Penguin.

Graeber, David. 2013. "It Is Value That Brings Universes into Being." *HAU: Journal of Ethnographic Theory* 32: 219–43.

Graeber, David. 2019. *Bullshit Jobs: A Theory.* New York: Simon and Schuster.

Grear, Anna. 2007. "Challenging Corporate 'Humanity': Legal Disembodiment, Embodiment and Human Rights." *Human Rights Law Review* 7, no. 3: 511–43.

Greenberg, Gary. 2010. "Inside the Battle to Define Mental Illness." *Wired*, December 27. Accessed February 3, 2015. http://www.wired.com/2010/12/ff _dsmv.

Greenberg, Gary. 2013. "The Psychiatric Drug Crisis." *New Yorker*, September 3. Accessed November 18, 2020. http://www.newyorker.com/Tech/Elements /The-Psychiatric-Drug-Crisis.

Greene, Jeremy A. 2014. *Generic: The Unbranding of Modern Medicine.* Baltimore: Johns Hopkins University Press.

Greenslit, Nathan. 2005. "Depression and Consumption: Psychopharmaceuticals, Branding, and New Identity Practices." *Culture, Medicine and Psychiatry* 29, no. 4: 477–502.

Gronfein, William. 1985. "Psychotropic Drugs and the Origins of Deinstitutionalization." *Social Problems* 32, no. 5: 437–54.

Gudeman, Stephen. 2016. *Anthropology and Economy*. Cambridge: Cambridge University Press.

Gumbrecht, Hans Ulrich. 2012. *Atmosphere, Mood, Stimmung: On a Hidden Potential of Literature*. Stanford, CA: Stanford University Press.

Habermas, Jürgen. 1971. *Knowledge and Human Interests*. Translated by Jeremy J. Shapiro. Boston: Beacon.

Hacking, Ian. 2007. "Kinds of People: Moving Targets." *Proceedings of the British Academy* 151: 285–318.

Hacking, Ian. 2013. "Lost in the Forest." *London Review of Books* 35, no. 15: 7–8.

Hale, Thomas, Anna Petherick, Toby Phillips, and Samuel Webster. 2020. "Variation in Government Responses to COVID-19: Version 4.0." Blavatnik School Working Paper, April 7. https://www.bsg.ox.ac.uk/sites/default/files/2021-06/BSG-WP-2020-032-v12_0.pdf.

Halliburton, Murphy. 2017. *India and the Patent Wars: Pharmaceuticals in the New Intellectual Property Regime*. Ithaca, NY: Cornell University Press.

Halliburton, Murphy. 2021. "The House of Love and the Mental Health Hospital: Zones of Care and Recovery in South India" In *The Movement for Global Mental Health*, ed. William S. Sax and Claudia Lang, 213–42. Amsterdam: Amsterdam University Press.

Halman, Loek, and John Gelissen. 2019. "Values in Life Domains in a Cross-National Perspective." *KZfSS Kölner Zeitschrift für Soziologie und Sozialpsychologie* 71: 519–43.

Halton, Eugene. 1995. *Bereft of Reason: On the Decline of Social Thought and Prospects for Its Renewal*. Chicago: University of Chicago Press.

Haraway, Donna J. 2008. *When Species Meet*. Minneapolis: University of Minnesota Press.

Haraway, Donna J. 2016. *Staying with the Trouble: Making Kin in the Chthulucene*. Durham, NC: Duke University Press.

Hardon, Anita, and Emilia Sanabria. 2017. "Fluid Drugs: Revisiting the Anthropology of Pharmaceuticals." *Annual Review of Anthropology* 46: 117–32.

Hardt, Michael, and Antonio Negri. 2017. *Assembly*. Oxford: Oxford University Press.

Harrington, Anne. 2019. *Mind Fixers: Psychiatry's Troubled Search for the Biology of Mental Illness*. New York: W. W. Norton.

Harris, John. 1985. *The Value of Life: An Introduction to Medical Ethics*. London: Routledge and Kegan Paul

Harvey, David, 2005. *A Brief History of Neoliberalism*. Oxford: Oxford University Press.

Harvey, David. 2018. *A Companion to Marx's Capital: The Complete Edition*. London: Verso.

Hausman, Daniel M. 2015. *Valuing Health: Well-Being, Freedom, and Suffering.* Oxford: Oxford University Press.

Hayden, Cori. 2007. "A Generic Solution? Pharmaceuticals and the Politics of the Similar in Mexico." *Current Anthropology* 48, no. 4: 475–95.

Hayden, Cori. 2011. "No Patent, No Generic: Pharmaceutical Access and the Politics of the Copy." In *Making and Unmaking Intellectual Property*, ed. Mario Biagioli, Peter Jaszi, and Martha Woodmansee, 285–304. Chicago: University of Chicago Press.

Hayden, Cori. 2013. "Distinctively Similar: A Generic Problem." uc *Davis Law Review* 47, no. 2: 601–32.

Hayek, Friedrich. 2011. *The Constitution of Liberty: The Definitive Edition*, ed. Ronald Hamowy. Chicago: University of Chicago Press.

Healy, David. 1997. *The Antidepressant Era*. Cambridge, MA: Harvard University Press.

Healy, David. 2008. "The Intersection of Psychopharmacology and Psychiatry in the Second Half of the Twentieth Century." In *History of Psychiatry and Medical Psychology*, eds. Edwin R. Wallace and John Gach, 419–42. New York: Springer.

Healy, David, Andrew Herxheimer, and David B. Menkes. 2007. "Antidepressants and Violence: Problems at the Interface of Medicine and Law." *International Journal of Risk and Safety in Medicine* 19, nos. 1–2: 17–33.

Heaton, Matthew M. 2013. *Black Skin, White Coats: Nigerian Psychiatrists, Decolonization, and the Globalization of Psychiatry*. Athens: Ohio University Press.

Heesterman, Johannes C. 1985. *The Inner Conflict of Tradition: Essays in Indian Ritual, Kingship, and Society*. Chicago: University of Chicago Press.

Heesterman, Johannes C. 1993. *The Broken World of Sacrifice: An Essay in Ancient Indian Ritual*. Chicago: University of Chicago Press.

Heidegger, Martin. [1927] 1993. *Sein und Zeit*, 17th ed. Tübingen, Germany: Max Niemeyer.

Heidegger, Martin. 1949. *Über den Humanismus*. Frankfurt am Main: Vittorio Klostermann.

Heim, Lale, and Susanne Schaal. 2014. "Rates and Predictors of Mental Stress in Rwanda: Investigating the Impact of Gender, Persecution, Readiness to Reconcile and Religiosity via a Structural Equation Model." *International Journal of Mental Health Systems* 8, no. 1: 37.

Heinz, Andreas. 2014. *Der Begriff der Psychischen Krankheit*. Frankfurt am Main: Suhrkamp.

Helm, Toby, Emma Graham-Harrison, and Robin McKie. 2020. "How Did Britain Get Its Coronavirus Response So Wrong?" *Guardian*, April 19.

Helman, Cecil. 2007. *Culture, Health and Illness*. London: Hodder Arnold.

Helmreich, Stefan. 2015. *Sounding the Limits of Life: Essays in the Anthropology of Biology and Beyond*. Princeton, NJ: Princeton University Press.

Henje Blom, Eva, Larissa G. Duncan, Tiffany C. Ho, Colm G. Connolly, et al. 2014. "The Development of an RDoC-Based Treatment Program for Adolescent

Depression: Training for Awareness, Resilience, and Action (TARA)." *Frontiers in Human Neuroscience* 8: 630. Accessed November 18, 2020. http://journal.frontiersin.org/article/10.3389/fnhum.2014.00630/full.

Herder, Johann Gottfried. 1965. *Ideen zur Philosophie der Geschichte der Menschheit, Band 1*, ed. Heinz Stolpe. Berlin: Aufbau.

Herzberg, David L. 2009. *Happy Pills in America: From Miltown to Prozac.* Baltimore: Johns Hopkins University Press.

Hickel, Jason, and Naomi Haynes, eds. 2018. *Hierarchy and Value: Comparative Perspectives on Moral Order.* Oxford: Berghahn.

Hidaka, Brandon H. 2012. "Depression as a Disease of Modernity: Explanations for Increasing Prevalence." *Journal of Affective Disorders* 140, no. 3: 205–14.

Hills, Michael D. 2002. "Kluckhohn and Strodtbeck's Values Orientation Theory." *Online Readings in Psychology and Culture* 4, no. 4. Accessed November 18, 2020. https://doi.org/10.9707/2307-0919.1040.

Hinton, Devon E., and Laurence J. Kirmayer, 2017. "The Flexibility Hypothesis of Healing." *Culture, Medicine, and Psychiatry* 41, no. 1: 3–34.

Hirose, Iwao, and Jason Olson, eds. 2015. *The Oxford Handbook of Value Theory.* Oxford: Oxford University Press.

Hobbes, Thomas. [1651] 1998. *Leviathan.* Oxford: Oxford University Press.

Hofstede, Geert. 2001. *Culture's Consequences: Comparing Values, Behaviors, Institutions, and Organizations across Nations.* Thousand Oaks, CA: SAGE.

Homans, George C. 1974. *Social Behavior: Its Elementary Forms.* Oxford: Harcourt Brace Jovanovich.

Homedes, Núria, and Antonio Ugalde. 2005. "Multisource Drug Policies in Latin America: Survey of 10 Countries." *Bulletin of the World Health Organization* 83, no. 1: 64–70.

Hornberger, Julia. 2018. "From Drug Safety to Drug Security: A Contemporary Shift in the Policing of Health." *Medical Anthropology Quarterly* 32, no. 3: 365–83.

Horwitz, Allan V., and Gerald N. Grob. 2011. "The Checkered History of American Psychiatric Epidemiology." *Milbank Quarterly* 89, no. 4: 628–57.

Horwitz, Allan V., and Jerome C. Wakefield. 2007. *The Loss of Sadness: How Psychiatry Transformed Normal Sorrow into Depressive Disorder.* Oxford: Oxford University Press.

Ingleby, David. 2014. "How 'Evidence-Based' Is the Movement for Global Mental Health?" *Disability and the Global South* 1, no. 2: 203–26.

Ingold, Tim. 2002. *The Perception of the Environment: Essays on Livelihood, Dwelling and Skill.* London: Routledge.

Ingold, Tim. 2014. "That's Enough about Ethnography!" *HAU: Journal of Ethnographic Theory* 4, no. 1: 383–95.

Insel, Thomas R. 2008. "Assessing the Economic Costs of Serious Mental Illness." *American Journal of Psychiatry* 165, no. 6: 663–65.

Insel, Thomas R. 2013. "Transforming Diagnosis." *NIMH Director's Blog*, April 29. Accessed November 18, 2020. https://www.nimh.nih.gov/About/Directors/Thomas-Insel/blog/2013/Transforming-Diagnosis.shtml.

Insel, Thomas R. 2014. "Mental Health in Davos." *NIMH Director's Blog*, January 27. Accessed November 18, 2020. https://www.nimh.nih.gov/About /Directors/Thomas-Insel/blog/2014/Mental-Health-In-Davos.shtml.

Insel, Thomas R., and Jeffrey A. Lieberman. 2013. "DSM-5 and RDoC: Shared Interests." Press release, National Institutes of Mental Health, May 13. Accessed November 18, 2020. http://www.nimh.nih.gov/news/science-news /2013/dsm-5-and-rdoc-shared-interests.shtml.

Insel, Thomas R., Valerie Voon, Jeffrey S. Nye, V. J. Brown, et al. 2013. "Innovative Solutions to Novel Drug Development in Mental Health." *Neuroscience and Biobehavioral Reviews* 37, no. 10: 2438–44.

International Monetary Fund (IMF). 2020. *World Economic Outlook: The Great Lockdown*. Washington, DC: International Monetary Fund.

Jadhav, Sushrut. 2007. "Dhis and Dhāt: Evidence of Semen Retention Syndrome amongst White Britons." *Anthropology and Medicine* 14, no. 3: 229–39.

Jain, Sumeet, and Sushrut Jadhav. 2009. "Pills That Swallow Policy: Clinical Ethnography of a Community Mental Health Program in Northern India." *Transcultural Psychiatry* 46, no. 1: 60–85.

Jenkins, Janis H. 2015. *Extraordinary Conditions: Culture and Experience in Mental Illness*. Berkeley: University of California Press.

Jenkins, Richard. 1982. "Pierre Bourdieu and the Reproduction of Determinism." *Sociology* 16, no. 2: 270–81.

Jevons, William S. [1871] 2004. "The Theory of Political Economy." In *The History of Economic Thought: A Reader*, ed. Steven G. Medema and Warren J. Samuels, 432–62. London: Routledge.

Johnson, Mark. 2017. *Embodied Mind, Meaning, and Reason: How Our Bodies Give Rise to Understanding*. Chicago: University of Chicago Press.

Johnston, Mark. 2006. "Hylomorphism." *Journal of Philosophy* 103, no. 12: 652–98.

Judson, D. H. 1989. "The Convergence of Neo-Ricardian and Embodied Energy Theories of Value and Price." *Ecological Economics* 1, no. 3: 261–81.

Kahneman, Daniel. 2011. *Thinking, Fast and Slow*. New York: Farrar, Straus and Giroux.

Kaiser, Bonnie N., Emily E. Haroz, Brandon A. Kohrt, Paul A. Bolton, et al. 2015. "'Thinking Too Much': A Systematic Review of a Common Idiom of Distress." *Social Science and Medicine* 147: 170–83.

Kaiser, Robert, and Heiko Prange. 2004. "The Reconfiguration of National Innovation Systems: The Example of German Biotechnology." *Research Policy* 33, no. 3: 395–408.

Kapur, Ravi L. 2004. "The Story of Community Mental Health in India." In *Mental Health: An Indian Perspective, 1946–2003*, ed. S. P. Agarwal, 92–100. New Delhi: Elsevier.

Kasper, Siegfried, and Göran Hajak. 2013. "The Efficacy of Agomelatine in Previously-Treated Depressed Patients." *European Neuropsychopharmacology* 23, no. 8: 814–21.

Katz, David. 2020. "Opinion: Is Our Fight Against Coronavirus Worse Than the Disease?" *New York Times*, March 20, 2020.

Keck, Frédéric. 2020. *Avian Reservoirs: Virus Hunters and Birdwatchers in Chinese Sentinel Posts*. Durham, NC: Duke University Press.

Kendell, Robert E. 1989. "Clinical Validity." In *The Validity of Psychiatric Diagnosis*, ed. L. N. Robins and J. E. Barrett, 305–21. New York: Raven.

Kessler, Ronald C., Martin B. Keller, and Hans-Ulrich Wittchen. 2001. "The Epidemiology of Generalized Anxiety Disorder." *Psychiatric Clinics of North America* 24, no. 1: 19–39.

Kierans, Ciara. 2020. *Chronic Failures: Kidneys, Regimes of Care, and the Mexican State*. New Brunswick, NJ: Rutgers University Press.

King, Marissa, and Connor Essick. 2013. "The Geography of Antidepressant, Antipsychotic, and Stimulant Utilization in the United States." *Health and Place* 20: 32–38.

Kirmayer, Laurence J. 2002. "Psychopharmacology in a Globalizing World: The Use of Antidepressants in Japan." *Transcultural Psychiatry* 39, no. 3: 295–322.

Kirmayer, Laurence J., and Daina Crafa. 2014. "What Kind of Science for Psychiatry?" *Frontiers in Human Neuroscience* 8: 1–12.

Kirmayer, Laurence J., Ana Gómez-Carrillo, and Samuel Veissière. 2017. "Culture and Depression in Global Mental Health: An Ecosocial Approach to the Phenomenology of Psychiatric Disorders." *Social Science and Medicine* 183: 163–68.

Kirmayer, Laurence J., and G. Eric Jarvis. 2007. "Depression across Cultures." In *Textbook of Mood Disorders*, ed. Dan J. Stein, Alan F. Schatzberg, and David J. Kupfer, 699–1218. Washington, DC: American Psychiatric Press.

Kirmayer, Laurence J., and Norman Sartorius. 2007. "Cultural Models and Somatic Syndromes." *Psychosomatic Medicine* 69, no. 9: 832–40.

Kirsch, Irving. 2010. *The Emperor's New Drugs: Exploding the Antidepressant Myth*. New York: Basic.

Kitanaka, Junko. 2011. *Depression in Japan: Psychiatric Cures for a Society in Distress*. Princeton, NJ: Princeton University Press.

Kleinman, Arthur. 1980. *Patients and Healers in the Context of Culture: An Exploration of the Borderland between Anthropology, Medicine, and Psychiatry*. Berkeley: University of California Press.

Kluckhohn, Clyde. 1951. "Values and Value-Orientations in the Theory of Action: An Exploration in Definition and Classification." In *Towards a General Theory of Action*, ed. Talcott Parsons and Edward A. Shils, 388–433. Cambridge, MA: Harvard University Press.

Kohn, Eduardo. 2013. *How Forests Think: Toward an Anthropology beyond the Human*. Berkeley: University of California Press.

Kopytoff, Igor. 1986. "The Cultural Biography of Things: Commoditization." In *The Social Life of Things: Commodities in Cultural Perspective*, ed. Arjun Appadurai, 65–91. Cambridge: Cambridge University Press.

KPMG. 2019. "CSR Audit Services." Accessed June 27, 2021. https://assets.kpmg /content/dam/kpmg/in/pdf/2019/01/CSR-Audit-Services.pdf.

Kramer, Peter D. 1993. *Listening to Prozac: A Psychiatrist Explores Antidepressant Drugs and the Remaking of the Self.* New York: Viking.

Kroeber, A. L., and Clyde Kluckhohn. 1952. *Culture: A Critical Review of Concepts and Definitions.* Papers, Peabody Museum of Archaeology and Ethnology, Harvard University, vol. 47, no. 1. Cambridge, MA: Harvard University.

Kuehner, Christine. 2017. "Why Is Depression More Common among Women Than among Men?" *Lancet Psychiatry* 4, no. 2: 146–58.

Kuhn, Thomas S. 1982. "Commensurability, Comparability, Communicability." *PSA: Proceedings of the Biennial Meeting of the Philosophy of Science Association 1982,* 2: 669–88.

Kumra, Gautam. 2006. "One Business's Commitment to Society: An Interview with the President of the Novartis Foundation for Sustainable Development." *McKinsey Quarterly,* no. 3. Accessed November 18, 2020. http://www .mckinseyquarterly.com/Article_Abstract.Aspx?Ar=1820&L2=33&L3=11.

Kupfer, David J., Michael B. First, and Darrel A. Regier. 2002. *A Research Agenda for DSM-V.* Washington, DC: American Psychiatric Association.

Kutchins, Herb, and Stuart A. Kirk. 1997. *Making Us Crazy: The Psychiatric Bible and the Creation of Mental Disorders.* New York: Free Press.

Lacina, Linda. 2020. "Nearly 3 Billion People around the Globe under COVID-19 Lockdowns." World Economic Forum, March 26. Accessed November 18, 2020. https://www.weforum.org/agenda/2020/03/todays-coronavirus -updates.

Laidlaw, James. 2014. *The Subject of Virtue: An Anthropology of Ethics and Freedom.* Cambridge: Cambridge University Press.

Lakoff, Andrew. 2004. "The Private Life of Numbers: Pharmaceutical Marketing in Post-welfare Argentina." In *Global Assemblages: Technology, Politics, and Ethics as Anthropological Problems,* edited by Aihwa Ong and Stephen J. Collier, 194–213. Oxford: Blackwell.

Lakoff, Andrew. 2017. *Unprepared: Global Health in a Time of Emergency.* Oakland: University of California Press.

LaMattina, John L. 2013. *Devalued and Distrusted: Can the Pharmaceutical Industry Restore Its Broken Image?* Hoboken, NJ: John Wiley and Sons.

Lambek, Michael. 2008. "Value and Virtue." *Anthropological Theory* 82: 133–57.

Latour, Bruno. 1987. *Science in Action: How to Follow Scientists and Engineers through Society.* Cambridge, MA: Harvard University Press.

Latour, Bruno. 1995. *We Have Never Been Modern.* Cambridge, MA: Harvard University Press.

Latour, Bruno. 2004. "Why Has Critique Run Out of Steam? From Matters of Fact to Matters of Concern." *Critical Inquiry* 302: 225–48.

Latour, Bruno. 2005. *Reassembling the Social: An Introduction to Actor-Network-Theory.* Oxford: Oxford University Press.

Latour, Bruno. 2009. "Spheres and Networks. Two Ways to Reinterpret Globalization." *Harvard Design Magazine* 30: 138–44.

Lemke, Thomas. 2001. "The Birth of Bio-Politics: Michel Foucault's Lectures at the Collège de France on Neo-Liberal Governmentality." *Economy and Society* 30: 190–207.

Lemke, Thomas. 2011. *Biopolitics: An Advanced Introduction.* New York: New York University Press.

Lenze, Eric J., Benoit H. Mulsant, M. Katherine Shear, Herbert C. Schulberg, et al. 2000. "Comorbid Anxiety Disorders in Depressed Elderly Patients." *American Journal of Psychiatry* 157, no. 5: 722–28.

Lévi-Strauss, Claude. 1963. *Structural Anthropology.* New York: Basic.

Lévi-Strauss, Claude. 1966. *The Savage Mind.* Chicago: University of Chicago Press.

Lexchin, Joel. 2018. "The Pharmaceutical Industry in Contemporary Capitalism." *Monthly Review* 69, no. 10: 37–50.

Leykin, Yan, and Robert J. DeRubeis. 2010. "Decision-Making Styles and Depressive Symptomatology." *Judgment and Decision Making* 5, no. 7: 506–15.

Liebert, Rachel, and Nicola Gavey. 2009. "'There Are Always Two Sides to These Things': Managing the Dilemma of Serious Adverse Effects from SSRIs." *Social Science and Medicine* 68, no. 10: 1882–91.

Lilienfeld, Scott O., and Michael T. Treadway. 2016. "Clashing Diagnostic Approaches: DSM-ICD versus RDoC." *Annual Review of Clinical Psychology* 12, no. 1: 435–63.

LiPuma, Edward, and Benjamin Lee. 2004. *Financial Derivatives and the Globalization of Risk.* Durham, NC: Duke University Press.

Littlewood, Roland, and Maurice Lipsedge. 1987. "The Butterfly and the Serpent: Culture, Psychopathology and Biomedicine." *Culture, Medicine, and Psychiatry* 11, no. 3: 289–335.

Livingston, Julie. 2019. *Self-Devouring Growth: A Planetary Parable as Told from Southern Africa.* Durham, NC: Duke University Press.

Lock, Margaret. 2001. "The Tempering of Medical Anthropology: Troubling Natural Categories." *Medical Anthropology Quarterly* 15, no. 4: 478–92.

Lock, Margaret, Wylie Burke, John Dupré, Hannah Landecker, et al. 2015. "Comprehending the Body in the Era of the Epigenome." *Current Anthropology* 56, no. 2: 163–77.

Lohoff, Falk W. 2010. "Overview of the Genetics of Major Depressive Disorder." *Current Psychiatry Reports* 12, no. 6: 539–46.

Lorant, Vincent, Christophe Croux, Scott Weich, Denise Deliège, et al. 2007. "Depression and Socio-economic Risk Factors: Seven-Year Longitudinal Population Study." *British Journal of Psychiatry* 190, no. 4: 293–98.

Lovell, Anne M. 2014. "The World Health Organization and the Contested Beginnings of Psychiatric Epidemiology as an International Discipline: One Rope, Many Strands." *International Journal of Epidemiology* 43, supp. 1: 16–18.

Luhmann, Niklas. 2006. "System as Difference." *Organization* 13, no. 1: 37–57.

Lund, Crick, Mary De Silva, Sophie Plagerson, Sara Cooper, et al. 2011. "Poverty and Mental Disorders: Breaking the Cycle in Low-Income and Middle-Income Countries." *The Lancet* 378, no. 9801: 1502–14.

Lupien, Sonia. J., M. Sasseville, Nathe François, Charles Édouard Giguère, et al. 2017. "The DSM5/RDoC Debate on the Future of Mental Health Research: Implication for Studies on Human Stress and Presentation of the Signature Bank." *Stress* 20, no. 1: 2–18.

Lutz, Catherine A. 2011. *Unnatural Emotions: Everyday Sentiments on a Micronesian Atoll and Their Challenge to Western Theory.* Chicago: University of Chicago Press.

Malabou, Catherine. 2008. "Addiction and Grace: Preface to Félix Ravaisson's 'Of Habit.'" In *Of Habit,* by Félix Ravaisson, vii–xx. London: Continuum.

Marcks, Brook A., Douglas W. Woods, and Jaime L. Ridosko. 2005. "The Effects of Trichotillomania Disclosure on Peer Perceptions and Social Acceptability." *Body Image* 2, no. 3: 299–306.

Marcus, George E. 1995. "Ethnography in/of the World System: The Emergence of Multi-sited Ethnography." *Annual Review of Anthropology* 24, no. 1: 95–117.

Markus, Hazel Rose, and Shinobu Kitayama. 1991. "Culture and the Self: Implications for Cognition, Emotion, and Motivation." *Psychological Review* 98, no. 2: 224–53.

Marmot, Michael. 2005. "Social Determinants of Health Inequalities." *The Lancet* 365, no. 9464: 1099–104.

Marriott, McKim. 1976. "Hindu Transactions: Diversity without Duality." In *Transaction and Meaning: Directions in the Anthropology of Exchange and Symbolic Behavior,* ed. Bruce Kapferer, 109–42. Philadelphia: Institute for the Study of Human Issues.

Marshall, Thomas H. [1949] 1991. "Citizenship and Social Class." In *Citizenship and Social Class,* ed. Thomas H. Marshall and Tom Bottomore, 3–51. London: Pluto.

Martin, Emily. 2009. *Bipolar Expeditions: Mania and Depression in American Culture.* Princeton, NJ: Princeton University Press.

Marx, Karl. 2016. *Collected Works of Karl Marx.* Hastings, UK: Delphi Classics.

Marx, Karl. [1845] 2016. *Theses on Feuerbach.* Marxists.org/archive/marx/works /1845/theses/theses.htm.

Marx, Karl, and Friedrich Engels. 1952. *Capital/Manifesto of the Communist Party.* Chicago: Encyclopedia Britannica.

Massie, Mary Jane. 2004. "Prevalence of Depression in Patients with Cancer." *JNCI Monographs* 2004, no. 32: 57–71.

Matten, Dirk, and Andrew Crane. 2003. "Corporate Citizenship: Towards an Extended Theoretical Conceptualization." International Centre for Corporate Social Responsibility Research Paper Series 4. Nottingham, UK: Nottingham University Business School.

Mauss, Marcel. 1973. "Techniques of the Body." *Economy and Society* 2, no. 1: 70–88.

Mayr, Ernst. [1942] 1982. *Systematics and the Origin of Species.* New York: Columbia University Press.

Mazzarella, William. 2003. *Shoveling Smoke: Advertising and Globalization in Contemporary India*. Durham, NC: Duke University Press.

Mazzucato, Mariana. 2018. *The Value of Everything: Making and Taking in the Global Economy*. London: Allan Lane.

McCracken, Harlan Linneus. [1933] 2001. *Value Theory and Business Cycles*. New York: Books for Business.

McCulloch, Warren S. 1945. "A Heterarchy of Values Determined by the Topology of Nervous Nets." *Bulletin of Mathematical Biophysics* 7, no. 2: 89–93.

McDaniel, June. 2004. *Offering Flowers, Feeding Skulls: Popular Goddess Worship in West Bengal*. Oxford: Oxford University Press.

McGoey, Linsey. 2012. "Strategic Unknowns: Towards a Sociology of Ignorance." *Economy and Society* 41, no. 1: 1–16.

McGoey, Linsey. 2015. *No Such Thing as a Free Gift: The Gates Foundation and the Price of Philanthropy*. London: Verso.

Médecins sans Frontiers (MSF). 2013. "Indian Supreme Court Delivers Verdict in Novartis Case." Press release, April 1. Accessed November 18, 2020. https://www.msf.org/Indian-Supreme-Court-Delivers-Verdict-Novartis-Case.

Menger, Carl. 1871. *Volkswirtschaftslehre: Erster, Allgemeiner Theil*. Vienna: Wilhelm Braumüller.

Menger, Carl. 1884. *Die Irrthümer des Historismus in der deutschen Nationalökonomie*. Vienna: Alfred Hölder.

Metzl, Jonathan. 2003. *Prozac on the Couch: Prescribing Gender in the Era of Wonder Drugs*. Durham, NC: Duke University Press.

Mezzich, Juan E., Laurence Kirmayer, Arthur Kleinman, Horacio Fabrega, et al. 1999. "The Place of Culture in DSM-IV." *Journal of Nervous and Mental Disease* 187, no. 8: 457–64.

Michaels, Axel. 1998. *Der Hinduismus: Geschichte und Gegenwart*. Munich: C. H. Beck.

Michaels, Axel. 2015. *Homo Ritualis: Hindu Ritual and Its Significance for Ritual Theory*. Oxford: Oxford University Press.

Miller, Greg. 2010. "Is Pharma Running Out of Brainy Ideas?" *Science* 329, no. 5991: 502–4.

Mills, China. 2014. *Decolonizing Global Mental Health: The Psychiatrization of the Majority World*. London: Routledge.

Mills, James. 2006. "Modern Psychiatry in India: The British Role in Establishing an Asian System, 1858–1947." *International Review of Psychiatry* 18, no. 4: 333–43.

Mills, James, and Sanjeev Jain. 2007. "Mapother of the Maudsley and Psychiatry at the End of the Raj." In *Psychiatry and Empire*, ed. Sloan Mahone and Megan Vaughan, 153–71. Basingstoke, UK: Palgrave Macmillan.

Mitchell, Philip B., and Dusan Hadzi-Pavlovic. 2014. "Psychopharmacology." In *Psychiatry: Past, Present, and Prospect*, ed. S. Bloch, S. A. Green, and J. Holmes, 335–54. Oxford: Oxford University Press.

Mol, Annemarie. 2002. *The Body Multiple: Ontology in Medical Practice.* Durham, NC: Duke University Press.

Moncrieff, Joanna. 2008. *The Myth of the Chemical Cure: A Critique of Psychiatric Drug Treatment.* London: Palgrave Macmillan.

Moon, Jeremy. 2014. *Corporate Social Responsibility: A Very Short Introduction.* Oxford: Oxford University Press.

Müller, F. Max. 1883. *India: What Can It Teach Us? A Course of Lectures Delivered before the University of Cambridge,* vol. 12. London: Longmans, Green.

Mullin, Rick. 2014. "Cost to Develop New Pharmaceutical Drugs Now Exceeds $2.5 B[illion]." *Scientific American,* November 24. Accessed November 18, 2020. https://www.scientificamerican.com/Article/Cost-To-Develop-New -Pharmaceutical-Drug-Now-Exceeds-2-5B.

Murphy, Michelle. 2017. *The Economization of Life.* Durham, NC: Duke University Press.

Murrough, James W., Chadi G. Abdallah, and Sanjay J. Mathew. 2017. "Targeting Glutamate Signalling in Depression: Progress and Prospects." *Nature Reviews Drug Discovery* 16: 472–86. Accessed November 18, 2020. http:// www.nature.com/Nrd/Journal/Vaop/Ncurrent/Abs/Nrd.2017.16.html.

Nagarajan, Rema. 2013. "India Fears Generic Woes as Drug Companies Fund Interpol." *Times of India,* March 27.

Nagel, Thomas. 1974. "What Is It Like to Be a Bat?" *Philosophical Review* 83, no. 4: 435–50.

Narayan, Deepa, Raj Patel, Kai Schafft, Anne Rademacher, and Sarah Koch-Schulte. 1999. *Can Anyone Hear Us? Voices from 47 Countries.* Washington, DC: World Bank.

Newman, Katinka B. 2016. *The Pill That Steals Lives: One Woman's Terrifying Journey to Discover the Truth about Antidepressants.* London: John Blake.

Nichter, Mark, and Mimi Nichter. 1996. *Anthropology and International Health: Asian Case Studies.* London: Routledge.

Nichter, Mark, and Nancy Vuckovic. 1994. "Agenda for an Anthropology of Pharmaceutical Practice." *Social Science and Medicine* 39, no. 11: 1509–25.

Nietzsche, Friedrich. [1887] 1968. *Zur Genealogie der Moral: Eine Streitschrift.* In *Nietzsche Werke: Kritische Gesamtausgabe,* vol. 2, ed. Giorgio Colli and Mazzino Montinari. Berlin: De Gruyter.

Novartis. 2012. *Novartis Group Annual Report 2012.* Accessed November 18, 2020. https://www.novartis.com/sites/www.novartis.com/files/novartis -annual-report-2012-en.pdf.

Obeyesekere, Gananath. 1985. "Depression, Buddhism, and the Work of Culture in Sri Lanka." In *Culture and Depression,* ed. Arthur Kleinman and Byron Good, 134–52. Berkeley: University of California Press.

Ong, Aihwa. 2006. *Neoliberalism as Exception: Mutations in Citizenship and Sovereignty.* Durham, NC: Duke University Press.

Opler, Marvin K. 1959. *Culture and Mental Health: Cross-Cultural Studies.* New York: Macmillan.

Organization for Economic Cooperation and Development (OECD). 2015. *Health at a Glance*. Paris: OECD Publishing.

Orsi, Francesco. 2015. *Value Theory*. London: Bloomsbury.

Ortner, Sherry B. 1984. "Theory in Anthropology since the Sixties." *Comparative Studies in Society and History* 26, no. 1: 126–66.

Östor, Akos. 2004. *The Play of the Gods: Locality, Ideology, Structure, and Time in the Festivals of a Bengali Town*. Delhi: Orient Blackswan.

Otto, Ton, and Rane Willerslev. 2013. "Introduction: Value *as* Theory: Comparison, Cultural Critique, and Guerilla Ethnographic Theory." *HAU: Journal of Ethnographic Theory* 3, no. 1: 1–20.

Padian, Kevin. 1999. "Charles Darwin's Views of Classification in Theory and Practice." *Systematic Biology* 48, no. 2: 352–64.

Parry, Jonathan P. 1994. *Death in Banaras*. Cambridge: Cambridge University Press.

Patel, Vikram. 2014. "Rethinking Mental Health Care: Bridging the Credibility Gap." *Intervention* 12, no. 1: 15–20.

Patel, Vikram, and Arthur Kleinman. 2003. "Poverty and Common Mental Disorders in Developing Countries." *Bulletin of the World Health Organization* 81, no. 8: 609–15.

Patel, Vikram, Mirja Koschorke, and Martin Prince. 2011. "Closing the Treatment Gap." In *Mental Health in Public Health: The Next 100 Years*, ed. Linda B. Cottler, 3–22. Oxford: Oxford University Press.

Patel, Vikram, Merlyn Rodrigues, and Nandita DeSouza. 2002. "Gender, Poverty, and Postnatal Depression: A Study of Mothers in Goa, India." *American Journal of Psychiatry* 159, no. 1: 43–47.

Patel, Vikram, Shekhar Saxena, Crick Lund, Graham Thornicroft, et al. 2018. "The Lancet Commission on Global Mental Health and Sustainable Development." *The Lancet* 392, no. 10157: 1553–98.

People's Health Movement, MedAct, Health Action International, Medicos International, and Third World Network. 2011. *Global Health Watch 3: An Alternative World Health Report*. London: Zed.

Perrett, Roy W., ed. 2013. *Theory of Value: Indian Philosophy*. London: Routledge.

Petryna, Adriana. 2002. *Life Exposed: Biological Citizenship after Czernobyl*. Princeton, NJ: Princeton University Press.

Petryna, Adriana. 2007. "Clinical Trials Offshored: On Private Sector Science and Public Health." *BioSocieties* 2: 21–40.

Pfeifer, Wolfgang. 1995. *Etymologisches Wörterbuch des Deutschen*. Munich: Deutscher Taschenbuch.

Pfizer. 2019. "Joy of Giving with Dignity Foundation." Accessed November 18, 2020. http://www.pfizerindia.com/Enewswebsite/Joy.aspx.

Phillips, James. 2013. "Conclusion." In *Making the DSM-5*, ed. Joel Paris and James Phillips, 159–75. New York: Springer.

Pickersgill, Martyn. 2013. "How Personality Became Treatable: The Mutual Constitution of Clinical Knowledge and Mental Health Law." *Social Studies of Science* 43, no. 1: 30–53.

Pickersgill, Martyn. 2019. "Psychiatry and the Sociology of Novelty: Negotiating the U.S. National Institute of Mental Health 'Research Domain Criteria' (RDoC)." *Science, Technology, and Human Values* (April 12). https://doi.org/10.1177/0162243919841693.

Pigg, Stacy Leigh. 2001. "Languages of Sex and AIDS in Nepal: Notes on the Social Production of Commensurability." *Cultural Anthropology* 16, no. 4: 481–541.

Pinto, Sarah. 2014. *Daughters of Parvati: Women and Madness in Contemporary India*. Pittsburgh: University of Pennsylvania Press.

Plato. 1952. *Timaeus*. In *The Dialogues of Plato*. Translated by Benjamin Jowett. Chicago: Encyclopedia Britannica.

Plessner, Helmuth. 1975. *Die Stufen des Organischen und der Mensch*. Berlin: De Gruyter.

Pollock, Anne. 2011. "Transforming the Critique of Big Pharma." *Biosocieties* 6, no. 1: 106–18.

Prakash, Gyan. 1999. *Another Reason: Science and the Imagination of Modern India*. Princeton, NJ: Princeton University Press.

President's Council on Bioethics. 2003. *Beyond Therapy: Biotechnology and the Pursuit of Happiness*. Washington, DC: President's Council on Bioethics.

Priebe, Stefan, Tom Burns, and Tom K. J. Craig. 2013. "The Future of Academic Psychiatry May Be Social." *British Journal of Psychiatry* 202, no. 5: 319–20.

Prince, Martin, Vikram Patel, Shekhar Saxena, Mario Maj, et al. 2007. "No Health without Mental Health." *The Lancet* 370, no. 9590: 859–77.

Przybylski, Andrew K., Kou Murayama, Cody R. DeHaan, and Valerie Gladwell. 2013. "Motivational, Emotional, and Behavioral Correlates of Fear of Missing Out." *Computers in Human Behavior* 29, no. 4: 1841–48.

Psychiatric News Alert. 2013. "Lieberman, Insel Issue Joint Statement about DSM-5 and RDoC." Press release, May 14. Accessed November 18, 2020. https://alert.psychnews.org/2013/05/lieberman-insel-issue-joint-statement.html.

Putnam, Hilary. 2002. *The Collapse of the Fact/Value Dichotomy and Other Essays*. Cambridge, MA: Harvard University Press.

Quine, Willard Van Orman. [1975] 2004. *Quintessence: Basic Readings from the Philosophy of W. V. Quine*, ed. Roger F. Gibson Jr. Cambridge, MA: Harvard University Press.

Rabinow, Paul. 2003. *Anthropos Today: Reflections on Modern Equipment*. Princeton, NJ: Princeton University Press.

Rabinow, Paul. 2009. *Anthropos Today: Reflections on Modern Equipment*. Princeton, NJ: Princeton University Press.

Raheja, Gloria Goodwin. 1988. *The Poison in the Gift: Ritual, Prestation, and the Dominant Caste in a North Indian Village*. Chicago: University of Chicago Press.

Rapp, Rayna. 2016. "Big Data, Small Kids: Medico-Scientific, Familial and Advocacy Visions of Human Brains." *BioSocieties* 11, no. 3: 296–316.

Ratcliffe, Matthew. 2014. *Experiences of Depression: A Study in Phenomenology.* Oxford: Oxford University Press.

Ravaisson, Félix. 2008. *Of Habit*, trans. Clare Carlisle and Mark Sinclair. London: Continuum.

Rawls, John. 1971. *A Theory of Justice.* Cambridge, MA: Harvard University Press.

Read, Rupert, and Phil Hutchinson. 2014. "Therapy." In *Wittgenstein: Key Concepts*, ed. Kelly Dean Jolly, 149–59. London: Routledge.

Redfield, Peter. 2013. *Life in Crisis: The Ethical Journey of Doctors Without Borders.* Berkeley: University of California Press.

Rees, Tobias. 2016. *Plastic Reason: An Anthropology of Brain Science in Embryogenetic Terms.* Berkeley: University of California Press.

Rees, Tobias. 2018. *After Ethnos.* Durham, NC: Duke University Press.

Regalado, Antonio. 2015. "Why America's Top Mental Health Researcher Joined Alphabet: Tom Insel Explains Why He's Ready to Give Silicon Valley a Try." *MIT Technology Review*, September 21. Accessed November 18, 2020. https://www.technologyreview.com/S/541446/Why-Americas-Top-Mental-Health-Researcher-Joined-Alphabet.

Reid, Thomas. [1778] 2011. *Essays on the Active Powers of Man.* Cambridge: Cambridge University Press.

Renteln, Alison Dundes. 1988. "Relativism and the Search for Human Rights." *American Anthropologist* 90, no. 1: 56–72.

Reuters. 2020a. "India's Coronavirus Relief Plan Could Leave Millions without Food Aid, Activists Say." Accessed November 18, 2020. https://www.reuters.com/Article/Us-Health-Coronavirus-India-Poverty-Iduskcn21S122.

Reuters. 2020b. "Wuhan Lockdown 'Unprecedented,' Shows Commitment to Contain Virus: WHO Representative in China." Accessed November 18, 2020. https://www.reuters.com/Article/Us-China-Health-Who-Iduskbn1Zm1G9.

Rice, Dorothy P., Sander Kelman, and Leonard S. Miller. 1992. "The Economic Burden of Mental Illness." *Psychiatric Services* 43, no. 12: 1227–32.

Ricoeur, Paul. [1950] 1966. *Freedom and Nature: The Voluntary and the Involuntary.* Evanston, IL: Northwestern University Press.

Ringmar, Erik. 2016. "Outline of a Non-deliberative, Mood-based, Theory of Action." *Philosophia* 77.

Robbins, Joel. 2013. "Monism, Pluralism, and the Structure of Value Relations: A Dumontian Contribution to the Contemporary Study of Value." *HAU: Journal of Ethnographic Theory* 3, no. 1: 99–115.

Rodrigues, Hillary Peter. 2018. "The Self in Hindu Philosophies of Liberation." In *Global Psychologies*, ed. Suman Fernando and Roy Moodley, 99–118. London: Palgrave Macmillan.

Rodseth, Lars. 2018. "Hegemonic Concepts of Culture: The Checkered History of Dark Anthropology." *American Anthropologist* 120, no. 3: 398–411.

Rogers, Adam. 2017. "Star Neuroscientist Tom Insel Leaves the Google-Spawned Verily for . . . a Startup?" *Wired*, May 11. Accessed November 18, 2020.

https://www.wired.com/2017/05/Star-Neuroscientist-Tom-Insel-Leaves
-Google-Spawned-Verily-Startup.

Rogers, Carl. 1990. *The Carl Rogers Reader*, ed. Howard Kirschenbaum and Valerie Land Henderson. London: Constable.

Romelli, Katia, Alessandra Frigerio, and Monica Colombo. 2016. "DSM over Time:
From Legitimisation of Authority to Hegemony." *BioSocieties* 11, no. 1: 1–21.

Rosa, Hartmut. 2016. *Resonanz: Eine Soziologie der Weltbeziehung*. Frankfurt
am Main: Suhrkamp.

Rose, Nikolas. 1990. *Governing the Soul: The Shaping of the Private Self*. London:
Routledge.

Rose, Nikolas. 2001. "The Politics of Life Itself." *Theory, Culture and Society* 18,
no. 6: 1–30.

Rose, Nikolas. 2006. *The Politics of Life Itself: Biomedicine, Power, and Subjectivity in the Twenty-first Century*. Princeton, NJ: Princeton University
Press.

Rose, Nikolas. 2010. "Normality and Pathology in a Biomedical Age." *Sociological Review* 57, no. 2 supp.: 66–83.

Rose, Nikolas. 2013. "What Is Diagnosis For?" Unpublished ms. https://
nikolasrose.com/wp-content/uploads/2013/07/Rose-2013-What-is-diagnosis
-for-IoP-revised-July-2013.pdf.

Rose, Nikolas. 2018. *Our Psychiatric Future*. Cambridge: Polity.

Rose, Nikolas, and Carlos Novas. 2004. "Biological Citizenship." In *Global Assemblages: Technology, Politics, and Ethics as Anthropological Problems*, ed.
Aihwa Ong and Stephen J. Collier. Oxford: Blackwell.

Rosenberg, Robin S. 2013. "Abnormal Is the New Normal." *Slate*, April 12. Accessed November 18, 2020. https://slate.com/technology/2013/04/diagnostic
-and-statistical-manual-fifth-edition-why-will-half-the-u-s-population
-have-a-mental-illness.html.

Rouvroy, Antoinette, and Thomas Berns. 2013. "Gouvernementalité algorith-
mique et perspectives d'émancipation: Le disparate comme condition d'in-
dividuation par la relation?" *Réseaux* 1, no. 177: 163–96.

Ruckenstein, Minna, and Natasha Dow Schüll. 2017. "The Datafication of
Health." *Annual Review of Anthropology* 46: 261–78.

Sadler, John Z. 2013. "Considering the Economy of DSM Alternatives." In *Making
the DSM-5: Concepts and Controversies*, ed. Joel Paris and James Phillips,
21–38. New York: Springer.

Sahlins, Marshall. 2013. *What Kinship Is—And Is Not*. Chicago: University of
Chicago Press.

Samuelson, Paul A., and William D. Nordhaus. 2010. *Economics*, 19th ed. New
York: McGraw-Hill.

Sanjek, Roger. 2009. "Ethnography." In *The Routledge Encyclopedia of Social
and Cultural Anthropology*, ed. Alan Barnard and Jonathan Spencer, 243–49.
London: Routledge.

Sankey, Howard. 1993. "Kuhn's Changing Concept of Incommensurability."
British Journal for the Philosophy of Science 44, no. 4: 759–74.

Sarbadhikary, Sunkaya. 2018. "The Body-Mind Challenge: Theology and Phenomenology in Bengal-Vaishnavisms." *Modern Asian Studies* 52, no. 6: 2080–108.

Sarkar, Sumit. 1992. "'Kaliyuga,' 'Chakri' and 'Bhakti': Ramakrishna and His Times." *Economic and Political Weekly* 27, no. 29: 1543–66.

Satel, Sally. 2013. "Why the Fuss over the DSM-5." *New York Times*, May 11.

Sax, William S. 2014. "Ritual Healing and Mental Health in India." *Transcultural Psychiatry* 51, no. 6: 829–49.

Schane, Sanford A. 1986. "The Corporation Is a Person: The Language of a Legal Fiction." *Tulane Law Review* 61: 563–609.

Scharff, Christina. 2016. "The Psychic Life of Neoliberalism: Mapping the Contours of Entrepreneurial Subjectivity." *Theory, Culture and Society* 33, no. 6: 107–22.

Schiebinger, Londa. 1993. "Why Mammals Are Called Mammals: Gender Politics in Eighteenth-Century Natural History." *American Historical Review* 98, no. 2: 382–411.

Schweitzer, Albert. [1936] 2009. *Albert Schweitzer's Ethical Vision: A Sourcebook*, ed. Predrag Cicovacki. Oxford: Oxford University Press.

Scull, Andrew. 2015. *Madness in Civilization: A Cultural History of Insanity, from the Bible to Freud, from the Madhouse to Modern Medicine*. Princeton, NJ: Princeton University Press.

Sedlacek, Tomas. 2011. *Economics of Good and Evil: The Quest for Economic Meaning from Gilgamesh to Wall Street*. Oxford: Oxford University Press.

Sewell, William H., Jr. 1992. "A Theory of Structure: Duality, Agency, and Transformation." *American Journal of Sociology* 98, no. 1: 1–29.

Shannon, Joel. 2019. "FDA Approves First Postpartum Depression Drug." *USA Today*, March 20.

Sharma, S. D. 2004. "Mental Health: The Pre-independence Scenario." In *Mental Health: An Indian Perspective, 1946–2003*, ed. S. P. Agarwal, 25–29. New Delhi: Elsevier.

Sharp, Lesley A. 2019. *Animal Ethos: The Morality of Human-Animal Encounters in Experimental Lab Science*. Oakland: University of California Press.

Shear, M. Katherine, Naomi Simon, Melanie Wall, Sidney Zisook, et al. 2011. "Complicated Grief and Related Bereavement Issues for DSM-5." *Depression and Anxiety* 28, no. 2: 103–17.

Shiva, Mira. 1985. "Towards a Healthy Use of Pharmaceuticals: An Indian Perspective." *Development Dialogue*, no. 2: 69–93.

Shorter, Edward. 1997. *A History of Psychiatry: From the Era of the Asylum to the Age of Prozac*. New York: John Wiley and Sons.

Shorter, Edward. 2013. *How Everyone Became Depressed: The Rise and Fall of the Nervous Breakdown*. Oxford: Oxford University Press.

Shukla, Nitin, and Tanushree Sangal. 2009. "Generic Drug Industry in India: The Counterfeit Spin." *Journal of Intellectual Property Rights* 14, no. 3: 236–40.

Simmel, Georg. [1900] 2011. *The Philosophy of Money*. Abingdon, UK: Routledge.

Sinclair, Simon. 2004. "Evidence-based Medicine: A New Ritual in Medical Teaching." *British Medical Bulletin* 69: 179–96.

Sloterdijk, Peter. 1998. *Sphären I: Blasen*. Frankfurt am Main: Suhrkamp.

Sloterdijk, Peter. 1999. *Sphären II: Globen*. Frankfurt am Main: Suhrkamp.

Sloterdijk, Peter. 2004. *Sphären III: Schäume*. Frankfurt am Main: Suhrkamp.

Sloterdijk, Peter. 2005. *Im Weltinnenraum des Kapitals: Für eine philosophische Theorie der Globalisierung*. Frankfurt am Main: Suhrkamp.

Smith, Adam. [1776] 1952. *An Inquiry into the Nature and Causes of the Wealth of Nations*. Chicago: Encyclopedia Britannica.

Snow, C. P. [1959] 2012. *The Two Cultures*. Cambridge: Cambridge University Press.

Solomon, Harry C. 1958. "The American Psychiatric Association in Relation to American Psychiatry." *American Journal of Psychiatry* 115, no. 1: 1–9.

Solt, Stephanie. 2016. "On Measurement and Quantification: The Case of *Most* and *More than Half*." *Language* 92, no. 1: 65–100.

Sovran, Tamar. 1992. "Between Similarity and Sameness." *Journal of Pragmatics* 18, no. 4: 329–44.

Sparrow, Tom, and Adam Hutchinson, eds. 2013. *A History of Habit: From Aristotle to Bourdieu*. Lanham, MD: Lexington.

Spellman, Barbara A., and Simone Schnall. 2009. "Embodied Rationality." *Queen's Law Journal* 35, no. 1: 117–64.

Spence, Ruth, Adam Roberts, Cono Ariti, and Martin Bardsley. 2014. "Focus on: Antidepressant Prescribing Trends in the Prescribing of Antidepressants in Primary Care." Project report. London: Nuffield Trust.

Spitzer, Robert L., Kurt Kroenke, Janet B. W. Williams, and the Patient Health Questionnaire Primary Care Study Group. 1999. "Validation and Utility of a Self-Report Version of PRIME-MD: The PHQ Primary Care Study." *Journal of the American Medical Association* 282, no. 18: 1737–44.

Stark, David, with Daniel Beunza, Monique Girard, and Janos Lukacs. 2009. *The Sense of Dissonance: Accounts of Worth in Economic Life*. Princeton, NJ: Princeton University Press.

Stein, Dan J., Crick Lund, and Randolph M. Nesse. 2013. "Classification Systems in Psychiatry: Diagnosis and Global Mental Health in the Era of DSM-5 and ICD-11." *Current Opinion in Psychiatry* 26, no. 5: 493.

Stern, David G. 1991. "Heraclitus' and Wittgenstein's River Images: Stepping Twice into the Same River." *The Monist* 74, no. 4: 579–604.

Stevens, S. S. 1946. "On the Theory of Scales of Measurement." *Science* 103, no. 2684: 677–80.

Stiegler, Bernard. 2013. *What Makes Life Worth Living: On Pharmacology*. Translated by Daniel Ross. Cambridge: Polity Press.

Strathern, Marilyn. 1990. *The Gender of the Gift: Problems with Women and Problems with Society in Melanesia*. Berkeley: University of California Press.

Strathern, Marilyn. [1991] 2004. *Partial Connections, Updated Edition.* Walnut Creek, CA: Altamira.

Sumathipala, Athula, Sisira H. Siribaddana, and Dinesh Bhugra. 2004. "Culture-Bound Syndromes: The Story of Dhat Syndrome." *British Journal of Psychiatry* 184, no. 3: 200–209.

Sumner, Andy, Chris Hoy, and Eduardo Ortiz-Juarez. 2020. "Estimates of the Impact of COVID-19 on Global Poverty." Working Paper 43. Helsinki: United Nations University World Institute for Development Economics Research.

Sunder Rajan, Kaushik. 2017. *Pharmocracy: Value, Politics, and Knowledge in Global Biomedicine.* Durham, NC: Duke University Press.

Supreme Court of India. 2013. *Novartis v. Union of India.* Accessed June 28, 2021. https://indiankanoon.org/doc/165776436/.

Taylor, Charles. 1991. *The Malaise of Modernity.* Toronto: Anansi.

Thaler, Richard H. 2015. *Misbehaving: The Making of Behavioral Economics.* New York: W. W. Norton.

Throop, C. Jason. 2010. *Suffering and Sentiment: Exploring the Vicissitudes of Experience and Pain in Yap.* Berkeley: University of California Press.

Timmermans, Stefan, and Marc Berg. 2003. *The Gold Standard: The Challenge of Evidence-Based Medicine and Standardization in Health Care.* Philadelphia: Temple University Press.

Tomasello, Michael. 2009. *Why We Cooperate.* Cambridge, MA: MIT Press.

Tone, Andrea. 2009. *The Age of Anxiety: A History of America's Turbulent Affair with Tranquilizers.* New York: Basic.

Tooze, Adam. 2020. "Coronavirus Has Shattered the Myth that the Economy Must Come First." *Guardian*, March 20.

Trautmann, Thomas R. 1995. "Indian Time, European Time." In *Time: Histories and Ethnologies*, ed. Diane Owen Hughes and Thomas R. Trautmann, 167–97. Ann Arbor: University of Michigan Press.

Tylor, Edward Burnett. 1871. *Primitive Culture*, 2 vols. London: John Murray.

Tyrer, Peter. 2012. "The End of the Psychopharmaceutical Revolution." *British Journal of Psychiatry* 201, no. 2: 168.

United Nations. 1998. "Unite Power of Markets with Authority of Universal Values, Secretary-General Urges at World Economic Forum." Press release SG/SN/6448, January 30.

US Department of Justice (DOJ). 2013. "Generic Drug Manufacturer Ranbaxy Pleads Guilty and Agrees to Pay $500 Million to Resolve False Claims Allegations, cGMP Violations and False Statements to the FDA." Press Release, May 13. Accessed November 18, 2020. https://www.justice.gov/opa/pr/generic-drug-manufacturer-ranbaxy-pleads-guilty-and-agrees-pay-500-million-resolve-false.

US Food and Drug Administration (FDA). 2019. "FDA Approves First Treatment for Post-partum Depression." News release, March 19. Accessed November 18, 2020. https://www.fda.gov/news-events/press-announcements/fda-approves-first-treatment-post-partum-depression.

Van der Veer, Peter. 2016. *The Value of Comparison*. Durham, NC: Duke University Press.

Van Dijk, Jan. 2012. *The Network Society*. Thousand Oaks, CA: SAGE.

Van Praag, Herman M. 1998. "Psychopharmacology and Biological Psychiatry: Pacemakers towards a Scientific Psychopathology." In *The Rise of Psychopharmacology and the Story of CINP*, ed. Thomas A. Ban, David Healy, and Edward Shorter. Budapest: Animula.

Varela, Francisco J., Evan Thompson, and Eleanor Rosch. 2016. *The Embodied Mind: Cognitive Science and Human Experience*. Cambridge, MA: MIT Press.

Vaughan, Megan. 2007. "Introduction." In *Psychiatry and Empire*, ed. Sloan Mahone and Megan Vaughan, 1–16. Basingstoke, UK: Palgrave Macmillan.

Vedantam, Shankar. 2001. "Renamed Prozac Fuels Women's Health Debate." *Washington Post*, April 29, 2001.

Veissière, Samuel P., Axel Constant, Maxwell J. D. Ramstead, Karl Friston, and Laurence J. Kirmayer. 2020. "Thinking through Other Minds: A Variational Approach to Cognition and Culture." *Behavioral and Brain Sciences* 43, no. e90. doi:10.1017/S0140525X19001213.

Ventimiglia, Jeffrey, and Amir H. Kalali. 2010. "Generic Penetration in the Retail Antidepressant Market." *Psychiatry (Edgmont)* 7, no. 6: 9–11.

Viveiros de Castro, Eduardo. 2015. *The Relative Native: Essays on Indigenous Conceptual Worlds*. Chicago: HAU.

Vivekananda, Swami. [1907] 2003. "Work and Its Secret." In *The Complete Works of Swami Vivekananda*, vol. 2. Calcutta: Advaita Ashrama.

Wahlberg, Ayo, and Nikolas Rose. 2015. "The Governmentalization of Living: Calculating Global Health." *Economy and Society* 44, no. 1: 60–90.

Wakefield, Jerome C. 2013. "The DSM-5 Debate over the Bereavement Exclusion: Psychiatric Diagnosis and the Future of Empirically Supported Treatment." *Clinical Psychology Review* 33, no. 7: 825–45.

Waldby, Catherine. 2002. "Stem Cells, Tissue Cultures and the Production of Biovalue." *Health* 63, no. 3: 305–23.

Walker, Peter. 2020. "No 10 Denies Claim Dominic Cummings Argued to 'Let Old People Die.'" *Guardian*, March 22.

Walwyn, David. 2013. "Patents and Profits: A Disparity of Manufacturing Margins in the Tenofovir Value Chain." *African Journal of AIDS Research* 12, no. 1: 17–23.

Walzer, Michael. 1983. *Spheres of Justice: A Defense of Pluralism and Equality*. New York: Basic.

Watzlawick, Paul, Janet Beavin Bavelas, and Don D. Jackson. 2011. *Pragmatics of Human Communication: A Study of Interactional Patterns, Pathologies, and Paradoxes*. New York: W. W. Norton.

Weber, Max. [1904–1905] 2010. *Die Protestantische Ethik und der Geist des Kapitalismus*. Munich: C. H. Beck.

Weber, Max. [1922] 2019. *Economy and Society: A New Translation*. Cambridge, MA: Harvard University Press.

Weber, Max. 1984. *Soziologische Grundbegriffe*. Tübingen, Germany: Mohr Siebeck.

Weber, Max. 2002. *Wirtschaft und Gesellschaft: Grundriss der verstehenden Soziologie*. Tübingen, Germany: Mohr Siebeck.

Wegener, Gregers, and Dan Rujescu. 2013. "The Current Development of CNS Drug Research." *International Journal of Neuropsychopharmacology* 16, no. 7: 1687–93.

Weiner, Annette B. 1992. *Inalienable Possessions: The Paradox of Keeping while Giving*. Berkeley: University of California Press.

Whitaker, Robert. 2010. *Anatomy of an Epidemic: Magic Bullets, Psychiatric Drugs, and the Astonishing Rise of Mental Illness in America*. New York: Crown.

Whitmarsh, Ian. 2013. "The Ascetic Subject of Compliance: The Turn to Chronic Diseases in Global Health." In *When People Come First: Critical Studies in Global Health*, ed. João Biehl and Adriana Petryna, 302–24. Princeton, NJ: Princeton University Press.

Whooley, Owen. 2016. "Measuring Mental Disorders: The Failed Commensuration Project of DSM-5." *Social Science and Medicine* 166: 33–40.

Whooley, Owen. 2019. *On the Heels of Ignorance: Psychiatry and the Politics of Not Knowing*. Chicago: University of Chicago Press.

Whyte, Susan Reynolds, Sjaak van der Geest, and Anita Hardon. 2002. *Social Lives of Medicines*. Cambridge: Cambridge University Press.

Widlok, Thomas. 2017. *Anthropology and the Economy of Sharing*. London: Routledge.

Wilde, Oscar. [1895] 1995. *The Importance of Being Earnest and Other Plays*. Oxford: Oxford University Press.

Wilkinson, Richard G. 2002. *Unhealthy Societies: The Afflictions of Inequality*. London: Routledge.

Wilkinson, Richard G., and Kate Pickett. 2010. *The Spirit Level: Why Equality Is Better for Everyone*. London: Penguin.

Williams, D. D. R., and Jane Garner. 2002. "The Case against 'the Evidence': A Different Perspective on Evidence-based Medicine." *British Journal of Psychiatry* 180, no. 1: 8–12.

Wilson, Elizabeth A. 2015. *Gut Feminism*. Durham, NC: Duke University Press.

Wittgenstein, Ludwig. 2017. *Philosophische Untersuchungen*. Frankfurt am Main: Suhrkamp.

Wohlleben, Peter. 2016. *The Hidden Life of Trees: What They Feel, How They Communicate—Discoveries from a Secret World*. Vancouver: Greystone.

Wolfe, Cary. 2010. *What Is Posthumanism?* Minneapolis: University of Minnesota Press.

World Bank. 1993. *World Development Report 1993: Investing in Health*. New York: Oxford University Press.

World Health Organization (WHO). 2001. *Mental Health: New Understanding, New Hope: The World Health Report 2001*. Geneva: World Health Organization.

World Health Organization (WHO). 2006. "Declaration of Rome: Conclusions and Recommendations of the WHO International Conference on Combating Counterfeit Medicines." Accessed November 18, 2020. https://www.who.int /medicines/services/counterfeit/RomeDeclaration.pdf.

World Health Organization (WHO). 2008. *mhGAP: Mental Health Gap Action Programme: Scaling Up Care for Mental, Neurological, and Substance Use Disorders.* Geneva: World Health Organization.

World Health Organization (WHO). 2010. *mhGAP Intervention Guide for Mental, Neurological and Substance Use Disorders in Non-specialized Health Settings.* Geneva: World Health Organization.

World Health Organization (WHO). 2013. *Mental Health Action Plan 2013–2020.* Geneva: World Health Organization.

World Health Organization (WHO). 2017. "WHO Global Surveillance and Monitoring System for Substandard and Falsified Medical Products." Accessed November 18, 2020. https://apps.who.int/iris/bitstream/handle/10665 /326708/9789241513425-eng.pdf?ua=1?

World Health Organization (WHO). 2019. "Substandard and Falsified Medicinal Products." Accessed November 18, 2020. https://www.who.int/En /News-Room/Fact-Sheets/Detail/Substandard-And-Falsified-Medical -Products.

World Health Organization (WHO). 2020. "Timeline: WHO's COVID-19 Response." Accessed June 18, 2021. https://www.who.int/emergencies/diseases /novel-coronavirus-2019/interactive-timeline.

World Health Organization World Mental Health Survey Consortium. 2004. "Prevalence, Severity, and Unmet Need for Treatment of Mental Disorders in the World Health Organization World Mental Health Surveys." *Journal of the American Medical Association* 291, no. 21: 2581–90.

Worrall, John. 2010. "Evidence: Philosophy of Science Meets Medicine." *Journal of Evaluation in Clinical Practice* 16, no. 2: 356–62.

Wurtzel, Elizabeth. 1994. *Prozac Nation: Young and Depressed in America.* Boston: Houghton Mifflin.

Yang, Lawrence Hsing, Arthur Kleinman, Bruce G. Link, Jo C. Phelan, et al. 2007. "Culture and Stigma: Adding Moral Experience to Stigma Theory." *Social Science and Medicine* 64, no. 7: 1524–35.

Zachar, Peter, Michael B. First, and Kenneth S. Kendler. 2017. "The Bereavement Exclusion Debate in the DSM-5: A History." *Clinical Psychological Science* 5, no. 5: 890–906.

Zarate, Carlos, Jr., Rodrigo Machado-Vieira, Ioline Henter, Lobna Ibrahim, et al. 2010. "Glutamatergic Modulators: The Future of Treating Mood Disorders?" *Harvard Review of Psychiatry* 18, no. 5: 293–303.

Zelizer, Viviana A. 2011. *Economic Lives: How Culture Shapes the Economy.* Princeton, NJ: Princeton University Press.

Zhou, Aileen J., Yena Lee, Giacomo Salvadore, Benjamin Hsu, et al. 2017. "Sirukumab: A Potential Treatment for Mood Disorders?" *Advances in Therapy* 34, no. 11: 78–90.

REFERENCES

Zuboff, Shoshana. 2019. *The Age of Surveillance Capitalism: The Fight for a Human Future at the New Frontier of Power.* New York: PublicAffairs.

Zumwalt, Rosemary Lévy. 2019. *Franz Boas: The Emergence of the Anthropologist.* Lincoln: University of Nebraska Press.

Index